UNIVERSITY
RNING F

oridd
101

BRITISH LIBERALISM

DOCUMENTS IN POLITICAL IDEAS

General editor: *Bernard Crick*

BRITISH LIBERALISM

Liberal thought from the 1640s to 1980s

Robert Eccleshall

Longman
London and New York

LONGMAN GROUP LIMITED
Longman House, Burnt Mill, Harlow
Essex CM20 2JE, England
Associated companies throughout the world

*Published in the United States of America
by Longman Inc., New York*

© Longman Group Limited 1986

First published 1986

BRITISH LIBRARY CATALOGUING IN PUBLICATION DATA

British liberalism : liberal thought from the
   1640s to 1980s.—(Documents in political ideas)
   1. Liberalism—Great Britain—History
   I. Eccleshall, Robert   II. Series
   320.5'1'0941   JA84.G7

   ISBN   0-582-29655-2

LIBRARY OF CONGRESS CATALOGING IN PUBLICATION DATA

Main entry under title:

British liberalism.
   (Documents in political ideas)
   1. Liberalism—Great Britain—History—
Addresses, essays, lectures. I. Eccleshall,
Robert.
JA84.G7B68   1986   320.5'1'0941   85-18063
ISBN 0-582-29655-2

Set in 10/11pt Comp/Set Plantin
Produced by Longman Group (FE) Limited
Printed in Hong Kong

CONTENTS

EDITOR'S PREFACE

Students of political ideas will be familiar with the debate among their teachers about texts and contexts, whether the study of political ideas primarily concerns the meaning of a text or an understanding of the main ideas of an epoch. Both should be done but not confused; and texts need setting in their context. But it is easier for the student to find and to read the texts of political philosophers than to be able to lay his hands upon the range of materials that would catch the flavour of the thinking of an age or a movement, both about what should be done and about how best to use common concepts that create different perceptions of political problems and activity.

So this series aims to present carefully chosen anthologies of the political ideas of thinkers, publicists, statesmen, actors in political events, extracts from State papers and common literature of the time, in order to supplement and complement, not to replace, study of the texts of political philosophers. They should be equally useful to students of politics and of history.

Each volume will have an authoritative and original introductory essay by the editor of the volume. Occasionally instead of an era, movement or problem, an individual writer will figure, writers of a kind who are difficult to understand (like Edmund Burke) simply by the reading of any single text.

B. R. C.

AUTHOR'S PREFACE

This book is intended to illustrate a tradition of political discourse which originated in the seventeenth century. It is not a history of the Liberal party which experienced a relatively brief period of political ascendancy: the party was not formally inaugurated until 1859 and there has been no Liberal Prime Minister since Lloyd George lost office in 1922. Some of the policy issues which preoccupied the party – the question of Irish Home Rule, for instance – have been ignored. Although the later extracts reflect the attitudes of Liberal party activists and supporters, leading politicians are not strongly represented. There are only short extracts, for example, from the speeches and writings of W. E. Gladstone, H. H. Asquith, David Lloyd George and Jo Grimond. Party leaders rarely provide the most succinct expression of particular ideas or themes. There are, in any case, plenty of books about Liberal Party policies and structure, as well as on the beliefs and influence of party statesmen. But there is no source book on British liberalism from its origins to the present day. This anthology is designed to fill the gap.

The book includes extracts from the principal exponents of liberalism – John Locke, J. S. Mill, T. H. Green, J. M. Keynes and so on – and also from the writings of many less familiar figures. The aim throughout has been to tell a coherent story and each extract has been chosen because it sheds light on some aspect of the ideology. My principles of selection have been either originality (especially with the more influential thinkers) or, more usually, clarity of argument. This latter criterion has occasionally given scope to opt for some neglected writers who, in my judgement, merit rehabilitation. Discussions of the utilitarian theory of democracy, for example, tend to focus on James Mill's *Essay on government*. But the lesser known George Grote presented the utilitarian case for democracy in a more structured and revealing manner. So I have chosen an extract from his *Essentials of parliamentary reform* rather than from Mill's *Essay*. Josiah Tucker, to take another example, was a witty and piquant writer who expressed Whiggish opinions on a range of issues. I have chosen a short extract from one of his many attacks upon Lockean radicals because he, too, has been badly served by historians. If this anthology encourages readers to find out more about liberalism, I hope that some of them will survey the neglected byways of the tradition. There is much to explore.

I should like to thank Bernard Crick for inviting me to produce this anthology and for sound advice on the way; and Vincent Geoghegan, David Gregg, Richard Jay, Christopher Shorley and Rick Wilford for help in its preparation. Margaret McCrum and Pauline McElhill typed the extracts with their usual speed and efficiency.

Robert Eccleshall

ACKNOWLEDGEMENTS

We are grateful to the following for permission to reproduce copyright material:

George Allen & Unwin (Publishers) Ltd for extracts from 'Liberty and Welfare' by G Elliott Dodds pp 14–15, 17–22, 25–26 *The Unservile State* ed George Watson; Associated Book Publishers (UK) Ltd for an extract from pp 187–190 *The Liberal Outlook* by Hubert Phillips (pub Methuen & Co); Association of Liberal Councillors for extracts from sections 4–10, 15 *The Theory and Practice of Community Politics* by Bernard Greaves & Gordon Lishman; the Beaverbrook Foundation for an extract from pp 6–9 *Slings and Arrows: sayings chosen from the speeches of David Lloyd George* ed Philip Guedalla; Liberal Publication Department, 1 Whitehall Place, SW1 for extracts from 'Liberalism & Industry' pp 205–209, 211–212 *Liberal Points of View* ed H L Nathan & H H Williams, pp xviii–xx, 63 *Britain's Industrial Future being the Report of the Liberal Industrial Inquiry*, 'Introduction' by Harry Cowie pp 7–8 *Partners to Progress*; Macmillan, London & Basingstoke and Cambridge University Press (NY) for an extract from pp 377–383 *The General Theory of Employment, Interest and Money* by J M Keynes; Times Newspapers Ltd for extracts from the article 'Liberalism means liberty, but it also means business' by John Rae *The Times* 13/9/76.

We have been unable to trace the copyright holder in *Why I am a Liberal by William Beveridge* and would appreciate any information that would enable us to do so.

INTRODUCTION

Histories of liberalism fall into two categories. There are, first, partisan accounts calculated to inspire the faithful and to win converts to the liberal creed. The story told is of a movement for individual emancipation from successive forms of arbitrary power and outworn privilege. It is an heroic tale in which bearers of the torch of freedom emerge as magnanimous individuals intent on creating a fairer, more tolerant and diversified society. Hence a tendency to designate liberalism as the mobilization of decent impulses on behalf of social progress: the spirit of 'liberality', as Lord Selborne put it, 'transferred only to the sphere of politics'.[1]* It is also a success story of battles won against such varied obstacles to individual liberty as absolute monarchy, religious conformity, economic protectionism, an undemocratic franchise and the degrading poverty which stems from unbridled capitalism. Each victory marks a consolidation of individual rights and, in consequence, an extension of opportunities for self-expression. Liberalism, on this assessment, has for three centuries spearheaded the transformation of society from semi-feudal despotism into a structure of liberties equally available to every citizen. It is this incessant opposition to the forces of privilege and oppression which is said to endow the liberal movement with coherence.[2]

But not every commentator is inclined to read the movement's history backwards from a checklist of policies successfully completed, and there are, secondly, more detached accounts intended to disclose the identity of liberalism as a body of ideas. In these commentaries a ragged story tends to unfold – often prefaced by acknowledgment of the ideology's apparent intellectual messiness.[3] Here is little sympathy

* References to material in this anthology are given in the text inside [square] brackets, indicating the number of the document in this book in which the extract occurs. Other references are given in the normal way, and are listed at the end of this introduction.

1

with the sanguine judgement that 'Liberalism has an advantage over other political creeds in being far more easily and more clearly defined'.[4] So numerous are the strands of liberalism, it is admitted, that the casual observer may dismiss the doctrine as essentially ambivalent. Sometimes it is concluded that even a detailed inspection can detect no unifying thread in the various arguments and objectives which constitute the liberal tradition. To search for such a nuclear identity, we are told, is to embark upon a misconceived and ultimately barren enterprise. We should be content instead to convey the full range of ideas which have been embraced by liberals down the centuries.[5]

What makes the character of liberalism elusive is the elasticity of its key concept. Liberals have championed the cause of freedom on the assumption that individuals are rational enough to shape their conduct and beliefs with minimal interference from State or Church. They have sought to disperse authority from the central agencies of society so that its members might exercise a degree of self-government or personal responsibility. But liberty is a flabby and ambiguous concept which yields neither a settled meaning nor consensus about the conditions in which it is secured.

Liberals certainly do not monopolize the different uses made of their prized idea. So versatile is the rhetoric of freedom that it features in most ideological accounts of society. In modern Britain, for example, it is central to the debate about the proper functions of the State. Conservatives tend to equate freedom with the unhindered pursuit by individuals of private ambition. Hence their demand for a competitive market economy in which the State is restricted to the provision of a system of law and order. Socialists, by contrast, believe that *laissez-faire* capitalism engenders a predatory and greatly unequal society in which the poor and unemployed are coerced by material insecurity. Hence their demand for an interventionist State which, through economic management and social welfare, establishes a platform of comfort upon which all citizens may freely shape their existence. Far from producing an undisputed set of political and economic prescriptions for organizing society, therefore, freedom is part of the shared language through which alternative ideological messages are proclaimed.

Liberalism itself has encompassed the contrary meanings which conservatives and socialists attach to freedom. Earlier liberals believed that liberty flourishes in a free-enterprise economy that imposes few restrictions on the accumulation of private property. From the end of the nineteenth century, however, liberals began to abandon the ideal of a minimal State in which individual property rights were sacrosanct. Gross inequalities of wealth and income, it was acknowledged, impaired the freedom of people whose struggle for survival afforded them little scope to make the best of their capacities. They now urged some political control of the economy to eliminate unemployment and low wages, as well as public provision of social welfare.

Commentators often treat the historical transformation of liberalism as an ideological shift of seismic proportions. They have conceptualized it as a transition from individualism to collectivism or, alternatively, as a rejection of negative liberty for a more positive conception of freedom – terms, in fact, which were coined by liberals at the end of the nineteenth century in an attempt to distinguish themselves from their predecessors. Early liberals, it is said, viewed society as an arena of self-sufficient and competitive individuals who were free in so far as they could pursue their private interests without coercion; whereas their successors envisage society as a collectivity of interdependent individuals who cannot fulfil their potentialities unless government assumes active responsibility for the public good. It is sometimes added that this shift from the ideal of a minimal State signified the moral decline or theoretical disintegration of liberalism. Right-wing critics, for example, argue that the concept of positive liberty is potentially despotic because it gives government licence to do whatever is considered expedient to transform subjects into good citizens.[6] Socialist commentators, by contrast, often suggest that liberalism has been stranded by the tide of history. The ideology was so inextricably tied to the age of *laissez-faire*, it is claimed, that subsequent liberals have failed to provide convincing arguments for an interventionist State.[7]

Within each historical half of liberalism, too, there emerge divergences of belief and policy. Many early liberals advocated a radical programme to secure various civil liberties – freedom of speech and assembly, religious toleration, freedom from arbitrary arrest or imprisonment and so forth – and to establish a much broader electoral franchise. They opposed every form of customary privilege and championed popular rights. But not every liberal was a populist. The principal carriers of the banner of British liberalism in the eighteenth century were the Whigs, who wished to curb the power of monarchy by means of parliamentary checks and balances. Though staunch defenders of limited and representative government, Whigs nevertheless supported the traditional social hierarchy of wealth and power in which their property rights were preserved. They resisted democratic pressures, and the 'rights of the people' for which they agitated was often little more than a euphemism for the privileges of the rich. Modern liberalism also reveals different emphases. Although twentieth-century liberals have advocated social and economic planning, many believe that individual liberty has been threatened by the growth of a centralized State.

If liberalism seems an ideology of infinite variety, part of the difficulty lies with the history of the concept itself. The adjective 'liberal' has for many centuries denoted a generous and tolerant disposition or habit of mind. Only at the beginning of the nineteenth century, however, was the epithet attached to European political creeds and parties. The noun 'liberalism' was coined soon afterwards to designate a political movement. Equipped with a novel term, historians refined it into a concept for classifying ideological strands associated with the evolution of the modern, capitalist world. Liberalism thus became a convenient label for an array of ideas and policies which often exhibited little in common beyond a general intention to liberate individuals from conventional economic and political constraints upon their activities. In modern usage, therefore, liberalism provides an ideological map of many of the major developments which have occurred in Britain and elsewhere since the seventeenth century. This means, of course, that the doctrine cannot be reduced either to timeless beliefs or to a single set of objectives and policies.

But the diversity of liberalism does not mean that it is essentially incoherent. The ideology, as the extracts in this anthology illustrate, does possess an unfolding identity which emerges in three recurrent themes: one conceptual; another related to liberalism's social roots; the third, a persistent image of society that derives from the other two. Conceptually, liberals have repeatedly affirmed an equal right to liberty. This claim that liberty ought to be shared equally throughout society is neither simple nor straightforward.[8] For one thing, it begs the question as to which particular freedoms should be made available to every citizen. Liberals have provided several answers. The early liberals were primarily concerned to safeguard all individuals against arbitrary government through the legal guarantee of various civil rights: security of property, religious liberty and so forth. Many later liberals favoured an equal distribution of political rights in the form of a democratic franchise. In this century the intention of most liberals has been to implement an equality of social or welfare rights: universal access to a minimum standard of comfort judged essential for a truly free existence.[9] So there has been little continuity of agreement about the measures required in order to enhance liberty. Historically, nevertheless, liberalism can be viewed as a succession of strategies for expanding the freedoms to which individuals are considered to be equally entitled.

The ideology, secondly, took shape from the particular social interests to which it was attached. 'In its living principle', wrote Harold Laski, liberalism 'was the idea by which the new middle class rose to a position of political dominance.'[10] Laski's statement requires qualification in so far as Britain never experienced clear-cut conflict between an ascendant middle class and an aristocracy in decline. The transition from agrarian to industrial society was relatively undramatic because the landed classes were themselves involved in commerce and industry. It would be mistaken, therefore, to suppose that liberalism originated as pure bourgeois ideology. Initially, in fact, there were two forms of liberalism: Whiggism embraced by owners of substantial property in commerce and finance, as well as land; and a more radical doctrine, whose earliest exponents were the Levellers in the middle of the seventeenth century, that was espoused by less prosperous social groups. Neither variants of liberalism constituted a eulogy of the middle classes. Whigs argued that the economic security enjoyed by men of rank and wealth gave them an interest in social stability while affording them sufficient leisure to acquire knowledge and political experience. The rich, in consequence, were entitled to wield political power since they were most likely to safeguard liberty against either the anarchic impulses of the masses or the despotic inclinations of the Crown. Radicals, by contrast, claimed that the privileges of inherited wealth sustained an exploitative aristocracy which frustrated the rights and freedoms of common people. Although these early radicals opposed monopolies, tithes and other economic practices which inhibited the transfer of aristocratic wealth to other social groups, they were hardly the ideologues of an aspirant middle class. Their ideal, rather, was a society of masterless men – smallholders of land, self-employed craftsmen, tradesmen and so forth – based upon a widespread distribution of property: a community in which great inequalities of wealth had been eroded and where, in consequence, everyone owned enough property to be independent of the political control of any social class. Liberalism, then, did not originate as the buoyant expression of the aspirations of a confident bourgeoisie.

But perhaps Laski's own phrase – 'in its living principle' – is sufficient to qualify the claim that liberalism is grounded in middle-class interests, for the ideology did convey ideas associated with the eventual triumph of capitalism. As society evolved, liberals increasingly denigrated the landed aristocracy and extolled the virtues of the commercial and industrial classes. The middle classes, wrote James Mackintosh in 1792, had pioneered the struggle to emancipate society from traditional constraints upon individual liberty:

> The commercial, or monied interest, has in all nations of Europe (taken as a body) been less prejudiced, more liberal, and more intelligent, than the landed gentry. Their views are enlarged by a wider intercourse with mankind, and hence the important influence of commerce in liberalizing the modern world. We cannot wonder then that this enlightened class of men ever prove the most ardent in the cause of freedom, the most zealous for political reform. It is not wonderful that philosophy should find in them more docile pupils; and liberty more active friends, than in a haughty and prejudiced aristocracy.[11]

Liberals believed that enlightened reforms would encourage everyone to acquire bourgeois habits. Therein lay the key to social progress.

In suggesting that liberals favoured the dispersal of bourgeois habits, however, we need to insert a cautionary note. Liberals, in the opinion of many commentators, have continually celebrated the acquisitive values associated with the pursuit of self-interest in a competitive capitalist economy. The 'emphasis on the asocial egoism of the individual', according to Anthony Arblaster, 'plays a permanently important part in liberalism. Without taking it into account it is impossible to understand the importance which liberalism attaches to the principles of personal freedom and privacy.'[12] Now it is true that liberals have always advocated a 'free zone' of individual rights within which people have ample scope to exercise private judgement and to manage their particular economic affairs. But it does not follow, as Arblaster and others contend, that liberalism is rooted in a form of bourgeois or 'possessive' individualism which sanctions the unrestricted pursuit of private goals – especially the accumulation of property – at the expense of wider social duties. Running through liberalism, in fact, is a persistent conviction that political stability presupposes a moral community of individuals who co-operate in the pursuit of common objectives. Early radicals and Whigs, notwithstanding their differences, shared the belief that private property tends to engender in its owners the moral discipline and mutual tolerance through which a free and integrated political order is sustained. And even later liberals, who were eager to demonstrate that economic prosperity flows from the ambitions of self-seeking individuals, believed that government should attend to the cultivation of socially responsible attitudes among its citizens. In endorsing the spread of bourgeois habits throughout society, therefore, liberals have wished to promote, not the 'asocial egoism' of atomistic individuals, but the civic virtues of people conscious of their obligations within the body politic.

In order to facilitate the process of *embourgeoisement*, liberals adopted a twofold strategy which has remained a hallmark of their ideology. They sought, on one side, to undermine the power of inherited wealth derived from ownership of land. The landed aristocracy was depicted as an idle and parasitic class which reaped an unearned income from rent. Its ethos of paternalism, moreover, was said to foster in others an attitude of deference incompatible with a free and independent existence. Liberals confronted aristocratic paternalism with an alternative social ideal - a meritocratic ideal of the self-made man whose wealth and status were achieved rather than conferred by birth and who embodied the productive energy from which flowed economic prosperity. On the other side, liberals wished to make the labouring classes virtuous. In becoming thrifty, prudent and self-reliant, it was claimed, the poor could alleviate their condition, and so free themselves from dependence upon aristocratic benevolence. They would, in addition, be law-abiding citizens who had abandoned any illusion that their future lay in class warfare. Hence, again, liberals endorsed policies intended to universalize bourgeois virtues. Historically, therefore, liberalism displays hostility to the undeserved benefits of aristocratic privilege and also wishes to promote the moral elevation of the labouring classes. This persistent impulse to construct society upon a bourgeois model provides a significant clue in the search for ideological coherence.

The image that emerges from the liberal desire to make everyone bourgeois through the implementation of equal rights is of a one-class society - a one-class society in that, notwithstanding inequalities of income which reflect the diversity of individual talent and achievement, there exist common habits of self-discipline and responsible citizenship. It differs from the conservative picture of a class-structured, hierarchical community in which the majority are guided and restrained by a powerful minority; and also from the socialist dream of an eventual classless society in which all capitalist inequalities of power and wealth have been eradicated. From this image, which surfaces in the various manifestations of liberalism, the ideology derives its identity.

The implication, contrary to the judgement of some commentators, is that liberalism is neither hopelessly multifarious nor split into two irreconcilable historical phases. Polar concepts such as individualism and collectivism, or negative and positive liberty, tend to conceal the continuities between earlier and later liberalism. We have, in fact, characterized the ideology in a similar – if less glamorous – manner to that of liberals, who view their movement as a continual endeavour to create a structure of equal liberties. To acknowledge the relative coherence of liberalism, however, is not necessarily to approve either its social vision or its political programme. Both can be judged inadequate and naive from alternative ideological perspectives. Our concern is to establish the intellectual identity of liberalism rather than to sell a particular ideological message.

ORIGINS

The period known as the English revolution began with civil war from 1642 to 1646, and ended with a constitutional settlement in 1688. Conflict was initially confined to factions within the ruling class, who either supported the personal rule of Charles I or wished to check his power through Parliament. But opposition to absolute monarchy soon broadened into an attack upon the paternalist control exercised over society by both aristocracy and the bishops of the Anglican Church. Civil war released a torrent of radical ideas that challenged the traditional image of a rigid social hierarchy, in which authority was the monopoly of a privileged minority.[13] Common people, it was now said, were entitled to use their own judgement in moral and religious matters and also to be involved in the political decisions that affected them. It was within these arguments for a structure of equal rights that the outlines of liberalism took shape.

Populist thinking during the civil war was facilitated by a collapse of censorship. Alternative ideas were not only widely discussed; they were, for the first time, printed in a mass of books and pamphlets. Much of this literature affirmed the Puritan conviction that individuals could understand scripture without help from either the priests or liturgy of the established Church. The poet, John Milton, spoke with the voice of radical Protestantism when he condemned a decision which Parliament took in 1643 to re-establish licensed printing. His *Areopagitica* celebrated the self-reliance of individual conscience, as well as religious nonconformity and diversity [1.1]. Religious truths were not to be discovered through deference to authority or subordination to tradition. Instead, the meaning of Christianity emerged from an open and tolerant exchange of ideas between ordinary people, who were rational enough to form valid opinions of their own. With the abolition of tyrannical monarchy, wrote Milton, people had been invigorated by a liberal atmosphere to search for enlightenment. It was incumbent upon Parliament to sustain this novel set of civil liberties – religious freedom, freedom of expression and so forth – which gave free rein to private judgement in matters of knowledge and belief.

Milton eloquently defended particular liberties. Others, however, produced a blueprint for a comprehensive structure of both civil and political rights. The Levellers, who formed a political party in 1646, represented the 'middle sort of people' – owners of small amounts of property, such as artisans and peasant farmers. They also drew support from the badly paid ranks of Oliver Cromwell's Parliamentary army. Parliamentary supremacy, the Levellers argued, had failed to transform a social order in which wealth conferred privileges of rank and birth. The poor, in consequence, were still oppressed by laws that enabled the rich to exact heavy taxes and rents, to inhibit fair economic competition, and to intimidate the exploited through a harsh criminal code. To explain why people endured unequal rights, the Levellers resorted to the theory of the Norman Yoke. William the Conqueror, it was alleged, had destroyed Anglo-Saxon liberties when he portioned the land amongst his nobility. Subsequent laws and customs had perpetuated the original theft of 1066 through a system of hereditary privilege. The time was ripe, however, for Englishmen to assert their birthright by liberating themselves from the shackles of history. This required the elimination of social and economic grievances by means of sweeping constitutional reforms.

The Leveller programme was designed to sever the link between aristocratic wealth and political power. *An agreement of the free people of England*, in consequence, urged three major sorts of reform to distribute authority among the common people [1.2]. It called, first, for a representative government in which monarchy and Lords were abolished and where supreme authority resided in a Parliament elected annually from a much wider electorate than had hitherto existed. Here, then, was a demand for a rough equality of political rights: rough because the Levellers wished to exclude from the franchise groups which they considered too economically dependent to exercise political judgement – women, servants, debtors and the unemployed. The Levellers appear to have made ownership of property, however small the amount, a criterion of political participation for two reasons: in part because it safeguarded electors against corrupting aristocratic influence; but also because economic independence bestowed a sense of personal autonomy from which was likely to flow the exercise of public virtue. Their proposed representative assembly was to have power to remove all the abuses of aristocratic privilege. It was, nevertheless, to possess only a limited authority that did not encroach upon religious worship and other issues of individual judgement. Hence, secondly, the Levellers demanded a constitutional guarantee of fully equal civil rights. Finally, their programme advocated a devolution of authority to local communities. Each parish, for example, was to have the right to elect its own minister; and legal trials were to be conducted entirely in the vernacular, rather than the customary mixture of English and Latin, with juries freely chosen by the people.

Some socialists, as well as liberals, count the Levellers amongst their ideological ancestors.[14] Yet they did not espouse the socialist ideal of common ownership of wealth. Their proposed Parliament was not intended to 'level mens Estates, destroy Propriety, or make all things Common' [1.2]. They were, nevertheless, opposed to vast inequalities of wealth and believed that the elimination of arbitrary power would enable more individuals to own property. Once people were released from dependence upon aristocratic paternalism, it was hoped, they would also acquire the virtues associated with economic self-reliance. The Leveller ideal was a society of free and independent citizens in which traditional distinctions between rulers and ruled had dissolved. It is this vision which, notwithstanding the failure of their programme, places the Levellers amongst the earliest liberals.

Radical aspirations were curbed even before the restoration of monarchy in 1660, which was accompanied by a reassertion of royal absolutism and Anglican orthodoxy. Hostility to authoritarianism in both State and Church converged in efforts made between 1679 and 1683 to exclude the future James II, a declared Catholic, from the English throne. This opposition marked the birth as a political group of the Whigs, foremost among whom was John Locke. Locke, who is often regarded as the father of liberalism, recounted some of the arguments that had been made against arbitrary power in the 1640s. His *Letter concerning toleration*, written in exile after the failure to exclude James, condemned the political enforcement of religious conformity [1.3]. Salvation, argued Locke, was a matter for individual conscience and people were entitled to their beliefs as equal members of society. Government, therefore, had no business to meddle in affairs of the soul. It should attend to civil interests, such as protection of life and property and not trespass upon that zone of private existence in which individual judgement was properly sovereign. This called for a policy of toleration rather than the arbitrary imposition of a State religion. Before he left England, however, Locke had probably already written the bulk of his most celebrated work, the *Two treatises of government*, which asserted a right of resistance to arbitrary power. If individuals were responsible for their own salvation, Locke believed, they were also competent to exercise political judgement. In the second *Treatise*, consequently, he sought to illustrate how legitimate government was grounded in the consent of those to whom its authority extended [1.4]. Here Locke made more explicit an idea that had also appeared in Leveller writings – the belief that God had equally endowed individuals with certain inalienable rights and had also given them reason to judge when these rights were infringed. In order to explain the idea, Locke postulated a natural condition in which individuals enjoyed the rights of life, liberty and property without political assistance. The state of nature, however, was unstable because each person was entitled to preserve his rights against encroachment by others. Government emerged when people agreed to resign to a central authority this power to judge in their disputes with one another.

Political authority, then, was based upon a trust or contract and its exercise was conditional upon the protection of natural rights. It existed to give people security as they pursued their private concerns. This required the executive, or Crown, to share power with a legislative assembly which represented the interests of the community. Arbitrary action by any part of government meant that it had broken its trust and had ceased to be an 'umpire' which impartially safeguarded inalienable human rights. It could then be overthrown and its authority returned to the 'body of the people' from whence it originated. From assumed equal rights, therefore, Locke had made a case for limited and accountable government which excluded absolute monarchy.

Locke was not a democrat and favoured a more restricted franchise than the Levellers advocated. He also said that the chief task of government was to preserve the rights of 'property' – though he used the word in a now unfamiliar sense, to include life and liberty as well as material possessions. This has persuaded some commentators to dub Locke a bourgeois ideologue whose primary concern was to uphold the interests of the propertied classes against arbitrary monarchy. His defence of equal rights, on this assessment, was little more than a subtle device to camouflage a structure of economic inequality in which political power was concentrated in the hands of the rich.[15] This interpretation is open to dispute. Incontestable, however, is the fact that even Locke was too radical for some subsequent liberals. The rhetoric of natural rights appealed to people in the eighteenth century who agitated, as the Levellers had done, for various constitutional reforms. For others, however, the suggestion that human beings were naturally free and equal contained dangerous political implications. The turmoil of the seventeenth century ended with the Glorious Revolution of 1688, which deposed James and limited the authority of monarchy through Parliament. The Whigs, who had engineered this destruction of arbitrary power, now began to undermine the egalitarian assumptions of Lockean political theory. They avoided the language of natural rights, and sought to sterilize the alleged right to resist tyrannical power. They produced, in consequence, a liberal justification of the State that suited the interests of the propertied classes in a more politically stable age.

Later liberals, then, inherited an ambivalent legacy from the seventeenth century. Some found in the arguments of the English revolution inspiration to continue the struggle for individual emancipation from existing social constraints; whereas others discovered a defence of parliamentary government that could be used in a post-revolutionary world to resist demands for further reform.

THE WHIGS

Even during the Glorious Revolution Whigs eschewed the doctrine of natural rights, which seemed to give power to the people in times of constitutional deadlock. They defended the deposition of James with historical, rather than abstract, arguments. By his arbitrary behaviour, it was alleged, James had broken his coronation oath which confirmed the limited authority of monarchy. Parliament, therefore, had invited William and Mary to occupy the throne in order to repair a temporary breach in England's ancient constitution. In so far as the events of 1688 occurred without extra-parliamentary activity, according to Whigs, they entailed neither a dissolution of government nor the exercise of political rights by the masses. The orthodox view of the Revolution – as the outcome of parliamentary supremacy rather than of popular sovereignty – was stated over a century later by Lord Erskine:

> Our ancestors, at that period, were well aware of the full right of the people, to have re-settled the whole frame of their Constitution, but they were wise enough to leave everything untouched, which, in principle and effect had not failed, and to provide only for the emergency of a vacant, or forfeited throne, by adhering as closely to ancient inheritance as the security of the Constitution would admit ... The people at large were not called upon to act for themselves, as if the whole frame of the ancient Government had been dissolved; but writs were sent to the Convention Parliament to supply the *single defect which had taken place*. In this manner, England preserved all the

ancient treasures of her freedom: her Laws and Constitution continued unshaken, whilst a principle of mutual obligation was solemnly established between the title of the sovereign and the stipulated rights of the people. This Revolution was, happily, not effected by an indignant and enraged multitude, but was slowly prepared by the most virtuous and best informed amongst the higher and enlightened classes of the people, who took prudent and effectual steps for securing its success without bloodshed; being confident of the support of a vast majority of the people: of all, indeed, who loved freedom and detested arbitrary power.[16]

English liberty had been secured against the threat of tyranny, then, because a propertied minority had acted on behalf of the nation. In this way Whigs could claim to be heirs of the Glorious Revolution without having to embrace the principles of democracy, which they equated with rule by the mob or rabble. For them, as Erskine indicated, the conduct of government was best left to an economically secure and leisured class: men of rank and fortune whose opportunity to seek enlightenment and to cultivate political virtue endowed them with a unique capacity to defend liberty.

Whigs in the early eighteenth century continued to condemn the extreme Tory belief that absolute monarchy was ordained by God, and also to support religious toleration. They were more anxious, however, to distance themselves from the radicalism of the previous century which attacked the power of inherited wealth and sought to extend popular rights.[17] The Glorious Revolution had ensured the Whigs a secure existence and under the leadership of Robert Walpole in the 1720s and 1730s they enjoyed a monopoly of political power. Landed and commercial interests now gained from an oligarchical political system that was held together by a web of patronage. Whiggism, therefore, ceased to be an oppositional ideology. It was transformed instead into a vindication of the established political order which sustained, in Professor Plumb's words, 'a paradise for gentlemen'.[18]

This ideological shift is apparent in the novel meaning assigned to the word liberty. The term was no longer used, as it had been in the seventeenth century, to urge the implementation of particular civil and political rights. It was now given a less precise connotation and equated with the political *status quo*. The English constitution, it was said, secured an ordered liberty by erecting a bulwark against both arbitrary power and anarchy. This balance was preserved by means of a mixed government in which King, Lords and Commons checked one another through their overlapping powers. Some Whigs now abandoned the claim that freedom had always been protected by the ancient constitution. Lord Hervey, a beneficiary of Walpolean patronage, argued that the Glorious Revolution heralded the dawn of real liberty in England. Magna Carta, according to his *Ancient and modern liberty stated and compar'd*, had failed to delineate the precise prerogatives and rights enjoyed by King and people in the mixed government [2.1]. Hence the political turmoil of the preceding century. But all had been resolved by the Bill of Rights. Even the residual right of popular resistance to tyranny was redundant, Hervey intimated, in a constitutional scheme which precluded every abuse of power.

Post-revolutionary Whiggism had side-stepped the Lockean theory of natural rights. In the second half of the eighteenth century, however, Whigs launched an explicit attack upon Locke. The offensive was in response to radicals, considered in the next section, who used Locke to demand an extension of political and civil rights – to be implemented by means of a wider franchise and by the disestablishment of the Church of England rather than the mere toleration of dissent. In *Four letters on important national subjects, addressed to the right honourable the Earl of Shelburne* (1783), Josiah Tucker dubbed Locke 'the Idol of the Levellers of *England*'. But the giddy multitude, which appeared in Lockean theory to be endowed with democratic rights, was not competent to exercise political power. Hence the need to restrict the franchise to the propertied classes and also to resist radical demands to dismantle the system of mixed government in which aristocratic privilege was crucial to the preservation of balance [2.2].

This defence of the power of inherited wealth was a world removed from the Leveller assault upon every form of customary privilege. The Whig defence of limited government and religious toleration provided a link, however tenuous, with earlier liberal themes. Yet the liberal kernel of aristocratic Whiggism was contained within a distinctly conservative shell. Indeed, there is a point at which Whiggism loses contact with its liberal heritage and is more properly labelled conservatism. It was a Whig, Edmund Burke, whose eloquent vindication of the established order has since earned him the sobriquet 'father' of British conservatism. His *Reflections on the revolution in France* (1790) repudiated the doctrine of natural rights, with its suggestion that common people were entitled to exercise political judgement. The outcome was a justification of traditional social hierarchy which firmly tied power to wealth.

There were nevertheless echoes of seventeenth-century liberalism in the plea which some Whigs made on behalf of civil liberties. Charles

James Fox, unlike Burke, gave qualified approval to the French revolutionaries. He also opposed those panic measures of the British government that were intended to stem the spread of republicanism at home. In a parliamentary speech delivered in 1792, therefore, he championed the rights of free speech and assembly, as well as religious dissent [2.3]. Fox suggested that discontent could be legitimately subdued only by an extension, rather than a contraction, of popular rights: by repeal of the Test and Corporation Acts which infringed the principle of religious toleration; by an improvement of the franchise; and by removal of other customary obstacles to individual freedom. So the heirs of the Glorious Revolution did not invariably uphold the political establishment. Their opposition to arbitrary power sometimes persuaded them to advocate a more equal structure of individual rights.

If Whigs endorsed equal civil rights, they still resisted an equality of political rights in the form of a democratic franchise. The self-image of Whigs as watchdogs of the constitution shaped their approach to parliamentary reform at the beginning of the nineteenth century. Various attempts to broaden the franchise, as well as to improve urban representation in the House of Commons, culminated in the 1832 Reform Act which incorporated the middle classes into the political nation. Whigs supported moderate reform in the belief that it was their task to steer a middle course between reactionary Tories and doctrinaire radicals. But this *via media*, which was intended to preserve the ordered liberty of the constitution, avoided democratic principles.

Lord John Russell spearheaded the reform movement, and subsequently led the Whig Party. Writing in the preface to a new edition of his *Essay on the history of the English government and constitution*, published in 1865, Russell explained his antipathy to universal suffrage forty years earlier [2.4]. He dismissed the radical claim that political rights could be deduced from an assumed equality of inalienable natural rights. The vote was a privilege to be enjoyed only by people with sufficient political wisdom to contribute to the national interest. The propertyless masses, judged by this criterion, were politically incompetent. Apart from their relative lack of education, the poor were likely to favour rash policies ultimately destructive of ordered liberty. Unequal political rights, therefore, fairly and necessarily reflected wider social and economic inequalities. Wise government, in this view, depended upon a propertied franchise that was exercised within a constitution designed to temper the passions of the lower orders.

This objection to democracy as an unstable form of government stemmed from the assumption that society was composed of various groups, each with its particular interests, rather than of individuals who were entitled to equal political rights. The landed and middle classes deserved the vote because their immediate interests coincided with the common good. But the poor, whose inclination was to confiscate the riches of the upper classes, pursued short-term policies inimical to the public interest. They failed to perceive that a system of private property was ultimately beneficial to all social classes and so were incompetent to participate in politics. Thomas Babington Macaulay, the great Whig historian, supported the admission of the middle classes to the franchise on the ground that, unlike the poor, they had demonstrated their political maturity. In an essay written in 1828 about another historian, Henry Hallam, Macaulay looked forward to an alliance between landed and commercial classes [2.5]. Without such an alliance, he believed, the country might be driven by revolutionary fervour into a crisis similar to that experienced in the seventeenth century. Hence the need for a judicious reformation of the electoral system in order to forestall constitutional subversion. Here was the Whig view of history in essence – the belief that constitutional equilibrium was perpetuated by periodic, yet cautious and pragmatic, renovation. It was not the task of statesmen to steer society towards some imaginary paradise; but rather to avoid political storms and thereby ensure a tranquil passage for the ship of State.

Macaulay's anticipated alliance between landed and commercial interests neither stifled pressure for a more democratic franchise, nor prevented the eventual 'passing of the Whigs' from the political stage.[19] Although the Liberal Party was not formally inaugurated until 1859, it took shape from the 1830s as an uneasy coalition of Whigs and Radicals. The emerging party provided an uncomfortable abode for aristocratic Whiggism. If Whigs endorsed the enfranchisement of the middle classes, they nevertheless clung to the ideal of a hierarchical society which secured them a natural function within the ruling elite. But their coalition partners – many of whom were beneficiaries of new forms of commercial and manufacturing capital – wished to purge society of every form of customary privilege and patronage associated with the ownership of land. To a much greater extent than the Whig grandees, therefore, Radicals were inclined to construct a popular party around social reforms designed to release the potential of everyone to lead a self-reliant and independent existence. The Whigs finally left the coalition in 1886 over the issue of Irish Home Rule. Now began the long process by which Whigs flowed into the

Conservative Party where their ideological peculiarities were submerged in a general justification of the interests of the propertied classes. It, rather than the Liberal Party, was to survive as the dominant voice of the alliance favoured by Macaulay. The heirs of the Glorious Revolution, in consequence, faded into obscurity two centuries after the event which had tossed them into the centre of politics.

FROM NATURAL TO DEMOCRATIC RIGHTS

Whereas mainstream Whigs retreated from the radicalism of the seventeenth century, others still derived inspiration from the 'Good Old Cause' against arbitrary power.[20] The heroes of these radical Whigs were men like John Milton and Algernon Sidney, who was executed in 1683 for plotting, as Locke had done, against tyrannical monarchy. The Glorious Revolution, they believed, had only partially curbed executive power and had also failed to consolidate individual rights. So they continued to assert a right of popular resistance to tyranny, as well as to oppose such threats to individual liberty as a standing army and the hierarchical authority of the Church of England. And, like Locke, they anchored their theory of limited and accountable government in inalienable natural rights.

The thrust of radical Whiggism is conveyed in a series of letters, written by John Trenchard and Thomas Gordon. *Cato's letters*, named after an opponent of Julius Caesar, opened with an assault upon the financial corruption of the Whig ascendancy during the early years of Walpole's leadership. But the authors quickly moved to broader themes [3.1]. Arguing from contractual premises, they based legitimate government on the protection of natural rights. This required stringent restraints upon the exercise of power, as well as maximum opportunity for individuals to shape their beliefs and conduct in peace and security.

Besides endorsing limited government and extensive civil liberties, Trenchard and Gordon regenerated the social ideal which had surfaced in Leveller writings – the image of a community of masterless and self-governing citizens. We have seen how aristocratic Whigs, though opposed to arbitrary power, clung to the traditional conception of a social hierarchy in which the propertied classes exercised tutelage over the lower orders. These custodial beliefs, which served to transform much of establishment Whiggism into conservatism in a liberal guise, were rejected by Trenchard and Gordon. Distinctions of rank and prestige, they argued, sprang from accidents of 'blood' or birth and inhibited the potential of everyone to attain virtue and to achieve economic independence. Vast concentrations of wealth, moreover, nurtured arbitrary power. Hence, where inequalities were so great as to impair liberty, government could ensure a more equitable distribution of wealth by means of an agrarian law. Both political stability and economic prosperity resulted from an impartial system of justice, they suggested, because free people were motivated to be industrious in an atmosphere of mutual respect. Individuals, once guaranteed moral and economic self-reliance through a structure of equal rights, were naturally disposed to be model citizens who pursued their private interests in harmony with the public good. Civil liberties, then, provided the bedrock of civic virtue. This ideal of a community of morally autonomous and politically responsible citizens had given ideological shape to the Leveller condemnation of hereditary privilege. Now revived in opposition to the rank commercialism of Walpolean Whiggism, it was to be a recurrent theme within later liberalism.

The radicalism of Trenchard and Gordon was not unbounded. Although hostile to the corruption of centralized executive power, they believed that its antidote lay in a mixed government which excluded the propertyless from the franchise. It was to be some time before radical liberals embraced democratic principles. Even religious dissenters, whom Josiah Tucker castigated for adopting Lockean premises [2.2], did not initially advocate universal male suffrage. For dissenters, who were victims of the Test and Corporation Acts against which Fox campaigned [2.3], a State religion violated the sovereignty of private judgement in matters of belief. It was the business of government, proclaimed Richard Price, 'to defend the *properties* of men, not to take care of their *souls* – And to protect *equally* all honest citizens of all persuasions, not to set up one religious sect above another.'[21] This opposition to the privileged position of the Church of England moulded radical Whiggism after 1750. In order to promote their ideal of voluntary and equal sects, the dissenters included religious freedom among the natural rights that should be preserved within a structure of civil liberties. In using contractual arguments, however, they were careful to distinguish civil from political liberties.

The distinction was made clear by Joseph Priestley in *An essay on the first principles of government*, published in 1768 [3.2]. Government, wrote Priestley, was intended to safeguard those individual rights which remained precarious in a state of nature. Hence the need for limited government which enshrined natural rights in an impartial system of civil liberties. Political liberties, by contrast, included the rights to stand for public office and to choose representatives. These, unlike civil liberties, could legitimately vary between nations. Perhaps only the wealthy should be eligible for important political posts, suggested Priestley, in an argument that echoed aristocratic Whiggism, because their education and economic security made them less likely than the poor to enact rash policies. He also believed, like the Levellers, that economic independence was an appropriate criterion of admission to the franchise. Yet, while not disposed towards fully equal political rights, Priestley conceded that the poor might participate in the election of humble public officials. He also acknowledged that civil and political liberties, though distinct, were mutually supportive. Their enjoyment served to foster in people a spirit of self-government – what Priestley described as 'a free, bold, and manly turn of thinking, unrestrained by the most distant idea of control'. Here was an argument that could be used to endorse equal political rights on the ground of their educative function. It was not long, in fact, before reformers urged a democratic franchise as a means of engendering civic virtue amongst the poor.

The demand for reform initially focused on support for American independence, which prompted opponents of colonialism to review the English constitution. But the clamour for political reconstruction reached a crescendo with the French Revolution of 1789, which provoked an upsurge of popular radicalism in Britain.[22] Thomas Paine, an active participant in both the American and French Revolutions, was the foremost publicist of late eighteenth-century radicalism. His widely read *Rights of man: being an answer to Mr Burke's attack on the French revolution* exploited the revolutionary potential of Lockean natural rights in order to advocate the establishment of a British democratic republic. Locke's contractual account of the origins of government had permitted the people to intervene in the political process only as a final resort against tyranny. Popular sovereignty for Locke did not imply that common people should be continually involved in public affairs through the exercise of democratic rights. Paine, by contrast, not only sanctioned a right of popular resistance to arbitrary power. He used contractual arguments to demand a renewal of the British political system on democratic principles.

British government, claimed Paine, was illegitimate because it had not emerged from an agreement among people to safeguard their natural rights through an appropriate polity [3.3]. It had arisen by conquest rather than consent, and had never been fundamentally revised since 1066. In referring to the Norman Yoke, as the Levellers had done, Paine could reject the Whig belief that liberty had been either restored or established in England by the Glorious Revolution. Whereas Trenchard, Gordon and Priestley had wished to preserve the outlines of the balanced constitution, he dismissed mixed government as a buttress of hereditary privilege and corruption. The British political system was designed to ensure the subordination of the majority to the propertied classes and was therefore incompatible with natural freedom and equality. It was now time for people to emancipate themselves from the inherited power of monarchy and aristocracy by constructing a constitution based upon their consent. This required sovereignty to be lodged in a representative assembly elected by manhood suffrage. People had to be involved in the decisions that jointly affected them, as well as to exercise private judgement in matters of individual belief and conduct, if they were to enjoy the rights to which they were naturally entitled. Paine's extension of the principles of self-government to the sphere of political – as well as civil – rights amounted to the fiercest rebuttal which aristocratic Whiggism had yet received.

Britain did not become a democratic republic modelled upon the rights of man. But the demand for democratic reform continued and was intensified by the failure of the 1832 Reform Act to extend the franchise to the working class. Religious dissenters were among the advocates of reform, as in the eighteenth century, and some of them based their case for manhood suffrage upon natural rights. Although the repeal of the Test and Corporation Acts in 1828 had removed the Anglican monopoly on many public offices, dissenters continued to suffer various disabilities. There emerged, in consequence, a form of radical Nonconformity that became both a focus of pressure for social reform and an important component of nineteenth-century liberalism. The outmoded privileges of the State Church, middle-class Nonconformists claimed, were part of a nexus of power and patronage which signified the social dominance of the landed interest. They therefore sought allies among the lower classes in an effort to build a common front against the Tory–Anglican Establishment. Such an alliance, Nonconformists believed, could be forged around the issue of the franchise. The *Nonconformist* weekly newspaper, founded in 1841 by the Reverend Edward Miall, mounted a campaign to disestablish and disendow the Church of England. This demand for religious equality was linked with support for an equality of political rights. The *Reconciliation between the middle and labouring classes*, which consisted of articles originally published in the *Nonconformist*, argued from contractual premises that men reserved a right to control the activities of government [3.4]. This required an equality of political participation through the ballot box. It was conceded, as the Levellers had done, that pauperism could be used as a test of political incompetence. It was nevertheless illegitimate to curtail the natural right of common labouring men to exercise the vote. Once admitted to the franchise, moreover, working men would acquire civic virtue. No longer inhibited by attitudes of deference and subordination, they would recognize that their future lay in moral and educational self-improvement rather than revolutionary activity. If Macaulay had anticipated an alliance between landed and commercial interests [2.5], it was now said that the key to social progress lay in a reconciliation between middle and working classes.

A democratic franchise, in Miall's opinion, was required on the ground of natural right and also because of its educative function for the masses. Many liberals, however, had begun to abandon contractual arguments. Some endorsed democracy as a device to safeguard individual interests; whereas others, like Miall, saw it as a means of disseminating that common morality of self-reliance and mutual respect considered essential for political stability. Few now resorted to the doctrine of natural rights which had shaped so much of radical liberalism since the time of Locke.

THE AGE OF *LAISSEZ-FAIRE*

An '*Englishman*, notwithstanding his boasted Liberty is, in regard to Commerce, still NOT FREE', proclaimed Josiah Tucker in *The elements of commerce and the theory of taxes* (1755). 'For he is still in Bondage, not to the Crown indeed, as formerly, but to his Fellow-Subjects; and we still want the GLORIOUS REVOLUTION in the Commercial System, which we have happily obtained in the Political.' The Leveller condemnation of hereditary privilege and economic monopolies had initiated a persistent strand of opposition to protectionist policies that gave unfair commercial advantage to a minority. An extension of opportunities for individuals to acquire wealth, ran the argument, would cultivate that spirit of civic responsibility associated with economic independence. By the time Tucker wrote his *Elements*, this demand for an equality of economic rights was directed against a mercantile system which attempted to balance trade by means of controls upon imports and exports, especially with regard to grain. Systematic arguments now began to unfold on behalf of a free-market economy unhampered by political intervention. The effect of this new science of political economy was to reinforce the liberal defence of limited government which preserved individual rights and liberties through the impartial provision of peace and security.

The most famous exponent of economic liberalism was a Scot, Adam Smith. He denounced mercantilism as both unjust and inefficient: unjust because it secured the interests of merchants and landed groups at the expense of other social ranks; and inefficient because it hindered economic growth. Once government refrained from meddling in commerce, Smith believed, everyone would be prompted to pursue their particular interests to a maximum extent. So much general prosperity would ensue that even the poor might benefit from unprecedented 'opulence'. In his *Wealth of nations*, published in 1776, Smith made a case for a minimal state whose business was neither to manage the economy nor to redistribute resources to the poor according to some criterion of public welfare. Its function, rather, was to sustain a free market in labour and commodities. This entailed a 'system of natural liberty', in which the primary responsibility of government was to safeguard its citizens against both internal and external aggression.

Smith is today regarded as the apostle of *laissez-faire* or self-regulating capitalism, and his authority is evoked by modern conservatives who wish to roll back the State from the economy. Despite his advocacy of unbridled commercialism, however, Smith was not hostile to government as such. He was one of several thinkers, writing at the time of the Scottish Enlightenment, who believed that social progress required wise statesmanship. Only if government promoted civic virtue, Smith believed, could the advantages of free enterprise be secured. Economic expansion entailed an elaborate division of labour which confined the bulk of the community to trivial occupational tasks. The effect was to undermine both individual responsibility and political stability. Common people, morally and intellectually enervated by monotonous work, were unlikely to acquire those habits of self-reliance and prudence which provided a safeguard against social conflict and fanciful political schemes. It was the responsibility of government, therefore, to combat these negative aspects of commercial activity. In particular, Smith included in the 'system of natural liberty' public provision of elementary education for the lower orders. Only if people were encouraged to be 'decent and orderly', he claimed, could the benefits of a free-market economy be enjoyed [4.1].

For some economic writers, the *embourgeoisement* of the lower ranks offered the only prospect of preserving that ordered liberty which Whigs acclaimed as the glory of the balanced constitution. This was an argument advanced by the Reverend Thomas Robert Malthus, the first British professor of political economy, in his *Essay on the principle of population*, originally published in 1798. Poverty, he argued, could tilt the constitution towards both anarchy and arbitrary power. It prompted the distressed to engage in insurrection, especially when they were deceived by such inflammatory writings as Paine's *Rights of man* into supposing that their condition was due entirely to oppressive government. This in turn gave the propertied classes a pretext to indulge in executive tyranny, thereby 'sacrificing the liberties of the subject on the altar of public safety'.

Malthus approved of Smith's proposal for a national system of education on the ground that enlightened people were unlikely to be swayed by wild political ideas. Once taught to be self-reliant, moreover, the lower classes could free themselves from the degradation of poverty. Pauperism, he suggested, stemmed from over-population which flooded the market with a superabundance of labour. It could be eliminated if the population expanded at a rate no faster than that of the economy. Hence the need for common people to exercise moral restraint and foresight and thereby postpone marriage until they could afford to support a family. In the labourer's capacity to acquire bourgeois habits, therefore, lay the prospect of greater prosperity and political equilibrium [4.2].

This message of self-help to the poor was proclaimed with fervour by nineteenth-century liberals. It held a particular attraction for the middle-class evangelical conscience. We have seen how religious dissenters advocated democracy as a stimulus to the moral elevation of the labouring classes. Political economy, too, was given a Christian gloss by the same optimistic belief in the capacity of ordinary people for self-improvement. Thomas Chalmers, a Presbyterian minister who became professor of theology at Edinburgh, was an enthusiastic Malthusian who believed that popular education could sustain indefinite social progress. Only when the masses were enlightened, he wrote in *The right christian and civic economy for a nation*, would they harvest the fruits of a commercial system which operated according to the 'unfettered principles of nature'.[23] Once the lower ranks acquired habits of sobriety and restraint, especially with regard to the size of their families, they would enjoy higher wages, greater leisure, and a generally civilized life-style. It was the particular responsibility of Christian ministers, he suggested in *The supreme importance of a right moral to a right economical state of the community*, to enable this paradise to unfold by providing a parochial scheme of education. Christian political economy, as depicted by Chalmers, appeared as a theodicy – the source of enlightened opinion through which citizens could co-operate with a benevolent divine mission [4.3]. A great deal of nineteenth-century liberalism was framed by this sort of theological optimism. In English Nonconformity, as well as Scottish Presbyterianism, individuals were accorded active responsibility for attaining salvation. Hence the appeal of a political doctrine in which the good life on earth was conceived as a reward for the exercise of moral self-discipline.

Many liberals without firm religious convictions also believed that a widespread 'spirit of independence', as Malthus put it, would serve to release the full potential of a free-enterprise economy. This belief inspired the creation of numerous organizations intended to instil in the working class both a thirst for edifying knowledge and a capacity for prudent economic management – institutions like the Society for the Diffusion of Useful Knowledge, the National Association for Promoting the Political and Social Improvement of the People, Mechanics Institutes, Public Libraries, Mutual Improvement Societies, Friendly Benefit Societies, and Savings Banks. The creed of *Self-help* – the title of an immensely popular book by Samuel Smiles, published in 1859 – would not have made such an impact upon Victorian society had it served merely as an ideological justification for the entrepreneurial success of a few capitalists. Self-improvement was a key component of radical liberalism for two reasons: in part because individual effort and self-discipline held the prospect of better living conditions for the mass of people; and also because the spread of bourgeois habits, it seemed, would remove those barriers between working and middle classes which inhibited the formation of a common front against aristocratic power and privilege.

These assumptions underpinned the Manchester School of economic liberalism, whose members spearheaded a free-trade movement which culminated in 1846 with the repeal of the Corn Laws. The leaders of the Anti-Corn Law League, formed in 1839, were two textile manufacturers who became Radical Members of Parliament – Richard Cobden and John Bright.[24] They objected to commercial monopolies, as Smith had done, on grounds of injustice and inefficiency. Protective tariffs on the import of grain, they claimed, inflated domestic bread prices and were, in consequence, an illegitimate tax on the poor for the benefit of a landed minority. Protectionism also inhibited economic growth. Once corn prices were fixed by the natural laws of supply and demand rather than by government, argued Cobden, both production and consumption would increase. More British commodities would be needed to exchange for imported grain; and at the same time the impact on the domestic labour market would result in higher wages, with which ordinary people could purchase a plentiful supply of food [4.4]. Only within the framework of a free market, then, might the labouring classes attain economic independence.

The campaign for free trade was linked with other familiar liberal themes. Cobden and Bright urged an extension of the franchise to every householder, as well as the introduction of a national scheme of education, as means of consolidating habits of self-government among the lower classes. In addition, they shaped political economy into an assault upon aristocratic privilege. They did not share Malthus' Whiggish enthusiasm for the balanced constitution in which the power of inherited wealth was preserved. The Glorious Revolution was described by Bright, in words that echoed Paine [3.3], as incomplete because it had secured the 'enthronisation of the great Norman territorial families', who proceeded to use their usurped power to unfair commercial advantage. It was the support given by landed classes to economic protectionism which now obstructed the progressive spirit of the age. The time was ripe, however, to remove these customary obstacles to the growth of commerce and industry.

The Anti-Corn Law League was intended to forge an alliance between middle and working classes in opposition to aristocratic privilege. Once the Corn Laws were repealed Cobden and Bright channelled their hostility to landed wealth into a condemnation of British foreign policy. Much of the initial opposition to mercantilism had concentrated upon the evils of colonialism. Adam Smith, for instance, linked his arguments for free trade with an attack upon the meddlesome commercial activities of the British East India Company. Other liberals, while advocating colonial emancipation, nevertheless believed that the possession of an empire gave Britain an opportunity to export enlightened reforms to India and elsewhere.[25] Their vision was of a global order of rationally administered states, each integrated by means of habits of self-reliance and independence throughout the native population. For Cobden and Bright, however, this dream could not be fulfilled until dynastic empires had been dismantled and the world transformed, in consequence, into a collection of self-governing nations.

Military conquest and colonial expansion, argued Bright, were a legacy of aristocratic ascendancy. The landed oligarchy, on the pretext of preserving an international balance of power, had, since the Glorious Revolution, initiated a succession of wars which burdened the nation with high rates of taxation. Their wealth and power had increased, in consequence, at the expense of other social classes [4.5]. With the introduction of free trade and the diminution of hereditary privilege, however, lay the prospect of international peace. The principles of political economy, once universally adopted, would not merely trigger national regeneration: they would also sustain a moral order between nations now united by economic reciprocity [4.6].

This belief in unimpeded economic exchange between peaceful nations supplied much of the ideological cement for binding the diverse groups which formed the Liberal Party in 1859. W. E. Gladstone used various tactics to unify the party which he led between 1868 and 1894. He consolidated Nonconformist support, for example, by disestablishing the Irish Church and eliminating some of the remaining privileges of the Church of England. Yet free trade was his most persistent theme. He firmly linked the economic case against protectionist tariffs with the liberal ideal of a society of autonomous citizens who were equal in their possession of basic rights [4.7]. By the end of the century, however, doubt had been cast on the efficacy of a *laissez-faire* economy. From now on, we shall see, most liberals wanted government to assume more active management of economic and social affairs.

UTILITARIANISM

If political economists reinforced the liberal defence of limited government, they nevertheless dislodged one of its original foundations. The State was depicted by economic liberals as a utilitarian device for safeguarding the particular interests of its members. In the doctrine of natural rights, too, government was called upon to provide impartial protection for all citizens. As Joseph Priestley put it: 'the good and happiness of the members, that is the majority of the members of any state, is the great standard by which every thing relating to that state must finally be determined' [3.2]. With the emergence of political economy, however, some writers extracted this pragmatic conception of government from its metaphysical shell of inalienable human rights. They now said simply that everyone had an equal interest in their own welfare, which meant that government had a duty to promote the greatest happiness of the greatest number. They added, however, that the language of natural rights should be discarded because it hindered the formulation of systematic policies in pursuit of this objective. These writers had learned from political economy that government should attend to the framework of security within which economic exchange occurred.

Only within a political order made stable by widespread habits of self-reliance, ran the argument, could the potential benefits of a free-market economy be delivered. The economic science of wealth, then, required obstetric assistance from a political science of happiness. The group of thinkers who sought to equip the age of *laissez-faire* with this science of political midwifery are known as utilitarians, foremost among whom was Jeremy Bentham.

Benthamite utilitarianism provided an impetus to social reform because it rejected historical experience as a measure of current political practice. The balanced constitution, in the orthodox Whig account, had withstood the test of time. It bore the weight of tradition and was, in consequence, an integral feature of an evolving social organism which gave shape and significance to the lives of individuals. Hence the need for gradual constitutional change and for members of the community to fulfil their various responsibilities within an intricate social hierarchy. Bentham, who believed that this tendency to genuflect towards the historical past resulted in antiquated and inefficient government, confronted Whiggism with a mechanistic conception of society as a collection of individuals, each of whom was motivated by similar desires. He intended utilitarianism to yield a deductive science of legislation, as certain as the laws of geometry, that would secure those individual interests with which everyone was equally concerned.

In his first published work, *A Fragment on Government* (1776), Bentham suggested that 'the indestructible prerogatives of mankind have no need to be supported upon the sandy foundation of a fiction'.[26] The fiction he had in mind was the Whig concept of an original contract, by which the coronation oath was supposed to symbolize an historical pact between King and community to respect constitutional privileges and rights. This idea, which surfaced during the Glorious Revolution, was part of the traditional defence of mixed government. But Bentham was no more sympathetic to the radical language of natural rights, which he later ridiculed, in *Anarchical fallacies* (1795), as 'rhetorical nonsense, – nonsense upon stilts'.[27] Government entailed some measure of coercion and it was therefore misleading to deduce political principles from an imaginary condition of natural freedom and equality. There was a need, instead, for a clear understanding of the particular rights which government should establish in order to confer benefits upon every citizen.

Elsewhere Bentham proposed the principle of utility as a scientific alternative to the 'sandy foundation' of government upon the fictions of an original contract and natural rights. The sole purpose of government was to promote a maximum of happiness throughout society. This was because human beings invariably pursued private well-being. But sometimes, through insufficient information or poor judgement, they suffered pain by miscalculating the consequences of their actions. It was the function of government, therefore, to assist the rational calculation of self-interest. This entailed a structure of rights and obligations through which individuals could shape their conduct without the pain of uncertainty and disappointment.

To clarify the proper scope of political activity, Bentham divided it into four categories [5.1]. Government's primary responsibility was to sustain individual initiative by securing the rights of private property. It ought, secondly, to favour equality because a more even spread of wealth would increase the total stock of happiness in society. But the overriding goal of security, Bentham argued, restricted what government could do in this area. Egalitarian measures, therefore, ought to be confined to taxes on the estates of dead people, who could no longer feel the pain of disappointment. In any case, he believed, the natural progress of a free-market society would steadily erode the vast inequalities characteristic of previous generations and enable more individuals to become economically independent. The other two ends of government – abundance and subsistence – concerned economic growth and social welfare. Here, as an advocate of *laissez-faire*, Bentham counselled political quiescence. He acknowledged, however, that neither private savings nor public charity were sufficient to cushion everyone against the misfortunes brought on by sickness, old age and economic recession. Government, therefore, had a responsibility to make provision for the relief of distress in a manner that fostered 'a spirit of economy and foresight in the lower classes of society'.

Bentham returned to this theme in his *Outline of a work entitled pauper management improved* (1798). Political economists attacked traditional outdoor parish-relief as an inefficient system which made recipients of charity dependent upon the benevolence of the wealthy and discouraged attitudes of self-reliance. Bentham's proposed remedy was a national network of workhouses where the destitute were to lead a frugal, closely supervised routine, designed to inculcate habits of thrift and prudence. These 'industry houses' were to be administered by a National Charity Company: a government-sponsored, joint-stock organization that was to operate as a profit-making concern.[28] Besides caring for indigent persons, the Company was to extend its activities to the independent poor outside workhouses. By managing, for example, employment exchanges and savings banks, as well as schemes of education, health care and social insurance, it could induce the lower classes to secure themselves against calamity.

The National Charity Company was intended to augment both the efficiency and the happiness of society. A central administrative framework would replace the ramshackle parochialism of English Poor Law; while the lower classes, having learned to calculate their long-term interests, would avoid the pain of pauperism. Bentham, who had an inventive mind, devised other administrative reforms which he also justified on grounds of utility. He was especially concerned with crime. Criminal activity, which was largely confined to the poorer classes, challenged government's primary responsibility to secure the rights of private property. Hence, for example, Bentham produced a blueprint for a prison in which a disciplined routine would teach inmates that illicit behaviour resulted in unhappiness. This panopticon – of circular design with a central tower of inspection – was presented as an architectural model for all institutions where large numbers of people required supervision: schools and factories, for example, as well as workhouses. Bentham also advocated a simpler system of criminal law so that potential offenders might be deterred by a clear understanding of the penalties attached to their intended crimes. In such ways, he believed, the labouring classes could be recast in a bourgeois mould. And, having acquired habits of rational calculation, the mass of people would find happiness in socially harmonious patterns of behaviour.

Although Bentham was often frustrated by official hostility to his schemes, his writings did influence the numerous administrative changes which followed the Reform Act of 1832. Benthamism 'fell in with the spirit of the time', as A. V. Dicey put it, because of the need for a more sophisticated political apparatus to regulate a rapidly expanding industrial society.[29] Utilitarians held key posts in government and administration, and they spearheaded the creation of central agencies to supervise areas of public life such as poor relief, factories, prisons, schools, health and sanitation. These reforms were intended to establish a political framework within which economic competition could flourish. Only if people inhabited a healthy environment with inducements to self-improvement, it was believed, could they fully participate in a *laissez-faire* society. Hence, like political economists, utilitarians stressed the importance of education in making the poor virtuous. John Austin, the Benthamite legal theorist, suggested that government was required by utilitarian considerations to acquaint working people with the elementary principles of the science of wealth. In this way, he claimed in *The province of jurisprudence determined*, the poor would appreciate the identity of interest which existed between capital and labour [5.2]. They would then refrain from crime and industrial unrest and instead seek material advance through habits of self-reliance. Thus, having learned to pursue their interests rationally, the labouring classes would behave in a manner which secured both their own happiness and the stability of society.

If utilitarians favoured the moral reformation of the poor, they also opposed the political power of inherited wealth. In his *Plan of parliamentary reform*, published in 1817, Bentham denounced the Whig defence of the balanced constitution and of mixed government [5.3]. The British constitution was corrupt, he wrote, because it secured the 'sinister interests' of a propertied minority at the expense of the general interest. He proposed as a remedy a 'virtual universality of suffrage', though he was vague as to whether women should be granted the vote. Bentham's radical case for democracy was conducted according to simple utilitarian logic. Government should register the fact that citizens had an equal interest in happiness. But given that each person pursued self-interest, it could only do so by means of equality of political participation through the ballot-box. Otherwise policies would inevitably reflect the interests of those privileged individuals to whom the franchise was restricted. Bentham also advocated secret ballots to avoid corruption, as well as annual parliaments in order to subject elected representatives to continual public scrutiny.

Bentham's *Plan of parliamentary reform* initiated a public controversy between utilitarians and Whigs as to the proper basis of representation.[30] The debate, which lasted until the passage of the Reform Act in 1832, revolved around the issue of a propertied franchise. Whigs such as Macaulay, we have seen, wished to extend the franchise to the middle classes in order to forge an alliance between them and landed wealth. The utilitarian proposal for universal suffrage, objected Macaulay, stemmed from an abstract mode of argument that was insensitive to the need for moderate and pragmatic constitutional evolution. Utilitarians retorted that a restricted franchise would produce sectional policies to the disadvantage of people without the vote.

Utilitarian Members of Parliament formed a group known as the Philosophic Radicals.[31] A member of the group was George Grote, a future historian of Greece, whose *Essentials of parliamentary reform* sought to demolish the Whig theory of representation [5.4]. Grote rejected the Whig assumption that property ownership was a test of political competence. The very rich, especially the owners of landed wealth, were responsible for political corruption and patronage; their leisured life-style inhibited any desire to seek political wisdom; and fearing that the lower orders would abandon those attitudes of deference and dependence by which aristocratic ascendancy was preserved, they opposed the moral elevation of the poor. If it was foolish to suppose that the wealthy were uniquely fitted to secure the public interest, it was also illegitimate to imagine that an enfranchised common people would disturb the social fabric. In so far as the rewards of labour flowed from the operations of capital, the working classes had as much interest as other social groups in upholding the system of private property. Here, however, Grote revealed his utilitarian credentials. He acknowledged that the poor did not always rationally calculate their interests. Hence, although the ideal was an equality of political rights, he conceded that for an interim period the vote might be extended only as far as the middle classes. Once they formed a political majority, he argued, traditional obstacles to social progress could be removed. Enlightened bourgeois government would foster economic competition, curb aggressive foreign policy and eliminate political corruption. Through social progress, too, working people would be stimulated to self-improvement. Then, having acquired bourgeois habits, they could be safely admitted to the franchise.

Liberals such as Edward Miall believed that the poor might be reconciled to the middle classes through the educative processes of democracy [3.4]. For Grote, by contrast, this alliance could be cemented only after a preliminary period of middle-class government had purged society of its legacy of aristocratic corruption. In order to comprehend the natural identity of interest which existed between capital and labour, the working classes had first to become morally and economically independent. Grote's belief that representative democracy should evolve in stages was consistent with the desire of utilitarians to promote the rational calculation of self-interest. Only after the mass of people had been remoulded by various administrative and political reforms, ran utilitarian logic, could they participate in the benefits of a post-aristocratic society. Utilitarian reforms were designed for the age of *laissez-faire*. The assumption that the State should be concerned with the moral development of its members was, nevertheless, to outlive the belief in a free-market economy. It became a corner-stone of the liberal endorsement of an enlarged state.

Introduction

JOHN STUART MILL

J. S. Mill is generally regarded as the greatest of British liberals. His father, James, was a close friend and ideological ally of Bentham. In 1826, aged twenty, the younger Mill suffered a mental breakdown which led him to question the creed of his childhood. He emerged from this experience convinced that Benthamism constituted a licence to selfishness, because it viewed the whole of human existence from the narrow ground of economic competition. It conceived the world, he wrote in his essay on 'Bentham' (1838), as 'a collection of persons pursuing each his separate interest or pleasure', where the responsibility of government was to facilitate the socially harmonious pursuit of rational self-interest.[32] Absent from this world-view was recognition of the human capacity for generosity, as well as for aesthetic appreciation of such essential features of civilization as music and poetry. Mill sought, in consequence, to broaden utilitarianism to include the cultivation of the inner life or 'individuality' in the pursuit of happiness. Mill probably exaggerated his distance from earlier utilitarians, who were also anxious to promote virtue throughout society. But even when presenting familiar arguments, he achieved new heights of eloquence and intellectual rigour. He succeeded, too, in introducing some unfamiliar themes into the liberal repertoire.

Mill made self-improvement the key theme of his various writings. It was incorporated into his defence of individual liberty. Individual actions were legitimately subject to either legal coercion or moral censorship, Mill argued in *On liberty*, only when they infringed the interests of other people [6.1]. Otherwise the sovereignty of private judgement ought to be enshrined in a cluster of civil liberties, which included the freedoms of belief, expression and association. To some extent, therefore, *On liberty* provided an orthodox justification of limited government. Mill extended traditional liberal arguments, however, when he elaborated on the need to preserve such a large area of individual conduct from social control. Whereas previous liberals had used the concept of individual freedom primarily to attack arbitrary government, Mill turned it into a condemnation of the social tyranny of public opinion. Citing the German philosopher, Wilhelm von Humboldt, he argued that individuality unfolded in so far as each person was free to experiment with life. In the modern world, however, spontaneity was crushed by pressures of social conformity. Individual character, in consequence, was overwhelmed by the despotism of custom. The effect of this 'collective mediocrity' was not merely to make the mass of people servile; it also deprived them of the leadership of original individuals, always in a minority, on whom depended the progress and ultimate happiness of society.

At first glance, *On liberty* stands the principle of utility on its head. Mill was less concerned to promote the welfare of the majority, it seems, than to protect an eccentric minority from mass mediocrity. On closer inspection, however, his arguments reveal something other than a snobbish obsession with talented individuals. Only through the public influence of an enlightened minority, he believed, might common people aspire to self-improvement. This belief also shaped his attitude to representative government. Although acknowledging that universal suffrage provided an essential safeguard of individual interests, he rejected the Benthamite proposition that everyone should exert an equal influence upon policies. Democracy, he feared, was potentially an elective dictatorship which failed to restrain the inclination of the majority to enact ignorant and capricious measures. It would thereby reinforce the tendency of the modern age to stifle individuality in mass conformity.

Mill formulated various proposals to forestall a democratic 'tyranny of the majority'. One measure, elaborated in *Thoughts on parliamentary reform*, was to reward educated citizens with extra votes by means of a graduated suffrage [6.2]. This system of plural voting was designed to weight the exercise of political power in favour of enlightened individuals. Mill nevertheless justified the scheme as a stimulus to self-development throughout society. If additional votes were rewarded for individual effort and achievement, he argued, the lower classes would wish to become educated. Once encouraged to reflect upon their political responsibilities, too, ordinary people would acquire that sense of civic virtue necessary to align them with the public interest.

Mill may have exhibited an almost Whiggish suspicion of the masses. Unlike Whigs, however, he considered it neither possible nor desirable for the poor to remain in permanent subjection to the rich. The alternative was to prepare the lower classes for a life of active citizenship. The objective of Mill's scheme for a scaled franchise, in fact, was not unlike that of earlier utilitarian proposals. Like Grote, whom he often visited as a child, Mill feared that bad government would ensue from rapid democratic reform. But like Grote, too, he favoured reforms to assist the moral elevation and political integration of working people. Hence his plan to incorporate meritocratic criteria into the exercise of democratic rights. If Mill recoiled from the Benthamite emphasis upon the universal calculation of self-interest, he retained the utilitarian faith in the potential of the masses to acquire responsible attitudes.

Mill's anxieties about democracy made him less radical than some liberals. But he was in advance of liberal opinion on the issue of female emancipation. The proposal for a scaled franchise, he made clear in *Considerations on representative government*, did not identify sex as a valid criterion for distributing votes [6.3]. Mill, unlike Bentham, argued without qualification for female suffrage, which he linked with support for equal legal rights for women. He was appalled by the subordinate social position of women as unpaid domestic labourers who enjoyed few rights independently of their husbands. Women's potentialities were frustrated by this servitude, he argued, while men were scarred by their despotic relationship to the opposite sex. In *The subjection of women*, Mill proclaimed that the 'moral regeneration' of people could not commence until household slavery had been abolished through the implementation of equal rights between the sexes.[33] It is to Mill's eternal credit that he placed women's emancipation firmly on the agenda of any worthwhile liberal programme of social reform.

In the area of political economy, too, Mill was not content to tread an orthodox liberal path. He accepted many of the assumptions of *laissez-faire*. As part of his reaction against the Benthamite celebration of self-interest, however, Mill rejected the acquisitive values associated with the private pursuit of individual ambition. His ideal remained a free-market economy, but one where self-seeking had yielded to a co-operative adventure in activities which led to self-development. The *Principles of political economy* contained two proposals to this end [6.4]. Mill advocated, first, a non-growth economy. Previous political economists had supposed that living standards would inevitably fall if production ever ceased to expand. Mill, by contrast, suggested that two measures might combine to secure affluence in a stationary economy: Malthusian habits of restraint to restrict population; and an inheritance tax to ensure an equitable distribution of available wealth. Enormous social benefits could be expected from the attainment of material comfort in a steady economy. People would lose the impulse endlessly to scramble for scarce resources. And, with greater leisure available, they would have opportunity to experiment in the art of living. Within this alternative economy, in short, individuality could flourish.

Mill proposed, secondly, measures to defuse class conflict. Whereas previous liberals expected democracy and education to cement an alliance between capital and labour, Mill argued that it was also necessary to reform industry. Capitalists had to be discouraged from treating employees as though they were still subordinates within an aristocratic hierarchy; at the same time workers had to be induced to abandon attitudes of hostility which had been fostered within them by the paternalism of their employers. Profit-sharing could partly resolve the feud between capital and labour, Mill believed, because it gave employees an additional stake in their industry. In the long run, however, he favoured the emergence throughout the economy of co-operatives, in which workers themselves owned capital and controlled management. Here lay the prospect of a 'moral revolution' that would transform the labouring classes into self-reliant and responsible citizens. This idea of workers' co-operatives was borrowed from some of the early socialists. But Mill was adamant that co-operatives ought to compete within a market economy which, unlike socialist planning, curbed inefficiency and monopoly.

Mill had an enormous impact on his own generation, and he remains among the most widely read of liberal writers. In the past few decades, for instance, his defence of individual liberty has been incorporated into arguments for decriminalizing such areas of personal conduct as soft drugs, pornography and homosexuality. Liberals themselves often cite his plea for individuality and variety as a bulwark against collective mediocrity. More interesting, perhaps, is the fact that few liberals prior to Mill were interested in grass-roots democracy, and the Levellers were exceptional in favouring a devolution of authority to local communities. Mill believed that communal participation in decisions about the issues of everyday life is both a stimulus to self-development and an education in citizenship. Hence his call for workers' co-operatives and also support for a revitalized system of local government. Most liberals now urge schemes of industrial democracy and a minority wish to refashion society by means of a massive decentralization of power to self-managed communities. It is ironical that Mill, a reluctant democrat, should have spawned an ideal of a participatory society which has since inspired some liberals to demand a radical extension of democratic procedures into every sphere of life.

TOWARDS AN ENLARGED STATE

Today it is not for individual freedom that we have to struggle against classes and privilege. That battle was fought by our ancestors and won. But we have to win a yet harder fight, a fight for emancipation from conditions which deny fair play to the collective energy for the good of

> society as a whole ... Over labour questions, over education, over the powers of municipal bodies, the struggle must take place as it did of yore, for freedom from hampering restrictions, but restrictions not of individual but of social liberty.[34]

So wrote R. B. Haldane in the first volume of the *Progressive Review*, a journal founded in 1896 by radicals who had discarded the ideal of *laissez-faire*. If Haldane and his associates represented the vanguard of liberal thinking, they nevertheless articulated a mood that had grown since the passage of the Second Reform Act in 1867. It was now generally considered neither possible nor desirable, Haldane indicated earlier in the article, to resist demands by a partly enfranchised and increasingly organized working class for new remedies to cure the ills of a complex industrial society. Hence the need for a liberal programme to eradicate, *inter alia*, illiteracy, urban squalor, and the exploitation of the labour force. It was essential to recognize that individuals were free only in so far as they could lead a worthwhile existence, liberals now argued, and also imperative to implement measures intended to emancipate people from degrading social conditions.

Haldane's 'new liberalism' was not as novel as he and other progressive thinkers imagined. Liberals tended to exaggerate their distance from the proponents of *laissez-faire*, who also assigned to government a responsibility to elevate the masses. Late nineteenth-century liberalism can be viewed, in part, as a synthesis of the two variants of utilitarianism. It combined a Benthamite passion for social reform with a Millian desire to foster individuality. Within the framework of an energetic state, it was suggested, individuals might co-operate to make the best of themselves. Yet progressive liberals were no mere closet utilitarians. Many of them rejected a doctrine which, they believed, was still tainted by the Benthamite obsession with self-interest. They now looked for firmer evidence of the material and moral progress of society to a stage where every citizen could contribute to the common good. Within a few decades, some liberals were to advocate extensive social and economic policies in order to consolidate this evolutionary trend towards a better tomorrow.[35]

This optimistic belief in the benevolent evolution of society preceded disenchantment with *laissez-faire*. Initially, indeed, it served to renew faith in a free-market economy. Alfred Marshall, who became professor of political economy at Cambridge, began a lecture on 'The future of the working classes' (1873) by acknowledging the influence of Mill's *Principles of political economy*. Marshall's projected future, in fact, differed little from that outlined by Mill in his account of a stationary economy [6.4]. Marshall envisaged a relatively prosperous and moderately populated society where much economic activity was conducted by workers' co-operatives and in which technological innovation had both increased leisure and eliminated the enervating work previously done by unskilled labour [7.1]. Here human effort could focus upon the quality of life. It would be a community, then, stocked with individuals of character who had a keen sense of civic virtue. There was nothing original in this rather precious vision of a community of 'gentlemen' – it was the familiar theme of the *embourgeoisement* of the masses but arranged, Millian style, as a paean to individuality.

Significantly, however, Marshall detached this vision from the non-growth economy anticipated by Mill. The future, according to Marshall, was already unfolding within the framework of a dynamic capitalist economy. Greater productive efficiency was constructing a foundation of material comfort upon which everyone could enjoy a decent existence. It was evident, too, that improved living standards were accompanied by moral regeneration. Skilled workers were attending to the cultivation of character and, with the eventual abolition of unskilled labour, there was nothing to hinder self-improvement throughout society. The duty of government was to provide a compulsory system of education in order to prepare the masses for this higher life.

Commentators often exaggerate the pessimism of earlier political economists. Writers like Smith and Malthus, it is said, saw little prospect of raising the living standards of the poor far above subsistence. If *bourgeois* habits could rescue the masses from pauperism, they believed, most of them would still need to toil for relatively meagre wages. Although there is some validity in this assessment, it nevertheless overlooks the faith which some political economists had in the evolutionary possibilities of society. There is, in fact, little difference between Marshall and Thomas Chalmers, for example, who also believed that a free-market economy could morally elevate the labouring classes by increasing their wages and reducing their hours of work [4.3]. Nor did Marshall's belief in education as a social panacea represent an advance on earlier political economy.[36] Yet it was not long before liberals began to advocate a more vigorous programme of reform in order to release the progressive potential of society. Many of them, including Haldane, had been influenced by the conceptual innovations of the Oxford philosopher and Liberal city councillor, Thomas Hill Green.

Green, like Marshall, looked to the benevolent march of history for confirmation of moral improvement among common people. Unlike Marshall, however, Green did not extract his conception of the future from Mill's sketch of a stationary economy. Utilitarianism was too deeply rooted in the Benthamite fixation with rational self-interest, Green believed, to make moral elevation a firm priority. Hence, seeking an alternative philosophical anchorage for self-improvement, Green turned to the German idealist, G. W. F. Hegel. He took from Hegel the idea that history registers an incessant struggle for human perfection. This struggle is revealed in successive attempts by human beings to create social institutions through which they can fulfil their rational and moral potentialities. The goal of history, then, is the formation of a society in which the good life is attainable for everyone. Moral goodness, in this conception, is manifested in that spirit of civic virtue by which people escape their own narrow, selfish concerns to co-operate in the pursuit of the common good. Herein lies true freedom.

German philosophy may appear to have provided a tortuous route by which to arrive at a conclusion long drawn by liberals – that government should foster habits of citizenship. Green's Hegelianism nevertheless helped to change the vocabulary of English liberalism. Liberals were now more inclined to argue that self-fulfilment was to be attained through participation in a shared way of life rather than by means of a utilitarian calculation of individual interest. The new terminology also added impetus to the reforming zeal of middle-class radicals who, convinced that altruism was the mark of true citizenship, sought to promote self-development among the less privileged members of society. Here they were influenced by Green's depiction of political reform as part of an unfolding attempt to purge society of obstacles to the formation of individual character.

Green's 'Lecture on liberal legislation and freedom of contract' (1881) defended various measures, either enacted or proposed by the Gladstone government, that included protection for landed tenants in Ireland, provision of compulsory education, regulation of public health, and control of conditions and hours of work in factories. Opponents of these measures claimed that they constituted unwarranted interference with the rights of landlords and employers. But freedom, retorted Green, did not give some individuals licence to frustrate the potential of others to make the best of themselves [7.2]. It included a shared capacity for self-improvement whereby everyone could contribute to the public good. Hence the State, as custodian of the national interest, had a duty to emancipate people from ignorance, disease, squalid housing, and exploitation at work. In these ways,

Green argued, government might assist the progressive unfolding of freedom in society.

Despite his novel vocabulary, Green did not extend the legitimate scope of legislation much beyond that already conceded by liberals. 'When Green posited the need for the state to do what cannot be left undone without damaging the interests of all', Melvin Richter perceived, 'he could have been rephrasing Adam Smith's views on education.'[37] Green, who read Hegel from the viewpoint of the Victorian evangelical conscience, believed that the middle classes had a mission to help the poor become more like themselves. Hence, for instance, he advocated restrictions on the sale of alcohol in order to discourage intemperance among the working classes. Once removed from its elaborate wrapping of German philosophy, in fact, individual fulfilment was equivalent to those bourgeois habits of self-reliance which liberals had always prized. Like earlier liberals, Green wanted government to assist social progress with measures designed to cultivate attitudes appropriate for a free-market economy. And, also like them, he blamed the moral degradation of the masses upon the persistence of aristocratic power.

Here Green, an admirer of John Bright, resorted to the now rather stale explanation that the Glorious Revolution had failed to rid society of the consequences of the Norman Conquest. This theme was pursued in *Lectures on the principles of political obligation*, where he argued, as liberals had always done, that economic independence breeds a sense of self-reliance [7.3]. It was therefore desirable that labourers should become small-scale property owners and, indeed, skilled workers had already done so. The fact that many of the 'proletariate' remained poor and improvident was due to a legacy of aristocratic conquest. Appropriation of the limited commodity of land by a few had turned the majority into serfs whose life-style engendered habits of deference and subordination. The new working classes, who had swarmed into towns under the impact of industrialization, were still marked by the servility to their rural ancestors. Aristocratic power, which had been undermined elsewhere in Europe by revolution, still frustrated attempts in England to curb those exploitative practices by which the proletariat were discouraged from becoming virtuous. This is why the sort of policies outlined in the 'Lecture on liberal legislation and freedom of contract' had not already been enacted. Hence the public interest required constraints upon the power of inherited wealth. But once society had been cleared of its feudal debris, Green believed, the goal of universal freedom could be attained within the framework of industrial capitalism.

It is tempting to dismiss Green as a philosophical sophisticate who was politically naive. Yet many liberals shared his obsession with the evils of semi-feudal landlordism. This antipathy to the landed Anglican establishment reflected the strength of liberalism in rural Nonconformity. It was reinforced by the rapid expansion of urban areas, which yielded enormous profits for landowners as well as aggravating a housing shortage. Central to Liberal Party policy at the beginning of the twentieth century were proposals to break the landed monopoly by means of taxation and compulsory purchase. Even liberals like Lloyd George, who favoured a more extensive programme of social reform than Green had envisaged, continued to attribute the condition of the poor primarily to the curse of intemperance coupled with the avarice of the landed classes [7.4].

Green was an old-fashioned liberal in a new conceptual outfit. He had assembled Hegelian ideas into an exploration of the moral potential of a free-market economy. Yet his positive conception of liberty, as a capacity for self-improvement, underpinned liberal arguments for further legislation to eliminate conditions which demoralized the poor. It also contributed to a growing conviction among liberals that they were formulating a new doctrine in conflict with the assumptions of *laissez-faire*.

This belief emerged in response to the opponents of social reform, who converted *laissez-faire* into an ideological weapon with which to attack the legislative activities of the Gladstone Government. Herbert Spencer claimed that liberals had betrayed their heritage in supporting laws to regulate, for example, housing, public health and conditions in factories. Whereas liberals had always sought to emancipate individuals from the clutches of government, they now delighted in the fact that Parliament meddled in every sphere of society. Spencer, who believed that the only proper function of government was to secure life and property, defended his ideal of a minimal State by invoking Charles Darwin's theory of natural selection. Society, argued Spencer, progressed through unbridled economic competition in which the fittest survived – and the weak and indolent perished. Yet proponents of legislation to assist the poor, he suggested in *The man versus the state*, were 'doing all they can to further the survival of the unfittest'.[38] Spencer was a brilliant maverick whose eulogy of dogmatic *laissez-faire* placed him outside the liberal mainstream and, indeed, separated him from earlier liberals, who had not imagined that society could operate according to the laws of the jungle. His ideas found a more comfortable home in the Conservative Party, whose members, like libertarian conservatives in modern Britain, sought an ideological justification for the wealth of an entrepreneurial minority. If Spencer distorted the liberal tradition, his writings were nevertheless immensely popular: partly because the idea of 'iron' laws of natural selection appealed to a sceptical generation for whom the theological certainties of earlier Victorians had crumbled; and also because Social Darwinism imparted scientific credibility to the entrepreneurial values of upwardly mobile, largely self-educated groups within an expanding capitalist society. This is why his claim to be the custodian of authentic liberalism provoked a counter-offensive among liberals who endorsed the growth of the State. In rejecting Social Darwinism, they also exaggerated their departure from the principles of *laissez-faire*.[39]

The influence of both Green and Spencer was evident in Herbert Samuel's *Liberalism: an attempt to state the principles of contemporary Liberalism in England*, published in 1902, which endeavoured to provide a philosophical framework for the legislative drift of recent years. H. H. Asquith wrote an introduction in the spirit of Green [7.5]. Samuel, like Asquith, argued that it was the duty of government to assist social progress by enhancing opportunities for individuals 'to lead the best life'. This entailed a comprehensive programme of social reform. Before elaborating its details, however, Samuel countered some of the objections to the growth of legislation. After dismissing the claim that government had already done enough to release people from debilitating conditions, he turned to the Social Darwinists. The major flaw in Spencer's theory of evolution was that it favoured a policy of State inaction which perpetuated the 'unfitness' of the masses [7.6]. But there was no need for the poor to perish in a harsh struggle for survival. Moral improvement provided an escape route from 'unfitness' and it was the duty of government in a civilized society to rescue people from an environment which fostered habits of idleness and imprudence. The third objection to social reform was that it undermined self-reliance. Samuel responded with the largely false – if now standard – claim that earlier liberals were hostile to government. Various factors, however, had eroded this suspicion in recent decades: it was generally acknowledged that the enactments of a democratic Parliament were far more likely to secure the public interest than those of a corrupt aristocratic government; the defects of *laissez-faire* had been exposed; and traditional mistrust of government had been undermined by a more positive conception of liberty, hence a climate of opinion now receptive to enlightened State activity. Samuel was adamant, however, that the purpose of legislation should be to encourage self-reliance throughout society – an objective with which previous liberals would have concurred.

Samuel was not the only liberal whose refutation of Spencer revealed the ghost of Green. For L. T. Hobhouse, too, social progress was marked by a greater readiness of individuals to co-operate in making 'the best lives' for themselves. Whereas Social Darwinism consecrated a harsh struggle for survival, Hobhouse was determined to demonstrate that society ascends through the mutual assistance of its members.[40] This alternative theory of evolution was outlined in an early article, 'The ethical basis of collectivism', published in 1898 [7.7]. Human history, according to Hobhouse, records a gradual shift from egoism and competitive individualism to altruism and social solidarity. An organic society was unfolding, in consequence, where citizens were conscious of their responsibility to help one another attain the good life. This higher morality was manifested in efforts to elevate evolutionary tendencies into deliberate policy. Hobhouse cited factory and sanitary legislation as evidence of social advance.

Despite its scientific gloss, Hobhouse's belief in the upward march of society was not original. Like Green, and also Marshall, whose discussion group he had attended as a student, Hobhouse equated progress with the growth of civic virtue and a concerted effort to improve the quality of life throughout society. He nevertheless used his theory of evolutionary collectivism to advocate a much more extensive programme of social reform than either Marshall or Green had envisaged. In *Liberalism* (1911), for example, he put evolutionary flesh on Green's positive conception of liberty as a capacity to contribute to the common good. It was the business of government to supervise the emergence of an organic society in which citizens could co-operate for their mutual advantage. A liberal political programme, therefore, should be designed to establish 'a living equality of rights' which afforded ample opportunities for individual fulfilment. It entailed, according to Hobhouse, a network of social welfare funded by means of graduated taxation.

Here Hobhouse was seeking to give ideological anchorage to some of the measures enacted by the Liberal Government between 1906 and 1911, which included provision of old-age pensions and an insurance scheme for sickness and unemployment. In the course of this ideological defence, however, Hobhouse revealed his distance from earlier liberals. He did not share the faith of Marshall and Green in the potential of a free-market economy to establish a platform of material security upon which everyone could lead a worthwhile life. Despite higher wages and thrifty habits among the working classes, he argued, numerous individuals were still impoverished. There were economic forces beyond the control of individuals. Poverty and unemployment, far from indicating merely a moral failure on the part of the poor, resulted from imperfections within market capitalism. Hence it was not enough simply to educate citizens and thereby enable them to participate in the benefits of free enterprise. Self-reliance, so prized by earlier liberals, was not a panacea for the ills of society. Government, as the organized intelligence of the community, had also to combat those defects of economic competition which deprived some people of the necessities of a civilized life [7.8]. Only in this way could liberty be made effective and the good life become available to everyone.

Although Hobhouse endorsed Liberal Government policies, he also favoured a more radical programme of social and fiscal reforms. In particular, he wanted redistributive taxation to be used to establish a guaranteed minimum standard of living. This prompted him to challenge the assumption that individual rights of property were sacrosanct. Property had a social dimension because wealth could be neither accumulated nor secured by isolated individuals. Society, therefore, was entitled to view part of individual income as unearned 'surplus' that was available for redistribution to the poor. Government, in short, could treat a portion of national wealth as a common stock to be used for the provision of a basic wage and other social benefits. Taxation of this surplus, argued Hobhouse, was justified on both moral and economic grounds. The working classes, once released from bad conditions, would become more economically efficient. Through a fiscal policy of redistribution, then, the productive energy of society could be increased.

The argument that the material necessities of life should be funded by public expenditure, Hobhouse conceded, derived from a socialist conception of justice. But he denied that the proposal for a minimum wage offended the liberal conviction that individual initiative ought to be properly rewarded. Everyone was to be comfortable; yet income differentials were to remain that reflected the diversity of human talent and achievement. Universal needs, then, were to be secured within a liberal framework of incentives which ensured that individual merit obtained its just deserts. Hobhouse was vague as to how government might determine the appropriate financial reward of each economic function. But once individuals were adequately remunerated for their particular work, he believed, there would remain a sufficient surplus of wealth for government to promote the public good [7.8].

Hobhouse may have operated largely with a conceptual apparatus constructed by Green. He nevertheless used evolutionary theory to free liberalism from its moorings in *laissez-faire*. Green, we said, was an old-fashioned liberal in a new intellectual outfit. Hobhouse, by contrast, was a modern liberal in a by now somewhat faded philosophical attire. Earlier liberals had not strayed far from the principles of *laissez-faire*, even when convinced that they were charting unfamiliar territory. Hobhouse, unlike them, favoured a comprehensive structure of social welfare to compensate for the imperfections of market capitalism. His writings cast doubt on the efficacy of a self-regulating economy and point towards a new kind of liberalism.

Hobhouse derived the idea of an unearned surplus from J. A. Hobson, a close friend and fellow journalist, who pursued the theme in a torrent of books.[41] Hobson, like Hobhouse, believed that an enlarged State signified the evolution of an organic society where everyone might lead a full life. Like Hobhouse, too, he wanted government to secure positive liberty by creating equal opportunities for individual fulfilment. His *Crisis of liberalism*, published in 1909, defended the social reforms of recent years and also castigated those liberals who remained nostalgic for a mythical golden age of *laissez-faire*. Hobson's exposure of the structural flaws within unregulated capitalism was more explicit than that of Hobhouse. Without government intervention, a market economy wasted enormous amounts of human energy. It generated unemployment and confined numerous individuals to socially useless economic functions. Nor could free enterprise direct technological knowledge towards greater productive efficiency. But the waste created by *laissez-faire* was most apparent in the persistence of poverty. Hobson, like Hobhouse, dismissed the conventional assumption that self-help was an adequate cure for material deprivation. Habits of thrift, unless accompanied by a political programme, were powerless to overcome the inherent defects of the economic system.

This programme, which Hobson proposed in the form of a 'People's Charter', included: some public ownership of land, to provide decent housing and permit ordinary people to acquire property; public ownership of transport, to facilitate freedom of movement; provision of State insurance and credit schemes, to encourage working people to establish businesses; public powers to eliminate monopolies; an improved system of public education; and a fairer legal system. Such a programme, in conjunction with a policy of redistributive taxation, would give everyone an opportunity to make the best of themselves. Besides eradicating poverty, it would lead to a 'prodigious increase of national productivity' [7.9]. Hence, again like Hobhouse, Hobson believed that the moral case against unbridled market forces was inseparable from a critique of their economic weaknesses.

One manifestation of these economic imperfections was aggressive foreign policy. Whereas Cobden and Bright had attributed militarism to aristocratic ambitions [4.5, 4.6], Hobson argued that colonial expansion resulted from a maldistribution of wealth within unreformed capitalism. Society was polarized by *laissez-faire* policies into two groups: a rich minority which, already bloated by luxuries, accumulated its excess wealth as savings; and an impoverished majority which lacked the capacity to purchase commodities. Domestic underconsumption prompted owners of capital to seek new markets for their products in the Third World. But the problem of underconsumption could be solved, Hobson suggested in *Imperialism* (1902), if the State channelled the unearned surplus wealth enjoyed by the rich into a living wage and decent conditions for common people. A comfortable working class, equipped with new purchasing power, would boost the demand for consumer goods. By creating equal opportunities through redistributive taxation, therefore, government could promote social justice and productive efficiency at home and also foster international harmony abroad [7.10].

Hobhouse and Hobson had travelled a fair distance from the liberalism of the 1870s and 1880s. A free-market economy, according to Marshall and Green, had the potential to abolish poverty and so create the material foundations of a society where everyone might acquire the virtues of citizenship. Although Hobson and Hobhouse shared this faith in the evolution of society to a higher material and moral stage, they nevertheless believed that the fruits of progress could not be harvested without more careful political husbandry than envisaged by their liberal predecessors. The task, as they saw it, was to reformulate liberalism in order to justify policies intended to create an equality of social or welfare rights. In their hands, therefore, evolution was used to underpin a system of social welfare and some political control of the economy. It was now possible for liberals to pronounce – with rather more justification than Haldane and others – the end of *laissez-faire*.

THE END OF *LAISSEZ-FAIRE*

Hobhouse and Hobson hoped that their proposed reforms would be implemented by a leftish Liberal Government. But in 1916 the party split for a period into two factions, led respectively by H. H. Asquith and David Lloyd George. Internal disharmony was followed by rapid electoral decline and the rise of the Labour Party as the major rival to Conservatives. It may be that the Liberal Party was electorally hamstrung by its desire to hold the middle ground between the competing claims of capital and labour. Liberals wished, on one hand, to abolish class privilege while preserving private enterprise; and, on the other, to elevate the poor while avoiding class conflict. Now that universal suffrage had been finally attained, however, class emerged as a major determinant of voting behaviour. The Conservative and Labour Parties, which were more closely aligned with sectional interests, reaped the electoral advantages of class politics. Despite its electoral misfortunes, however, liberalism was by no means ideologically exhausted. The classless image of the party appealed to intellectuals anxious to make capitalism both more productive and more just. Their goal was a conflict-free and technically efficient society, where people could make the best of themselves in a context of economic growth and ample consumer choice. From this vision of a more humane capitalism, tamed by means of an enlarged State, was to emerge an ideological consensus which shaped the programmes of both Labour and Conservative Governments in the decades after the Second World War. Ironically, therefore, liberalism underwent an ideological renaissance during the years of its electoral downfall.[42]

The Liberal Party became an intellectual power-house largely through the influence of its Summer Schools, held annually in the 1920s, which attracted people eager to explore the possibilities of further State intervention in the economy. J. M. Keynes, who is today recognized as the principal architect of the mixed economy, regularly attended the Schools. The unregulated pursuit of self-interest, Keynes believed, was inefficient. Hence the need for government to assume responsibility for those economic activities that could not be entrusted to private enterprise. *The end of laissez-faire*, published in 1926, outlined some of the areas in which political management of the economy was legitimate. Keynes began by absolving political economists from the charge that they had propagated the dogmatic free-market principles popularized by the Social Darwinists. He then demolished the philosophical arguments for unbridled market forces [8.1]. Keynes argued that the political 'agenda' – a term borrowed from Bentham – should be settled on pragmatic rather than metaphysical grounds. High on the agenda was public control of credit and investment in order to stimulate demand and so reduce unemployment. Government should aim to balance the economy through central supervision, according to Keynes, while leaving sufficient scope for the exercise of individual initiative. This entailed socialization of investment rather than of production.

Keynes sought an evolutionary route towards a more productive and humane capitalism. The Liberal Party, he believed, was most likely to nurture the non-ideological expertise required for this orderly transition. He explained his antipathy to the other two parties in 'Liberalism and industry', a lecture given in 1927 at the National Liberal Club [8.2]. The Conservative Party was full of die-hards still wedded to an ideal of unregulated capitalism. Socialists, by contrast, shared with liberals a concern to promote social justice. But among them were too many dogmatists obsessed with class warfare and nationalization. Only liberals, therefore, could be expected to steer between the extremes of *laissez-faire* capitalism and revolutionary socialism. It was their business, as intelligent occupants of a halfway house of moderation, to strike a balance between efficiency and justice. This, as he had indicated in *The end of laissez-faire*, entailed a centrally managed economy which did not stifle private enterprise.

Keynes returned to this theme in his *General theory of employment, interest, and money*, published in 1936, the most influential economic treatise since Adam Smith's *Wealth of nations*. Much of the book consists of technical arguments illustrating why free-market capitalism is unable to sustain growth and is therefore powerless to eliminate want and unemployment. It was the function of government, therefore, to boost demand to a level at which full employment is created. In the concluding chapter, however, Keynes clarified the political implications of his economic theory [8.3]. Keynes insisted, as he had done in previous writings, that a centrally co-ordinated economy did not involve widespread socialist ownership of the means of production. Although the State should manage overall levels of consumption and investment, economic activities were still to remain largely in the hands of private capital. Otherwise individual choice and variety would be crushed. Here Keynes argued, in words which echoed J. S. Mill [6.1], that personal liberty could not be preserved, nor social progress prolonged, unless individuals had opportunities to experiment with life. If capitalism was not salvaged by some measure of State intervention, however, people might be driven by the experience of mass employment towards totalitarianism. Finally, like Hobson [7.10], Keynes believed that a buoyant economy provided an antidote to the militaristic search for fresh markets. The political orchestration of economic prosperity, then, would produce both domestic stability and international harmony.

Much of the groundwork for the *General theory* had been done at the Liberal Summer Schools. In 1926 Lloyd George financed a Summer School inquiry into the British economy. Keynes and Herbert Samuel were executive members of the inquiry, and L. T. Hobhouse participated in its specialist committees. The result was *Britain's industrial future*, known from the colour of its cover as the Yellow Book, which appeared in 1928. It contained five hundred pages of detailed analysis, as well as an elaborate programme of social reconstruction. Keynes' influence was especially evident in the various proposals for a national policy of credit and investment. The Bank of England was to be made more publicly accountable, for example, and a Board of National Investment was to channel the flow of capital into areas likely to generate employment. This was to be accomplished through extensive public works, which included road construction, slum clearance, electrification, improvement of docks and waterways, a revitalized coal industry, and the reclamation of unused land for agriculture. There were also plans to abolish the 'propertyless proletariat' by diffusing ownership, for ' "to have a bit of property" safeguards personal liberty, buttresses self-respect, and teaches responsibility'. This familiar theme of the *embourgeoisement* of the masses was linked with the traditional condemnation of inherited wealth. Hence accumulation of unearned fortunes was to be curbed by means of an inheritance tax and progressive taxation was to be coupled with measures to encourage popular habits of saving and investment. The intention was to 'advance towards that goal of Liberalism in which everybody will be a capitalist, and everybody a worker, as everybody is a citizen'. One means of spreading the ownership of property was, as Mill had advocated [6.4], through industrial profit-sharing schemes. The Yellow Book linked this proposal with other reforms intended to remove class hostilities from industrial relations. The State was to supervise a network of agencies for mediating between employers and employees, and there was to be a statutory minimum wage for each industry.

The document amounted to one of the most comprehensive programmes devised by a political party. Not unnaturally its authors believed that they occupied the middle ground between the extremes of individualism and collectivism. Pragmatic – rather than doctrinaire – State intervention in the economy would promote positive liberty and thereby enable individuals to co-operate in the pursuit of the common good [8.4]. This may sound like Green. Yet late nineteenth-century liberalism had been refined to accommodate a form of managed capitalism.

The Yellow Book did not secure electoral victory for the Liberal

Party, but it did renew confidence amongst liberals. The report was followed by a number of writings which, for the most part, merely presented its prescriptions in more accessible prose. What these less impressive books conveyed, however, was the conviction that economic planning could secure the liberal goal of a one-class society of autonomous individuals: a community in which economic prosperity was both sustained and fairly distributed, and where, in consequence, everyone could acquire the virtues associated with independence and responsible citizenship [8.5, 8.6].

The dominant theme of the Yellow Book and satellite writings was the necessity of State intervention to release the productive potential of capitalism. Little was said about the need to reform social welfare. With the Second World War, however, the defects of existing social services were exposed, and the government established a committee to devise remedies. The outcome was a *Report on social insurance and allied services*, published in 1942, which recommended the creation of a comprehensive system of social insurance, as well as the provision of child allowances and free medical treatment. Chairman of the committee was Sir William Beveridge, a former Director of the London School of Economics.[43] His intention, like that of Hobhouse in proposing a minimum wage [7.8], was to secure universal needs without undermining individual responsibility and incentive. Every individual, in return for compulsory contributions from earnings, was to receive sufficient benefits to withstand the misfortunes of life. The effect would be the elimination of poverty through the creation of a national minimum. Yet State provision was not to exceed a safety net of subsistence. Although safeguarded against want, therefore, people were not to be discouraged from cultivating habits of thrift and independence.

Beveridge had stood outside the liberal mainstream in the 1930s because of his disagreement with Keynesian policies, but he was now convinced of the desirability of widespread social and economic planning. Hence, as a private citizen, he produced in 1944 a sequel to his report on the social services. Whereas it had been concerned to eliminate want, the *Report on full employment in a free society* contained a blueprint for eradicating idleness. It was written in a Keynesian spirit. Private enterprise would still control the bulk of production but the State was to manage demand. Beveridge endorsed the Yellow Book's proposal for a National Investment Board to direct spending on public works, such as roads, housing, schools and hospitals. He also favoured fiscal policies for stimulating private consumption by means of redistributive taxation and expenditure on the social services. Once government assumed responsibility for economic stability and expansion, argued Beveridge, mass unemployment would disappear.

In 1944 Beveridge was adopted as Liberal candidate for Berwick-upon-Tweed. During the election campaign he depicted his reports as the twin pillars of a liberal programme of radical social reconstruction, in which Britain would be cleansed of the five 'evils of Want, Disease, Ignorance, Squalor and Idleness'. These and other speeches, together with various articles, were collected in a book, entitled *Why I am a liberal* [8.7]. Beveridge, like Keynesians in the previous decade, characterized liberalism as a *via media* between intransigent conservatism and Clause Four socialism. The Liberal Party, untainted by identification with sectional interests, was uniquely competent to balance public control with private enterprise. Only it, therefore, could be trusted to improve living conditions without impairing individual freedom.

This was fairly ritual stuff. In distinguishing liberalism from its rivals, however, Beveridge made an interesting comparison between primary and secondary liberties. Essential liberties embraced traditional civil rights, as well as the freedoms to choose an occupation and to spend personal income. Lesser liberties included the unimpeded pursuit of economic self-interest. If collectivists were implacably hostile to these secondary liberties, individualists made the mistake of treating them as essential. Here Beveridge reproved Friedrich von Hayek – whose *Road to freedom* (1944) is still in vogue among free-market conservatives – for suggesting that any interference with private enterprise is tyrannical. Beveridge, citing Mill, argued that lesser liberties could be sacrificed if they harmed other people. The unrestricted right of businessmen to invest capital, for example, had resulted in urban squalor and mass unemployment. It thereby constituted a privilege which a minority enjoyed at the expense of the majority. The task of liberal policy, therefore, was to determine the point at which non-essential liberties should be discarded for the sake of social justice. For, in eliminating injustice, the State enhanced liberty throughout society. The drift of Beveridge's argument was similar to that of liberals since Green. In delineating primary and secondary freedoms, however, he provided an alternative defence of State action from the stock liberal assertion that it was the duty of government to secure positive liberty.

Beveridge lost his parliamentary seat in 1945, when only twelve Liberal candidates were returned at the general election. Yet many of his proposals for the creation of a Welfare State were implemented by the new Labour Government. And Keynesian economic strategy influenced the policies of Labour and Conservative Governments until the 1960s. 'If we cannot carry out our policies ourselves', announced Keynes in 1927, 'we can at least develop them and hope with some confidence that others will steal them' [8.2]. Keynes, had he lived, would have been delighted that political theft occurred on such a massive scale in post-war Britain.

A DECENTRALIZED STATE

Liberals had invested a great deal of ideological capital in the formation of a mixed economy and Welfare State. With many of their policies implemented by Labour and Conservative Governments, however, liberals faced a dilemma. They had to find a niche within the edifice of a post-war consensus which, notwithstanding their electoral misfortunes, had been constructed upon essentially liberal foundations. Although liberals have agreed on the need for progressive policies, especially with regard to issues like race and civil liberties, they have differed as to whether they should seek to be a party of government or a vehicle of social protest. Liberals in Parliament, particularly after Jo Grimond became leader of the party in 1956, have wished to dislodge the Labour Party as the only effective alternative to the Conservatives. The Lib-Lab parliamentary pact of 1977–8 and, more recently, the Alliance with Social Democratic defectors from the Labour Party, have reflected the aspirations of David Steel to make his party a powerful influence on the centre-left of the political spectrum. For many party activists, by contrast, the intention has been to build a protest movement for people disillusioned with Parliament and who, in consequence, are unlikely to respond to the moderate rhetoric of the liberal middle way. Ideologically, however, this tension between parliamentary liberalism and liberal activism has been partially resolved by a shared antipathy to concentrated power. Liberals remain committed to some form of political control of the economy and also to the public provision of basic welfare needs. Yet they also condemn what they regard as the excessive bureaucracy and centralization of the modern State. Their vision has been of a participatory society where responsibility and power are dispersed from central agencies to individuals and local communities. Liberals have attached different meanings to this concept of grass-roots democracy. Yet their common anti-statist position has given them a distinctive ideological role in post-war Britain.

The threat of bureaucratic regimentation was conveyed in Elliott

Dodds's introduction to a collection of essays by various writers, *The unservile state: essays in liberty and welfare*, published in 1957 [9.1]. Liberals, according to Dodds, acknowledged that individual freedom was enhanced by economic planning and social welfare. Yet they were alert to the dangers of an overbearing nanny-State which undermined private endeavour and sapped self-reliance. In regard to welfare, therefore, they wished to encourage greater private provision by extending voluntary schemes of self-help and mutual aid. In other areas, too, their aim was a wider spread of power and responsibility. This is why liberals advocated, for example, devolution of authority from Westminster, a revitalized system of local government, and co-partnership in industry. The intention was to transform the Welfare State into a welfare society – as Beveridge put it – in which there were equal opportunities for responsible citizenship. Hence, although committed to the positive aspects of modern collectivism, liberals remained vigilant against the tendency of an enlarged State to erode individual initiative. With such a strategy, suggested Dodds, the Liberal Party might again become the dominant voice of British radicalism.

Liberalism, as portrayed in *The unservile state*, was primarily about distributing power, property and responsibility throughout society. This was a variation on the old theme of *embourgeoisement*. It was nevertheless a fruitful theme to pursue because it enabled liberals to project – as Keynes and Beveridge had done – a classless image of their party. Hence, in the spirit of J. S. Mill, there now began to flow a series of proposals intended to heal social divisions. Industrial democracy was to be established by means of profit-sharing and shareholding schemes, as well as through extended opportunities for employees to participate in boardroom decisions. Greater political democracy, on the other hand, was to be achieved through a decentralization of power to local and regional government.

These policies were summarized in *Partners for progress*, a booklet published in 1964. Liberals, argued Harry Cowie in a short introduction [9.2], wished to create a participatory society in which conflict was displaced by a sense of partnership. This required radical policies distinct from those of the Conservative and Labour Parties. For the need was to erode class privilege but also to arrest the statist developments within post-war Britain. Cowie, like Mill [6.4], emphasized the material benefits to be expected from greater self-government in industry and politics. The productive capacity of society was impaired by inadequate decision-making procedures, as well as by a failure to harness individual initiative. Once power had been dispersed outwards and downwards, however, people could co-operate in the pursuit of economic efficiency. The nation would then reap the harvest of a technological revolution.

Policies designed to redistribute power and responsibility have given modern liberalism a distinctive flavour. In opposing a centralized state, however, liberals walk a perilous tightrope from which it is easy to topple towards one or other of the rival ideological camps. Both conservatives and socialists, especially since the breakdown in the 1970s of ideological consensus, have also condemned modern bureaucracy. Once Margaret Thatcher became party leader in 1975, conservatives launched an assault upon economic planning and widespread social welfare. The post-war settlement, as depicted by conservatives, was a collectivist nightmare in which individual choice and private enterprise were stifled – hence their attempt to restore a free-market economy and to revive habits of self-reliance. Conservatives aim to construct the kind of minimal State which, according to liberals, entrenches class privilege and increases social inequality. In stressing the need to emancipate people from the stranglehold of bureaucracy, however, liberals occasionally sound like the new Social Darwinists of the Conservative Party. Other liberals, by contrast, share much in common with libertarian socialists. People on the Labour Left now emphasize the need for popular participation in socialist planning. Their goal is a socialist democracy where power and wealth have been transferred from a minority who control private capital to the mass of ordinary citizens. In recent years, however, some liberals have urged a radical programme of decentralization which resembles aspects of the 'alternative economic strategy' favoured by socialists.

The tendency of some liberals to drift towards conservatism is illustrated by an article which Dr John Rae, headmaster of Westminster School, wrote for *The Times* in 1976 [9.3]. The liberal tradition, Rae believes, has been severely threatened by post-war collectivism. Egalitarian measures have engendered a nursemaid State which pampers to every human need and have also lodged power in corporate groups such as trade unions. Individual liberty, in consequence, has been undermined by a massive concentration of power which far exceeds that achieved in the seventeenth century by absolute monarchy. In order to establish an identity, therefore, liberals should no longer attempt to forge an alliance between moderate people on the centre–left of the political stage. They ought instead to challenge the Conservative Party as the champion of freedom against 'the protective totalitarianism of the left'. Tories, according to Rae, are too concerned to further the interests of private property to be trusted with this task. Read in perspective, however, his article appears to fly a kite on behalf of the policies and ideology since espoused by most conservatives.

More radical liberals wish to dismantle centralized bureaucracy through community politics. Young Liberals in the late 1960s spearheaded a movement intended to mobilize the frustration of people who feel powerless in the modern State. The outcome was a form of 'pavement' politics in which party activists, especially in deprived inner cities, sought to articulate and resolve local grievances through techniques like advice centres, newsletters and petitions. From these activities, which brought some electoral advantages, has emerged an ideal of self-managed communities in which people control the decisions that affect their everyday lives.

Community politics has made some impact on more orthodox liberals. Jo Grimond, for example, believes that disenchantment with the political process offers an opportunity to fortify the practice and ideology of liberalism on the basis of 'fraternalism', a concept traditionally associated with socialism [9.4]. It is radical activists outside Parliament, however, who are most eager to provide a blueprint for a more participatory society. In *The theory and practice of community politics* Bernard Greaves and Gordon Lishman depict, Millian fashion, a society which submerges individuality in mass conformity [9.5]. The solution is to release the potential for individual self-expression through a variety of co-operative ventures. This would entail a redistribution of power from the remote bureaucracies of central, and even local, government to a plurality of smaller communities. Although there should remain widespread provision of social welfare, for instance, responsibility for its administration ought to devolve to self-help and mutual support groups, which, runs the argument, are more likely than the statutory services to respond to particular needs. And the competitive units of the economy should consist, as Mill believed, of autonomous co-operatives. The intention is to create multiple centres of power with ample opportunities for individual fulfilment and mutual co-operation. These numerous neighbourhood and regional communities are to be co-ordinated by means of a federal structure that transcends national boundaries.

Such a radical vision of the future belies the image of liberalism as an ideology of the dead centre. With some justification, however, Greaves and Lishman ground their ideal of a participatory society within the liberal tradition. They evidently derive little inspiration from Bentham's model of democracy as merely a protective device for individuals who would otherwise be exploited by vested interests. The need for fairer and more effective policies is only one of the arguments for giving people greater access to the power structure. Advocates of community politics also believe that involvement in participatory structures enables individuals to fulfil themselves in the pursuit of shared objectives – that it cultivates individuality and is therefore an education in citizenship. Not surprisingly, therefore, Greaves and Lishman list Mill and Green among their intellectual forebears.

It remains to be seen how far liberalism will be renewed by the theory and practice of community politics. Most parliamentary liberals, encouraged by some election successes, are eager to maintain their alliance with the Social Democratic Party. Yet Social Democrats have sparse roots in local communities. Although hostile to bureaucratic centralism, they appear to be moving towards the conservative ideal of a minimal State – where free-market principles have been revived and in which there is no longer public provision of universal needs. It may be that the Liberal Party, tempted by the prospect of political power for the Alliance, will lose touch with the radical features of its ideological heritage. Within that heritage, however, lies the prospect of a different kind of alliance. The intention of democratic socialists is to disperse wealth and power from private capital to ordinary people. This is why socialists like Tony Benn, as well as liberals, are inspired by the struggles of the English revolution to construct a more accountable and decentralized community. But there is little sign of the formation of a partnership between democratic socialists and radical liberals; still less that such an alliance would be electorally successful. Without such a broad front, however, Britain is unlikely to approximate the vision initially explored by the Levellers: a society in which, to use the words of modern liberals, 'all people have an equal right to take part in the process by which decisions that affect their lives are taken' [9.5].

POSTSCRIPT

The story began in the seventeenth and eighteenth centuries with a broad and progressive current of thought: broad in so far as liberal ideas were embraced by radicals who rejected hierarchical assumptions, as well as by a property-owning Whig minority concerned to protect its rights against executive tyranny and the propertyless multitude; progressive because liberals confronted arbitrary power and outworn privilege. From the middle of the nineteenth century the story revolved around the ideas of members of the Liberal Party. As an organized political movement, however, liberalism has shrunk during the last sixty years from a party of government to a parliamentary rump. Is it therefore fitting to conclude in the fashion of one of those *Times* obituarists, who, anticipating the death of a distinguished person now in his dotage, writes a short appreciation of his long life and numerous achievements? Maybe. Yet the premature epitaphs composed at the end of the age of *laissez-faire* provide a cautionary lesson for anyone inclined to pronounce the terminal condition of liberalism. If the liberal creed appears fatigued, it nevertheless continues to inspire a minority of citizens to strive for a more decentralized and participatory community. The beliefs of members of the Liberal Party, moreover, do not comprise the whole story of modern liberalism in so far as many of its assumptions and values spill into society at large. So perhaps it is not inappropriate to finish as we began – by identifying a flow of progressive thought which, although detached from a specific political group, can be described as broadly liberal.

There is a sense, of course, in which it is not misleading to suggest that the disintegration of the Liberal Party signifies the triumph of liberalism. We saw that the ideal of reformed capitalism, from which Labour and Conservative Governments constructed electorally successful manifestoes, was shaped by liberal arguments about the efficacy of a mixed economy and Welfare State. Keynes and Beveridge were the intellectual architects of the post-war social democratic consensus. If that consensus has been shattered since the early 1970s by the impact of economic recession, there are numerous people who remain convinced that capitalism can be tamed through partial management of the economy and adequate social welfare. A few, with a clear perception of their ideological pedigree, remain faithful to the Liberal Party; while the rest either cluster in the Social Democratic Party, gravitate towards the centre-right of the Labour Party, or else shiver on the wet wing of the Conservative Party. Nor has the appropriation of liberal ideas been confined to the period since 1945. Given its intimate association with the progressive unfolding of capitalist society, liberalism has been vulnerable to ideological pillage since its inception. Civil liberties; representative and accountable government; democracy; economic competition; the greatest happiness of the greatest number; and eventually social welfare and the mixed economy: each concept has been clarified and defended by liberals and subsequently incorporated into alternative political perspectives and programmes. If liberalism is now partly invisible, this is because so many of its assumptions and ideals have infiltrated political practice and public awareness.

But a catalogue of the successes of liberalism is hardly an indication of its present vitality. There is one area, however, in which people are motivated by recognizably liberal principles to urge further political reforms. In contemporary Britain there is an energetic campaign to give substance to the claim – initially formulated and persistently sustained by liberals – that citizens have an equal right to liberty. It crystallizes around various demands to reinforce and extend civil liberties in order to cushion individuals against the exigencies of State power: repeal of the Official Secrets Act to curtail the arbitrary activities of the security forces; enactment of a Freedom of Information Act to make government more accountable for decisions allegedly taken on our behalf; repeal of the Prevention of Terrorism Act and other statutes which infringe such rights as freedom from arbitrary arrest; removal of remaining obstacles to freedom of speech and assembly; abolition of immigration laws which discriminate against citizens on racial grounds. Organizations like the National Council for Civil Liberties, from which such demands emanate, recruit support from across the political divide because 'taking rights seriously', to use Professor Dworkin's phrase,[44] is not a preoccupation of liberals alone. But in so far as liberalism has persistently generated strategies for enlarging the freedoms to which citizens are judged to be equally entitled, today's civil libertarians should not object to being called its heirs.

Indeed, recent proposals for fortifying the rights of citizens against an overmighty State echo earlier liberal schemes. We saw how Whigs were prompted to jettison a contractual account of government because of their conviction that individual rights and liberties were safeguarded against executive abuse by the Act of Settlement. What some people now recommend, in effect, is a revised constitutional settlement to cope with the massive extension of political power since the Glorious Revolution. One suggestion is to replace the Bill of Rights of 1688 by a modern charter of civil liberties, which could be implemented through parliamentary enactment of the European Convention for the Protection of Human Rights. If basic freedoms were legally entrenched and judicially assessed, it is claimed, government would be less likely to drift towards authoritarianism or degenerate into new forms of absolutism. And it is sometimes added, in an argument which J. S. Mill might have found attractive, that an accessible code of basic rights would serve an educative function by alerting citizens to the value and fragility of liberty.[45] But the mere statutory enactment of a Bill of Rights, according to others, would fail to secure it against future parliamentary appeal; nor would such a Bill be sufficient to consolidate individual liberties in an age of encroaching government. Like Tom Paine, who believed that the Glorious Revolution had failed to purge the legacy of the Norman Conquest [3.3], these people have little faith in the capacity of either Parliament or the common law to eradicate arbitrary power. Their solution is a new form of social contract: a written constitution, as Paine advocated, that would accommodate a Bill of Rights within a framework of fundamental law which firmly bounded the legitimate scope of government.

In searching for liberal fragments across the political spectrum, however, we run the risk of stretching liberalism so far that it loses all coherence. Some of the current arguments for constraining government, in fact, should warn us against including everyone in the liberal fold, especially some people most anxious to assert their right of admission. Among enthusiasts for a Bill of Rights and a written constitution are free-market conservatives, who imagine that the post-war mixture of Keynesian economic management and ample social welfare has unleashed a form of creeping collectivism which, unless checked, will terminate in a totalitarian centralization of State power.[46] But their radicalism is a world removed from the progressive sentiments of earlier liberals. Paine's proposal for a written constitution was part of a package of reforms intended to open the political process to popular participation and control. Parliament was corrupt, he believed, because it operated within a system of mixed government which gave expression to the arbitrary will of the landed classes. Paine's solution was to eliminate those antiquated constitutional arrangements which undermined the supremacy of the Commons, while making the latter institution democratically accountable to the whole community. Modern conservatives, by contrast, fear that arbitrary decisions will emerge from too much rather than too little democracy: from the will of the majority articulated in an unbridled Parliament that is determined to extend public controls over private enterprise. A Bill of Rights enshrined in a written constitution, they suppose, would throw a barrier across the parliamentary road to socialism, thereby impeding any reckless exercise of popular sovereignty. The apparently benign advocacy of a new constitutional settlement as a means of safeguarding individual rights and liberties, therefore, does not necessarily indicate a characteristically liberal belief in the capacity of ordinary people for self-government; but may conceal a mistrust of the masses on the ground of their susceptibility to the allegedly poisonous attractions of an interventionist nanny-State.

This desire to confine a potentially unruly Parliament within the straitjacket of a written constitution, then, must be set in the context of the New Right's mission to roll back the State from the economy. Whereas post-war collectivism crushed enterprise and incentive, according to conservatives, the revival of a market economy will enhance individual freedom by facilitating the unfettered pursuit of private ambition. The advocates of a minimal State derive encouragement from the writings of such economists as F. A. Hayek, whom Beveridge reproved for failing to grasp that unregulated capitalism yields riches for the few at the expense of poverty and squalor for a much larger section of the community [8.7]. Yet 'we find in Hayek', a devotee imagines, 'a restatement of classical liberalism in which it is purified of errors'.[47] So it is not surprising that some conservatives either extol the virtues of thrift and self-reliance associated with the age of *laissez-faire* or, more boldly, profess to be born-again liberals of the Manchester School variety. Although people are entitled to label themselves as they wish, there are nevertheless grounds for suggesting that the latter-day apostles of free-market capitalism have misread their liberal texts.

The free market was a conceptual device by which nineteenth-century liberals condemned landed privilege and also promulgated the ideal of a society where everyone possessed enough resources to live a morally autonomous existence. But *laissez-faire* has never been an exclusively liberal concept: it was appropriated by Edmund Burke from the writings of Adam Smith and has remained a prominent theme within the conservative repertoire for two hundred years.[48] Economic stagnation, claim free-market conservatives, issues from two principal causes: a lack of incentives for potential wealth-creators; and the capacity of organized labour artificially to inflate wages, and thereby prices, beyond the natural laws of supply and demand. Entrepreneurial drive and a competitive national economy can be sustained or restored, in this view, only if the rich are stimulated to become richer and the poor are discouraged from seeking too much affluence. Hence the evils of an interventionist State which imposes bureaucratic controls and punitive taxation upon private enterprise, while sapping the self-reliance of common people through, for example, wages councils and bountiful welfare benefits. Whereas *laissez-faire* was once an ideologically useful weapon for liberals intent on destroying privilege and patronage, then, it continues to appeal to conservatives eager to defend the privileges of an economically successful minority.

In conservative usage, moreover, the free market is usually

associated with social authoritarianism. If libertarian conservatives aim to preserve private enterprise from the clutches of the State, they nevertheless tend to be firm disciplinarians on moral and social issues. In a competitive economy, they assume, many individuals will fail either to exercise entrepreneurial initiative or to acquire the bourgeois virtues of restraint and self-discipline. People who spurn the message of self-help, it is imagined, are likely to indulge in morally dubious and politically disruptive conduct. In rolling back the State from the economy, therefore, conservatives also wish to expand some of its other activities. They are far more inclined than liberals to extend the frontiers of State surveillance of private citizens through, for example, vigorous use of the Official Secrets Act, to endorse an enlargement of police powers, to approve of censorship, to restrict freedom of speech and assembly and to curb the rights of trade unions. The free market, conservatives judge, needs to be framed by a strong 'law and order' state.

Those conservatives who now purport to be the bearers of a purified liberalism are heirs of the Social Darwinists. Even a century ago, however, Herbert Spencer's sterilized doctrine of the minimal State was considered to place him outside the pale of liberalism. Without some public supervision of private enterprise, liberals acknowledged, many individuals would be deprived of a secure and worthwhile existence. The story of liberalism this century has been of a growing recognition that every citizen has a right to enjoy cultural and economic benefits – that individuals require access to education, decent housing, adequate health care and a minimum wage in order to make effective choices and thereby experience freedom in any concrete and meaningful sense. The myth of a golden age of unsullied *laissez-faire* may serve the ideological purposes of conservatives intent on cleansing society of every trace of post-war collectivism; it has nothing to do with mainstream liberalism.

If conservatives are too quick to unfurl the banner of liberalism, socialists are too prone to view it as a remnant of former ideological battles. Not that most socialists have qualms about accepting the liberal values of liberty and equality. Socialists seek a sufficiently even spread of material resources to enable everyone to make the best of themselves: a society in which, to use the language of J. S. Mill, individuality is given maximum opportunity to flourish. As Marx and Engels put it:

> We are not among those communists who are out to destroy personal liberty, who wish to turn the world into one huge barrack or into a gigantic workhouse. There are certainly some communists who, with an

easy conscience, refuse to countenance personal liberty and would like to shuffle it out of the world because they consider that it is a hindrance to complete harmony. But we have no desire to exchange freedom for equality. We are convinced . . . that in no social order will personal freedom be so assured as in a society based upon communal ownership.[49]

The stumbling-block has been communal ownership. Socialists contend that the liberal objective of an equal right to freedom remains frozen as an unfulfilled potential within capitalism: that a system of private property necessarily congeals into a class structure in which the rhetoric of freedom masks the privileges of an exploitative minority. It follows that liberal values can only be given substance outside liberal society – in a community which displaces the competitive struggle for scarce resources by a co-operative pursuit of human needs and so resolves the age-old antagonism between capital and labour. Hence a tendency of socialists to dismiss liberalism as a congenitally bourgeois ideology which, having once performed a useful function in marshalling opposition to aristocratic power, is now historically exhausted; and to suppose that their mission is to salvage liberal values after torpedoing the capitalist vessel which conveys liberalism.

As the ideology of a competitive economy, in this account, liberalism will be negated when capitalism itself is finally transcended. One problem with this tidy conception of social progress – tidy because it packages historical development into neat stages – is that it tends to caricature the doctrine which is supposed to be buried in the ashes of capitalism. Underlying much of the socialist distaste for liberalism is the assumption that it is rooted in the kind of bourgeois individualism which is most sharply expressed in pure *laissez-faire*. Socialists misconceive liberalism, in consequence, in the same manner as those libertarian conservatives who now use the doctrine as a flag of convenience – as sanctioning the removal of public constraints upon the pursuit of self-interest or, as socialists would put it, as licensing the rich to rip off the poor. But liberalism has always been far more complex and progressive than it appears from this strange conspiracy between the proponents and opponents of Social Darwinism.

In practice, of course, most socialists do not anticipate an imminent revolutionary leap into a post-capitalist future. Notwithstanding their thunder against bourgeois ideology, they often attempt to implement the kind of political programme favoured by liberals since the time of Hobson and Hobhouse. If socialists condemn capitalist freedom as counterfeit, they nevertheless seek to defend and expand the popular rights that have been gained in the centuries since the breakdown of feudalism. Besides advocating a greater redistribution of income and wealth in order to give everyone a secure existence, socialists can usually be relied upon to champion civil liberties. Many socialists act, in fact, as progressive liberals.

The collapse of the Liberal Party does not necessarily signify the decline of liberalism as a flow of values and principles embraced by people who wish to give substance to the claim that citizens have an equal right to freedom. It does mean, however, that the survival of liberalism in this broad sense largely depends upon the activities of individuals who are often anxious to proclaim their distance from the liberal camp. To a greater extent than they concede, the task of creating a more liberal society now lies with those people who strive to lay the foundations of a socialist future within the existing framework of capitalism: with socialists who recognize, in the words of Marx and Engels, 'that mankind advances, not by leaps, but only step by step . . . Only by degrees can private property be transformed into social property'.

NOTES

1. In Andrew Reid (ed.), *Why I am a liberal: being definitions and confessions of faith by the best minds of the Liberal Party*, Cassell: London, 1885, p. 82.

2. See for example W. Lyon Blease, *A short history of English liberalism*, T. Fisher Unwin: London, 1913.

3. Alan Bullock and Maurice Shock (eds), *The liberal tradition from Fox to Keynes*, Adam and Charles Black: London, 1956, p. xix; John Dunn, *Western political theory in the face of the future*, CUP: Cambridge, 1979, p. 28.

4. Austin Hopkinson, 'The future of the Liberal Party', *Edinburgh Review*, **247**, Jan. 1928, p. 51.

5. See W. H. Greenleaf, *The British political tradition*, vol. 2: *The ideological heritage*, Methuen: London, 1983.

6. Isaiah Berlin, 'Two concepts of liberty', in *Four essays on liberty*, OUP: Oxford, 1967.

7. Harold Laski, *The decline of liberalism*, L. T. Hobhouse Memorial Lecture No. 10, OUP: Oxford, 1940.

8. A good discussion of the several problems entailed by the claim is provided by Amy Gutmann, *Liberal equality*, CUP: Cambridge, 1980. For an attempt to articulate a liberal theory of equality see Ronald Dworkin, 'Liberalism', in Stuart Hampshire (ed.), *Public and private morality*, CUP: Cambridge, 1978.

9. An interesting historical account of these various rights is given by T. H. Marshall, *Citizenship and social class and other essays*, CUP: Cambridge, 1950, pp. 1–85.

10. Harold Laski, *The rise of European liberalism*, Allen and Unwin: London, 1936, p. 17.

11. James Mackintosh, *Vindiciae Gallicae: defence of the French revolution and its English admirers, against the accusations of the Right Hon. Edmund Burke*, G. G. J. and J. Robinson: London, 1792.

12. Anthony Arblaster, *The rise and decline of western liberalism*, Basil Blackwell: Oxford, 1984, p. 43.

13. See especially Brian Manning, *The English people and the English revolution*, Penguin Books: Harmondsworth, 1978.

14. Tony Benn, 'The inheritance of the labour movement', in Chris Mullin (ed.), *Arguments for socialism*, Penguin Books: Harmondsworth, 1980.

15. See C. B. Macpherson, *The political theory of possessive individualism: Hobbes to Locke*, OUP: Oxford, 1968.

16. Thomas Erskine, 1st Baron, *A short defence of the Whigs*, Ridgway: London, 1819, pp. 3–4.

17. The fullest account of Whig ideology is H. T. Dickinson, *Liberty and property: political ideology in eighteenth-century Britain*, Weidenfeld and Nicolson: London, 1977.

18. J. H. Plumb, *The growth of political stability in England 1675–1725*, Macmillan: London, 1967, p. 187.

19. Donald Southgate, *The passing of the Whigs 1832–1886*, Macmillan: London, 1962.

20. The classic account of radical Whiggism is Caroline Robbins, *The eighteenth-century commonwealthman: studies in the transmission, development and circumstance of English liberal thought from the restoration of Charles II until the war with the thirteen colonies*, Harvard UP: Cambridge, Massachusetts, 1959.

21. Richard Price, *The evidence for a future period of improvement in the state of mankind*, London, 1787, p. 23.

22. See Albert Goodwin, *The friends of liberty: the English democratic movement in the age of the French revolution*, Hutchinson: London, 1979.

23. Thomas Chalmers, *The right Christian and civic economy for a nation, with a more special reference to its large towns* (1821), in *The works of Thomas Chalmers*, William Collins: Glasgow, 1836–42, Vol. 14, p. 29.

24. See Donald Read, *Cobden and Bright: a Victorian political partnership*, Edward Arnold: London, 1967.

25. See E. T. Stokes, *The English utilitarians and India*, OUP: Oxford, 1959.

26. Jeremy Bentham, *A fragment on government*, ed. F. C. Montague, Clarendon Press: Oxford, 1891, p. 154.

27. Jeremy Bentham, *Anarchical fallacies: being an examination of the declarations of rights issued during the French revolution*, in *The works of Jeremy Bentham*, ed. John Bowring, William Tait: Edinburgh, 1843, Vol. 2, p. 501.

28. See Charles F. Bahmueller, *The National Charity Company: Jeremy Bentham's silent revolution*, University of California Press: Berkeley and Los Angeles, 1981.

29. A. V. Dicey, *Lectures on the relation between law and public opinion in England during the nineteenth century*, Macmillan: London, 1905, p. 169. Dicey believed that the growth of state administration from 1830 to 1870 signified the triumph of a coherent Benthamite ideology. Since the 1950s, however, Dicey's thesis has generated a heated controversy among historians. Some commentators contend that Benthamites had little influence upon administrative changes which emerged, rather, as pragmatic responses to particular social problems – e.g. Oliver MacDonagh, 'The nineteenth-century revolution in government: a reappraisal', *Historical Journal*, 1 (1958), pp. 52–67; David Roberts, 'Jeremy Bentham and the Victorian administrative State', *Victorian Studies*, 2 (1959), pp. 193–210. Other historians accept the thrust of Dicey's argument – e.g. Henry Parris, 'The nineteenth-century revolution in government: a reappraisal reappraised', *Historical Journal*, 3 (1960), pp. 17–37; Jennifer Hart, 'Nineteenth-century social reform: a Tory interpretation of history', *Past and Present*, 31 (1965), pp. 39–61. Whatever the precise relationship between Benthamite ideology and political practice in mid-Victorian England, Professor Finer is surely right to suggest that in respect 'to penology and to health, education, and to the protection of paupers and factory workers, to financial administration, fiscal policy and the machinery of central and local administration ... Bentham's thoughts and attitudes played a predominant role'. S. E. Finer, 'The transmission of Benthamite ideas 1820–50', in Gillian Sutherland (ed.), *Studies in the growth of nineteenth-century government*, Routledge and Kegan Paul: London, 1972, pp. 11–32.

30. Some of the principal articles in the debate are reprinted in Jack Lively and John Rees (eds), *Utilitarian logic and politics: James Mill's 'essay on government', Macaulay's critique and the ensuing debate*, Clarendon Press: Oxford, 1978.

31. William Thomas, *The philosophic radicals: nine studies in theory and practice 1817-1841*, Clarendon Press: Oxford, 1979.

32. J. S. Mill, 'Bentham', in *Dissertations and discussions political, philosophical and historical reprinted chiefly from the Edinburgh and Westminster Reviews*, Parker and Son: London, 1859, Vol. 1, p. 362.

33. J. S. Mill, *The subjection of women*, Longmans, Green, Reader, and Dyer: London, 1869, pp. 147, 177.

34. R. B. Haldane, 'The new liberalism', *Progressive Review*, 1 (1896), pp. 141-42.

35. See generally Peter Clarke, *Liberals and Social Democrats*, CUP: Cambridge, 1978; Michael Freeden, *The new liberalism: an ideology of social reform*, Clarendon Press: Oxford, 1978.

36. In his later writings, however, Marshall dissociated himself from the ideal of unregulated capitalism. He now favoured limited state intervention in the economy and a redistribution of wealth from rich to poor. And his *Principles of economics*, published in 1890, attempted to lay the theoretical foundations for a programme of social welfare.

37. Melvin Richter, *The politics of conscience: T. H. Green and his age*, Weidenfeld and Nicolson: London, 1964, p. 271.

38. Herbert Spencer, *The man versus the State*, Williams and Norgate: London, 1885, p. 69.

39. See generally Greta Jones, *Social Darwinism and English thought: the interaction between biological and social theory*, Harvester Press: Brighton, 1980.

40. See Stefan Collini, *Liberalism and political argument in England 1880-1914*, CUP: Cambridge, 1979.

41. See John Allett, *New liberalism: the political economy of J. A. Hobson*, University of Toronto Press: Toronto, 1981.

42. See John Campbell, 'The renewal of liberalism: liberalism without liberals', in Gillian Peele and Chris Cook (eds), *The politics of reappraisal 1918-1939*, Macmillan: London, 1975, pp. 88-113.

43. See José Harris, *William Beveridge: a biography*, Clarendon Press: Oxford, 1977.

44. Ronald Dworkin, *Taking rights seriously*, Duckworth: London, 1977.

45. See Peter Wallington and Jeremy McBride, *Civil liberties and a bill of rights*, Cobden Trust: London, 1976.
46. This thesis is eloquently argued by Nevil Johnson, *In search of the constitution: reflections on State and society in Britain*, Pergamon Press: Oxford, 1977.
47. John Gray, *Hayek on liberty*, Basil Blackwell: Oxford, 1984, p. viii.
48. See Robert Eccleshall, 'Conservatism', in R. Eccleshall, V. Geoghegan, R. Jay and R. Wilford, *Political ideologies*, Hutchinson: London, 1984, pp. 79–114.
49. *Communist Journal*, **1**, Sept. 1847, in *The communist manifesto of Karl Marx and Friedrich Engels*, intro. D. Ryazanoff, Martin Lawrence: London, 1930, App. E, p. 292.

Part one
ORIGINS

1.1 JOHN MILTON (1608-1674)

From *Areopagitica; a speech of John Milton for the liberty of unlicensed printing, to the Parliament of England* (1644), in *Tracts for the people, designed to vindicate religious and christian liberty*, E. Wilson and J. Smallfield: London, 1840, no. X, pp. 29-30, 33, 39, 41-2.

Milton was vehemently opposed to an authoritarian State and Church, and wrote radical pamphlets on politics, theology, education and divorce. Following the execution of Charles I, the almost blind Milton was appointed in 1649 to the secretariat for foreign tongues in the new republic. *Areopagitica* reproved those Presbyterians in Parliament who favoured the kind of censorship of opinions formerly imposed by Anglican prelates. It is an eloquent expression of a belief shared by Radicals during the ferment of civil war: that truth emerges from unfettered debate between free and independent individuals.

Truth and understanding are not such wares as to be monopolized and traded in by tickets, and statutes, and standards. We must not think to make a staple commodity of all the knowledge in the land, to mark and license it like our broad-cloth and our wool-packs. What is it but a servitude like that imposed by the Philistines, not to be allowed the sharpening of our own axes and coulters, but we must repair from all quarters to twenty licensing forges! Had any one written and divulged erroneous things and scandalous to honest life, misusing and forfeiting the esteem had of his reason among men, if after conviction this only censure was adjudged him, that he should never henceforth write but what were first examined by an appointed officer, whose hand should be annexed to pass his credit for him, that now he might be safely read, it could not be apprehended less than a disgraceful punishment. Whence to include the whole nation, and those that never yet thus offended, under such a diffident and suspectful prohibition, may plainly be understood what a disparagement it is. So much the more, whenas debtors and delinquents may walk abroad without a keeper, but unoffensive books must not stir forth without a visible gaoler in their title. Nor is it to the common people less than a reproach; for if we be so jealous over them, as that we dare not trust them with an English pamphlet, what do we but censure them for a giddy, vicious and ungrounded people, in such a sick and weak estate of faith and discretion, as to be able to take nothing down but through the pipe of a licenser! That this is care or love of them, we cannot pretend, whenas in those popish places where the laity are most hated and despised, the same strictness is used over them. Wisdom we cannot call it, because it stops but one breach of license, nor that neither; whenas those corruptions which it seeks to prevent, break in faster at other doors which cannot be shut ...

Well knows he who uses to consider, that our faith and knowledge thrives by exercise, as well as our limbs and complexion. Truth is compared in scripture to a streaming fountain; if her waters flow not in a perpetual progression, they sicken into a muddy pool of conformity and tradition. A man may be a heretic in the truth; and if he believe things only because his pastor says so, or the assembly so determines, without knowing other reason, though his belief be true, yet the very truth he holds becomes his heresy ...

Where there is much desire to learn, there of necessity will be much arguing, much writing, many opinions; for opinion in good men is but knowledge in the making. Under these fantastic terrors of sect and schism, we wrong the earnest and zealous thirst after knowledge and understanding which God hath stirred up in this city. What some lament of, we rather should rejoice at, should rather praise this pious forwardness among men, to re-assume the ill-deputed care of their religion into their own hands again. A little generous prudence, a little forbearance of one another, and some grain of charity might win all these diligences to join, and unite into one general and brotherly search after truth; could we but forego this prelatical tradition of crowding free consciences and Christian liberties into canons and precepts of men ...

What should ye do then? Should ye suppress all this flowery crop of knowledge and new light sprung up, and yet springing daily in this city? Should ye set an oligarchy of twenty engrossers over it to bring a famine upon our minds again, when we shall know nothing but what is measured to us by their bushel? Believe it, Lords and Commons, they who counsel ye to such a suppressing, do as good as bid ye suppress yourselves; and I will soon shew how. If it be desired to know the immediate cause of all this free writing and free speaking, there cannot be assigned a truer than your own mild and free and humane government; it is the liberty, Lords and Commons, which your own valorous and happy counsels have purchased us – liberty, which is the nurse of all great wits: this is that which hath rarefied and enlightened our spirits like the influence of heaven; this is that which hath enfranchised, enlarged and lifted up our apprehensions degrees above themselves. Ye cannot make us now less capable, less knowing, less eagerly pursuing of the truth, unless ye first make yourselves, that made us so, less the lovers, less the founders of our true liberty. We can grow ignorant again, brutish, formal and slavish, as ye found us; but you then must first become that which ye cannot be – oppressive, arbitrary and tyrannous, as they were from whom ye have freed us. That our hearts are now more capacious, our thoughts more erected to the search and expectation of greatest and exactest things, is the issue of your own virtue propagated in us; ye cannot suppress that, unless ye reinforce an abrogated and merciless law, that fathers may dispatch at will their own children ... Give me the liberty to know, to utter, and to argue freely according to conscience, above all liberties.

1.2 THE LEVELLERS

From *An agreement of the free people of England* (1649), in William Haller and Godfrey Davies (eds), *The Leveller tracts 1647–1653*, Columbia University Press: New York, 1944, pp. 320–1, 323–8.

This, the third and final Leveller *Agreement*, summarizes their constitutional programme. It was signed by John Lilburne, William Walwyn, Thomas Prince and Richard Overton, all of whom had been sent to the Tower of London at the instigation of Oliver Cromwell.

After the long and tedious prosecution of a most unnaturall cruel, homebred war, occasioned by divisions and distempers amongst ourselves, and those distempers arising from the uncertaintie of our Government, and the exercise of an unlimited or Arbitrary power, by such as have been trusted with Supreme and subordinate Authority, wherby multitudes of grievances and intolerable oppressions have been brought upon us. And finding after eight yeares experience and expectation all indeavours hitherto used, or remedies hitherto applyed, to have encreased rather then diminished our distractions, and that if not speedily prevented our falling againe into factions and divisions, will not only deprive us of the benefit of all those wonderful Victories God hath vouchsafed against such as sought our bondage, but expose us first to poverty and misery, and then to be destroyed by forraigne enemies.

And being earnestly desirous to make a right use of that opportunity God hath given us to make this Nation Free and Happy, to reconcile our differences, and beget a perfect amitie and friendship once more amongst us, that we may stand clear in our consciences before Almighty God, as unbyassed by any corrupt Interest or particular advantages, and manifest to all the world that our indeavours have not proceeded from malice to the persons of any, or enmity against opinions; but in reference to the peace and prosperity of the Common-wealth, and for prevention of like distractions, and removall of all grievances; We the free People of England, to whom God hath given hearts, means and opportunity to effect the same, do with submission to his wisdom, in his name, and desiring the equity thereof may be to his praise and glory; Agree to ascertain our government, to abolish all arbitrary Power, and to set bounds and limits both to our Supreme, and all Subordinate Authority, and remove all known Grievances.

And accordingly do declare and publish to all the world, that we are agreed as followeth,

I. That the Supreme Authority of England and the Territories therewith incorporate, shall be and reside henceforward in a Representative of the People consisting of four hundred persons, but no more; in the choice of whom (according to naturall right) all men of the age of one and twenty years and upwards (not being servants, or receiving alms, or having served the late King in Arms or voluntary Contributions) shall have their voices; and be capable of being elected to that Supreme Trust, those who served the King being disabled for ten years onely. All things concerning the distribution of the said four hundred Members proportionable to the respective parts of the Nation, the severall places for Election, the manner of giving and taking of Voyces, with all Circumstances of like nature, tending to the compleating and equall proceedings in Elections, as also their Salary, is referred to be setled by this present Parliament, in such sort as the next Representative may be in a certain capacity to meet with safety at the time herein expressed: and such circumstances to be made more perfect by future Representatives ...

VIII. And for the preservation of the supreme Authority (in all times) entirely in the hands of such persons only as shal be chosen thereunto – we agree and declare: That the next & al future Representatives, shall continue in full power for the space of one whole year: and that the people shall of course, chuse a Parliament once every year ...

IX. And that none henceforth may be ignorant or doubtful concerning the power of the Supreme authority, and of the affairs, about which the same is to be conversant and exercised: we agree and declare, that the power of Representatives shall extend without the consent or concurrence of any other person or persons,

1. To the conservation of Peace and commerce with forrain Nations.

2. To the preservation of those safe guards, and securities of our lives, limbes, liberties, properties, and estates, contained in the Petition of Right, made and enacted in the third year of the late King.

3. To the raising of moneys, and generally to all things as shall be evidently conducing to those ends, or to the enlargement of our freedom, redress of grievances, and prosperity of the Common-wealth.

For security whereof, having by wofull experience found the prevalence of corrupt interests powerfully inclining most men once entrusted with authority, to pervert the same to their own domination, and to the prejudice of our Peace and Liberties, we therefore further agree and declare.

X. That we do not impower or entrust our said representatives to continue in force, or to make any Lawes, Oaths, or Covenants, whereby to compell by penalties or otherwise any person to any thing in or about matters of faith, Religion or Gods worship or to restrain any person from the profession of his faith, or exercise of Religion according to his Conscience, nothing having caused more distractions, and heart burnings in all ages, then persecution and molestation for matters of Conscience in and about Religion:

XI. We doe not impower them to impresse or constrain any person to serve in war by Sea or Land every mans Conscience being to be satisfied in the justness of that cause wherein he hazards his own life, or may destroy an others.

And for the quieting of all differences, and abolishing of all enmity and rancour, as much as is now possible for us to effect.

XII. We agree, That after the end of this present Parliament, no person shall be questioned for any thing said or done in reference to the late Warres, or publique differences; otherwise then in pursuance of the determinations of the present Parliament, against such as have adhered to the King against the Liberties of the people: And saving that Accomptants for publick moneys received, shall remain accomptable for the same.

XIII. That all priviledges or exemptions of any persons from the Lawes, or from the ordinary course of Legall proceedings, by vertue of any Tenure, Grant, Charter, Patent, Degree, or Birth, or of any place of residence, or refuge, or priviledge of Parliament, shall be henceforth void and null; and the like not to be made nor revived again.

XIIII. We doe not impower them to give judgement upon any ones person or estate, where no Law hath been before provided, nor to give power to any other Court or Jurisdiction so to do, Because where there is no Law, there is no transgression, for men or Magistrates to take Cognisance of; neither doe we impower them to intermeddle with the execution of any Law whatsoever.

XV. And that we may remove all long setled Grievances, and thereby as farre as we are able, take away all cause of complaints, and no longer depend upon the uncertain inclination of Parliaments to remove them, nor trouble our selves or them with Petitions after Petitions, as hath been accustomed, without fruit or benefit; and knowing no cause why any should repine at our removall of them, except such as make advantage by their continuance, or are related to some corrupt Interests, which we are not to regard.

We agree and Declare,

XVI. That it shall not be in the power of any Representative, to punish, or cause to be punished, any person or persons for refusing to answer to questions against themselves in Criminall cases.

XVII. That it shall not be in their power, after the end of the next Representative, to continue or constitute any proceedings in Law that shall be longer then Six months in the final determination of any cause past all Appeal, nor to continue the Laws or proceedings therein in any other Language then English, nor to hinder any person or persons from pleading their own Causes, or of making use of whom they please to plead for them.

The reducing of these and other the like provisions of this nature in this Agreement provided, and which could not now in all particulars be perfected by us, is intended by us to be the proper works of faithful Representatives.

XVIII. That it shall not be in their power to continue or make any Laws to abridge or hinder any person or persons, from trading or merchandizing into any place beyond the Seas, where any of this Nation are free to Trade.

XIX. That it shall not be in their power to continue Excise or Customes upon any sort of Food, or any other Goods, Wares, or

Commodities, longer then four months after the beginning of the next Representative, being both of them extreme burthensome and oppressive to Trade, and so expensive in the Receipt, as the moneys expended therein (if collected as Subsidies have been) would extend very far towards defraying the publick Charges; and forasmuch as all Moneys to be raised are drawn from the People; such burthensome and chargeable wayes, shall never more be revived, nor shall they raise Moneys by any other ways (after the aforesaid time) but only by an equal rate in the pound upon every reall and personall estate in the Nation.

XX. That it shall not be in their power to make or continue any Law, whereby mens reall or personall estates, or any part thereof, shall be exempted from payment of their debts; or to imprison any person for debt of any nature, it being both unchristian in it self, and no advantage to the Creditors, and both a reproach and prejudice to the Commonwealth.

XXI. That it shall not be in their power to make or continue any Law, for taking away any mans life, except for murther, or other the like hainous offences destructive to humane Society, or for endevouring by force to destroy this our Agreement, but shall use their uttermost endeavour to appoint punishments equall to offences: that so mens Lives, Limbs, Liberties, and estates, may not be liable to be taken away upon trivial or slight occasions as they have been; and shall have speciall care to preserve, all sorts or people from wickedness misery and beggery: nor shall the estate of any capitall offendor be confiscate but in cases of treason only; and in all other capitall offences recompence shall be made to the parties damnified, as well out of the estate of the Malifactor, as by loss of life, according to the conscience of his jury.

XXII. That it shall not be in their power to continue or make any Law, to deprive any person, in case of Tryals for Life, Limb, Liberty, or Estate, from the benefit of witnesses, on his, or their behalf; nor deprive any person of those priviledges, and liberties, contained in the Petition of Right, made in the third yeer of the late King Charls.

XXIII. That it shall not be in their power to continue the Grievance of Tithes, longer then to the end of the next Representative; in which time, they shall provide to give reasonable satisfaction to all Impropriators: neither shall they force by penalties or otherwise, any person to pay towards the maintenance of any Ministers, who out of conscience cannot submit thereunto.

XXIV. That it shall not be in their power to impose Ministers upon any the respective Parishes, but shall give free liberty to the parishioners of every particular parish, to chuse such as themselves shall approve; and upon such terms, and for such reward, as themselves shall be willing to contribute, or shall contract for. Provided, none be chusers but such as are capable of electing Representatives.

XXV. That it shall not be in their power, to continue or make a law, for any other way of Judgments, or Conviction of life, limb, liberty, or estate, but onely by twelve sworn men of the Neighbor-hood; to be chosen in some free way by the people; to be directed before the end of the next Representative, and not picked and imposed, as hitherto in many places they have been.

XXVI. They shall not disable any person from bearing any office in the Common-wealth for any opinion or practice in Religion, excepting such as maintain the Popes (or other forraign) Supremacy.

XXVII. That it shal not be in their power to impose any publike officer upon any Counties, Hundreds, Cities, Towns, or Borroughs; but the people capable by this Agreement to chuse Representatives, shall chuse all their publike Officers that are in any kinde to administer the Law for their respective places, for one whole yeer, and no longer, and so from yeer to yeer: and this as an especial means to avoyd Factions, and Parties.

And that no person may have just cause to complain, by reason of taking away the Excise and Customs, we agree,

XXVIII. That the next, and all future Representatives shall exactly keep the publike Faith, and give ful satisfaction, for all securities, debts, arrears or damages, (justly chargeable) out of the publike Treasury; and shall confirm and make good all just publike Purchases and Contracts that have been, or shall be made; save that the next Representative may confirm or make null in part or in whole, all gifts of Lands, Moneys, Offices, or otherwise made by the present Parliament, to any Member of the House of Commons, or to any of the Lords, or to any of the attendants of either of them.

And for as much as nothing threateneth greater danger to the Common wealth, then that the Military power should by any means come to be superior to the Civil Authority,

XXIX. We declare and agree, That no Forces shal be raised, but by the Representatives, for the time being; and in raising thereof, that they exactly observe these Rules, namely, That they allot to each particular County, City, Town, and Borrugh, the raising, furnishing, agreeing, and paying of a due proportion, according to the whole number to be levyed; and shall to the Electors or Representatives in each respective place, give Free liberty, to nominate and appoint all

Officers appertaining to Regiments, Troops, and Companies, and to remove them as they shall see cause, Reserving to the Representative, the nominating, and appointing onely of the General, and all General-Officers; and the ordering, regulating, and commanding of them all, upon what service shall seem to them necessary for the Safety, Peace, and Freedom of the Common-wealth.

And in as much as we have found by sad experience, That generally men make little or nothing, to innovate in Government, to exceed their time and power in places of trust, to introduce an Arbitrary, and tyrannical power, and to overturn all things into Anarchy and Confusion, where there are no penalties imposed for such destructive crimes and offences,

XXX. We therefore agree and declare, That it shall not be in the power of any Representative, in any wise, to render up, or give, or take away any part of this Agreement, nor level mens Estates, destroy Propriety, or make all things Common: And if any Representative shall endevor, as a Representative, to destroy this Agreement, every Member present in the House, not entering or immediately publishing his dissent, shall incur the pain due for High Treason, and be proceeded against accordingly; and if any person or persons, shall by force endevor or contrive, the destruction thereof, each person so doing, shall likewise be dealt withal as in cases of Treason.

And if any person shall by force of Arms disturb Elections of Representatives, he shall incurr the penalty of a Riot; and if any person not capable of being an Elector, or Elected, shall intrude themselves amongst those that are, or any persons shall behave themselves rudely and disorderly, such persons shall be liable to a presentment by a grand Inquest and to an indictment upon misdemeanor; and be fined and otherwise punish'd according to the discretion and verdict of a Jury. And all Laws made, or that shall be made contrary to any part of this Agreement, are hereby made null and void.

Thus, as becometh a free People, thankfull unto God for this blessed opportunity, and desirous to make use thereof to his glory, in taking off every yoak, and removing every burthen, in delivering the captive, and setting the oppressed free; we have in all the particular Heads forementioned, done as we would be done unto, and as we trust in God will abolish all occasion of offence and discord, and produce the lasting Peace and Prosperity of this Common wealth: and accordingly do in the sincerity of our hearts and consciences, as in the presence of Almighty God, give clear testimony of our absolute agreement to all and every part hereof by subscribing our hands thereunto. Dated the first day of May, in the Yeer or our Lord 1649.

1.3 JOHN LOCKE (1632-1704)

From *A letter concerning toleration* (1689), in *The works of John Locke, in four volumes*, 7th edn, London, 1768, vol. 2, pp. 347, 351-3.

Born into a Puritan family in Somerset, Locke was for some time a don at Christ Church, Oxford. In 1667 he entered the household of Lord Ashley, first Earl of Shaftesbury, who from 1679 to 1683 spearheaded a Whig movement to curb the growth of royal absolutism. Following the failure of the Rye House Plot to kidnap Charles II and his Catholic brother, the future James II, Locke fled to Rotterdam in 1683. He returned to England in 1689 once Parliament had replaced James by William of Orange. *A letter concerning toleration* was written in Latin and published anonymously in Holland during April 1689; translated into English by William Popple, a Unitarian, it was published in London during October of the same year. It was written in order to warn a European audience that the spread of Catholicism would result in political absolutism and religious intolerance. Locke proposed to withold toleration from two categories of people: Catholics because their religion subverted individual liberty; and atheists on the ground that belief in God provided the only foundation upon which individuals could make moral judgements.

OUR government has not only been partial in matters of religion; but those also who have suffered under that partiality, and have therefore endeavoured by their writings to vindicate their own rights and liberties, have for the most part done it upon narrow principles, suited only to the interests of their own sects.

THIS narrowness of spirit on all sides has undoubtedly been the principal occasion of our miseries and confusions. But whatever have been the occasion, it is now high time to seek for a thorough cure. We have need of more generous remedies than what have yet been made use of in our distemper. It is neither Declarations of Indulgence, nor Acts of Comprehension, such as have yet been practised or projected amongst us, that can do the work. The first will but palliate, the second increase our evil.

ABSOLUTE LIBERTY, JUST AND TRUE LIBERTY, EQUAL AND IMPARTIAL LIBERTY, IS THE THING THAT WE STAND IN NEED OF. Now though this has indeed been much talked of, I doubt it has not been much understood; I am sure not at all practised, either by our governors towards the people in general, or by any dissenting parties of the people towards one another ...

THE commonwealth seems to me to be a society of men constituted only for the procuring, preserving, and advancing their own civil interests.

CIVIL interests I call life, liberty, health, and indolency of body; and the possession of outward things, such as money, lands, houses, furniture, and the like.

IT is the duty of the civil magistrate, by the impartial execution of equal laws, to secure unto all the people in general, and to every one of his subjects in particular, the just possession of these things belonging to this life. If any one presume to violate the laws of publick justice and equity, established for the preservation of these things, his presumption is to be checked by the fear of punishment, consisting in the deprivation or diminution of those civil interests, or goods, which otherwise he might and ought to enjoy. But seeing no man does willingly suffer himself to be punished by the deprivation of any part of his goods, and much less of his liberty or life, therefore is the magistrate armed with the force and strength of all his subjects, in order to the punishment of those that violate any other man's rights.

NOW that the whole jurisdiction of the magistrate reaches only to these civil concernments; and that all civil power, right and dominion, is bounded and confined to the only care of promoting these things; and that it neither can nor ought in any manner to be extended to the salvation of souls; these following considerations seem unto me abundantly to demonstrate.

FIRST, Because the care of souls is not committed to the civil magistrate, any more than to other men. It is not committed unto him, I say, by God; because it appears not that God has ever given any such authority to one man over another, as to compel any one to his religion. Nor can any such power be vested in the magistrate by the consent of the people; because no man can so far abandon the care of his own salvation, as blindly to leave it to the choice of any other, whether prince or subject, to prescribe to him what faith or worship he shall embrace. For no man can, if he would, conform his faith to the dictates of another. All the life and power of true religion consists in the outward and full persuasion of the mind; and faith is not faith without believing. Whatever profession we make, to whatever outward worship we conform, if we are not fully satisfied in our own mind that the one is true, and the other well pleasing unto God, such profession and such practice, far from being any furtherance, are indeed great obstacles to our salvation. For in this manner, instead of expiating other sins by the exercise of religion, I say, in offering thus unto God Almighty such a worship as we esteem to be displeasing unto him, we add unto the number of our other sins, those also of hypocrisy, and contempt of his Divine Majesty.

IN the second place. The care of souls cannot belong to the civil magistrate, because his power consists only in outward force: but true and saving religion consists in the inward persuasion of the mind, without which nothing can be acceptable to God. And such is the nature of the understanding, that it cannot be compelled to the belief of any thing by outward force. Confiscation of estate, imprisonment, torments, nothing of that nature can have any such efficacy as to make men change the inward judgment that they have framed of things.

IT may indeed be alledged, that the magistrate may make use of arguments, and thereby draw the heterodox into the way of truth, and procure their salvation. I grant it; but this is common to him with other men. In teaching, instructing, and redressing the erroneous by reason, he may certainly do what becomes any good man to do. Magistracy does not oblige him to put off either humanity or christianity. But it is one thing to persuade, another to command; one thing to press with arguments, another with penalities. This the civil power alone has a right to do; to the other goodwill is authority enough. Every man has commission to admonish, exhort, convince another of error, and by reasoning to draw him into truth: but to give laws, receive obedience, and compel with the sword, belongs to none but the magistrate. And upon this ground I affirm, that the magistrate's power extends not to the establishing of any articles of faith, or forms of worship, by the force of his laws. For laws are of no force at all without penalties, and penalties in this case are absolutely impertinent; because they are not proper to convince the mind. Neither the profession of any articles of faith, nor the conformity to any outward form of worship, as has been already said, can be available to the salvation of souls, unless the truth of the one, and the acceptableness of the other unto God, be thoroughly believed by those that so profess and practise. But penalties are no ways capable to produce such belief. It is only light and evidence that can work a change in mens opinions; and that light can in no manner proceed from corporal sufferings, or any other outward penalties.

IN the third place, The care of the salvation of mens souls cannot belong to the magistrate; because, though the rigour of laws and the force of penalties were capable to convince and change mens minds, yet would not that help at all to the salvation of their souls. For, there being but one truth, one way to heaven: what hopes is there that more men would be led into it, if they had no other rule to follow but the religion of the court, and were put under a necessity to quit the light of their own reason, to oppose the dictates of their own consciences, and blindly to resign up themselves to the will of their governors, and to the religion, which either ignorance, ambition, or superstition had chanced to establish in the countries where they were born? In the variety and contradiction of opinions in religion, wherein the princes of the world are as much divided as in their secular interests, the narrow way would be much straitened; one country alone would be in the right, and all the rest of the world put under an obligation of following their princes in the ways that lead to destruction: and that which heightens the absurdity, and very ill suits the notion of a deity, men would owe their eternal happiness or misery to the places of their nativity.

THESE considerations, to omit many others that might have been urged to the same purpose, seem unto me sufficient to conclude, that all the power of civil government relates only to mens civil interests, is confined to the care of the things of this world, and hath nothing to do with the world to come.

1.4 JOHN LOCKE

From *Two treatises of government ... Of civil government* (1689), in *The works of John Locke, in four volumes*, 7th edn, London, 1768, vol. 2, pp. 250, 255, 265–6, 268–73, 301–2.

Although Locke wrote widely on such subjects as economics, education, epistemology and theology, his reputation as one of Britain's greatest political thinkers rests upon the *Two treatises*. The book, which was probably written during the Exclusion Crisis of 1679 to 1683, attacked Sir Robert Filmer whose *Patriarcha* provided an extreme defence of royal absolutism. Locke responded to absolutists by arguing that government arose from consent, which meant that the community was entitled to resist and ultimately overthrow unjust power. The *Two treatises* appeared anonymously in 1689.

Sec. 87. MAN being born, as has been proved, with a title to perfect freedom, and uncontrouled enjoyment of all the rights and privileges of the law of nature, equally with any other man, or number of men in the world, hath by nature a power, not only to preserve his property, that is, his life, liberty and estate, against the injuries and attempts of other men; but to judge of, and punish the breaches of that law in others, as he is persuaded the offence deserves, even with death itself, in crimes where the heinousness of the fact, in his opinion, requires it.

But because no political society can be, nor subsist, without having in itself the power to preserve the property, and in order thereunto, punish the offences of all those of that society; there, and there only is political society, where every one of the members hath quitted this natural power, resigned it up into the hands of the community in all cases that exclude him not from appealing for protection to the law established by it. And thus all private judgment of every particular member being excluded, the community comes to be umpire, by settled standing rules, indifferent, and the same to all parties; and by men having authority from the community, for the execution of those rules, decides all the differences that may happen between any members of that society concerning any matter of right; and punishes those offences which any member hath committed against the society, with such penalties as the law has established: ...

Sec. 97. AND thus every man, by consenting with others to make one body politick under one government, puts himself under an obligation, to every one of that society, to submit to the determination of the majority, and to be concluded by it; or else this original compact, whereby he with others incorporate into one society, would signify nothing, and be no compact, if he be left free, and under no other ties than he was in before in the state of nature. For what appearance would there be of any compact? what new engagement if he were no farther tied by any decrees of the society, than he himself thought fit, and did actually consent to? This would be still as great a liberty, as he himself had before his compact, or any one else in the state of nature hath, who may submit himself, and consent to any acts of it if he thinks fit ...

Sec. 123. IF man in the state of nature be so free, as has been said; if he be absolute lord of his own person and possessions, equal to the greatest, and subject to no body, why will he part with his freedom? why will he give up this empire, and subject himself to the dominion and controul of any other power? To which it is obvious to answer, that though in the state of nature he hath such a right, yet the enjoyment of it is very uncertain, and constantly exposed to the invasion of others: for all being kings as much as he, every man his equal, and the greater part no strict observers of equity and justice, the enjoyment of the property he has in this state is very unsafe, very unsecure. This makes him willing to quit a condition, which, however free, is full of fears and continual dangers: and it is not without reason, that he seeks out, and is willing to join in society with others, who are already united, or have a mind to unite, for the mutual preservation of their lives, liberties and estates, which I call by the general name, property.

Sec. 124. THE great and chief end, therefore, of men's uniting into commonwealths, and putting themselves under government, is the preservation of their property ...

Sec. 134. THE great end of men's entering into society, being the enjoyment of their properties in peace and safety, and the great instrument and means of that being the laws established in that society; the first and fundamental positive law of all commonwealths is the establishing of the legislative power; as the first and fundamental natural law, which is to govern even the legislative itself, is the preservation of the society, and (as far as will consist with the publick good) of every person in it. This legislative is not only the supreme power of the commonwealth, but sacred and unalterable in the hands where the community have once placed it; nor can any edict of any body else, in what form soever conceived, or by what power soever backed, have the force and obligation of a law, which has not its sanction from that legislative which the publick has chosen and appointed: for without this the law could not have that, which is absolutely necessary to its being a law, the consent of the society, over whom no body can have a power to make laws, but by their own consent, and by authority received from them. And therefore all the obedience, which by the most solemn ties any one can be obliged to pay, ultimately terminates in this supreme power, and is directed by those laws which it enacts: nor can any oaths to any foreign power whatsoever, or any domestick subordinate power, discharge any member of the society from his obedience to the legislative, acting pursuant to their trust; nor oblige him to any obedience contrary to the laws so enacted, or farther than they do allow; it being ridiculous to imagine one can be tied ultimately to obey any power in the society, which is not the supreme.

Sec. 135. THOUGH the legislative, whether placed in one or more, whether it be always in being, or only by intervals, though it be the supreme power in every commonwealth; yet,

FIRST, It is not, nor can possibly be absolutely arbitrary over the lives and fortunes of the people: for it being but the joint power of every member of the society given up to that person, or assembly, which is legislator; it can be no more than those persons had in a state of nature before they entered into society, and gave up to the community: for no body can transfer to another more power than he has in himself; and no body has an absolute arbitrary power over himself, or over any other, to destroy his own life, or take away the life or property of another. A man, as has been proved, cannot subject himself to the arbitrary power of another; and having in the state of nature no arbitrary power over the life, liberty, or possession of another, but only so much as the law of nature gave him for the preservation of himself, and the rest of mankind; this is all he doth, or can give up to the commonwealth, and by it to the legislative power, so that the legislative can have no more than this. Their power, in the utmost bounds of it, is limited to the publick good of the society. It is a power, that hath no other end but preservation, and therefore can never have a right to destroy, enslave, or designedly to impoverish the subjects. The obligations of the law of nature cease not in society, but only in many cases are drawn closer, and have by human laws known penalties annexed to them, to inforce their observation. Thus the law of nature stands as an eternal rule to all men, legislators as well as others. The rules that they make for other man's actions, must, as well as their own and other man's actions, be conformable to the law of nature, i.e. to the will of God, of which that is a declaration, and the 'fundamental law of nature being the preservation of mankind', no human sanction can be good, or valid against it.

Sec. 136. SECONDLY, The legislative or supreme authority, cannot assume to itself a power to rule, by extemporary, arbitrary decrees, but is bound to dispense justice, and to decide the rights of the subject, by promulgated, standing laws, and known authorized judges. For the law of nature being unwritten, and so no where to be found, but in the minds of men; they who through passion, or interest, shall miscite, or misapply it, cannot so easily be convinced of their mistake, where there is no established judge: and so it serves not, as it ought, to determine the rights, and fence the properties of those that live under it, especially where every one is judge, interpreter, and executioner of it too, and that in his own case: and he that has right on his side, having ordinarily but his own single strength, hath not force enough to defend himself from injuries, or to punish delinquents. To avoid these inconveniences, which disorder men's properties in the state of nature, men unite into societies, that they may have the united strength of the whole society to secure and defend their properties, and may have standing rules to bound it, by which every one may know what is his. To this end it is that men give up all their natural power to the society which they enter into, and the community put the legislative power into such hands as they think fit; with this trust, that they shall be governed by declared laws, or else their peace, quiet, and property will still be at the same uncertainty, as it was in the state of nature ...

Sec. 138. THIRDLY, The supreme power cannot take from any man part of his property without his own consent: for the preservation of property being the end of government, and that for which men enter into society, it necessarily supposes and requires, that the people should have property, without which they must be supposed to lose that, by entering into society, which was the end for which they entered into it; too gross an absurdity for any man to own. Men therefore in society having property, they have such right to the goods, which by the law of the community are their's, that no body hath a right to take their substance or any part of it from them, without their own consent: without this they have no property at all; for I have truly no property in that, which another can by right take from me, when he pleases against my consent. Hence it is a mistake to think, that the supreme or legislative power of any commonwealth, can do what it will, and dispose of the estates of the subject arbitrarily, or take any part of them at pleasure ...

Sec. 140. IT is true, governments cannot be supported without great charge, and it is fit every one who enjoys his share of the protection, should pay out of his estate his proportion for the maintenance of it. But still it must be with his own consent, i.e. the consent of the majority, giving it either by themselves, or their representatives chosen by them: for if any one shall claim a power to lay and levy taxes on the people, by his own authority, and without such consent of the people, he thereby invades the fundamental law of property, and subverts the end of government: for what property have I in that, which another may by right take, when he pleases, to himself?

Sec. 141. FOURTHLY, The legislative cannot transfer the power of making laws to any other hands: for it being but a delegated power from the people, they who have it cannot pass it over to others. The people alone can appoint the form of the commonwealth, which is by constituting the legislative, and appointing in whose hands that shall be. And when the people have said, we will submit to rules, and be governed by laws made by such men, and in such forms, no body else can say other men shall make laws for them; nor can the people be bound by any laws, but such as are enacted by those whom they have chosen, and authorized to make laws for them. The power of the legislative being derived from the people by a positive voluntary grant and institution, can be no other than what that positive grant conveyed, which being only to make laws, and not to make legislators, the legislative can have no power to transfer their authority of making laws and place it in other hands ...

Sec. 222. THE reason why men enter society, is the preservation of their property; and the end why they chuse and authorize a legislative, is, that there may be laws made, and rules set, as guards and fences to the properties of all the members of society; to limit the power, and moderate the dominion, of every part and member of the society: for since it can never be supposed to be the will of society, that the legislative should have a power to destroy that which every one designs to secure, by entering into society, and for which the people submitted themselves to legislators of their own making; whenever the legislators endeavour to take away, and destroy the property of the people, or to reduce them to slavery under arbitrary power, they put themselves into a state of war with the people, who are thereupon absolved from any farther obedience, and are left to the common refuge, which God hath provided for all men, against force and violence. Whensoever therefore the legislative shall transgress this fundamental rule of society; and either by ambition, fear, folly or corruption, endeavour to grasp themselves, or put into the hands of any other, an absolute power over the lives, liberties, and estates of the people; by this breach of trust they forfeit the power the people had put into their hands for quite contrary ends, and it devolves to the people, who have a right to resume their original liberty, and, by the establishment of a new legislative, (such as they shall think fit) provide for their own safety and security, which is the end for which they are in society. What I have said here, concerning the legislative in general, holds true also concerning the supreme executor, who having a double trust put in him, both to have a part in the legislative, and the supreme execution of the law, acts against both, when he goes about to set up his own arbitrary will as the law of the society.

Part two
THE WHIGS

2.1 JOHN, LORD HERVEY (1696-1743)

From *Ancient and modern liberty stated and compar'd*, London, 1734,
pp. 3, 40-1, 43-7.

Hervey, eldest son of the first earl of Bristol, entered Parliament in 1725
and eventually became a beneficiary of Robert Walpole's patronage
(being granted a pension, and appointed successively vice-chamberlain
of the household and lord privy seal). By vindicating the Glorious
Revolution as a fresh departure in English constitutional history, Hervey
was seeking to purge Whiggism of any lingering association with the
radicalism of the previous century.

And as it must be granted, that all Peace, all Order in Society is
maintain'd by some Restrictions on natural Liberty, and that the
Anarchy of natural Liberty wholly unrestrain'd, would be as great an
Evil as the Slavery of no Liberty at all allow'd; so the best regulated
and best concerted Form of Government must be that which avoids
the Inconveniences of both these Extremes, and at once preserves
Mankind from the Oppressions consequent to an absolute Submission
to the Will of another, and from the Confusion that would result from
an unlimited Indulgence of their own ...

From King *James* the Second's Banishment, Abdication, Deposition, or whatever People please to call it, I date the Birth of real Liberty
in this Kingdom, or at least the Establishment, if not the
Commencement, of every valuable Privilege we now enjoy.

The *Bill of Rights* ascertain'd all those disputable Points of
Prerogative and Liberty, that had hitherto been insisted on either by
the Crown or the People, just as the Power of the one, or the other, at
different *Era's*, had prevail'd.

For notwithstanding *the Great Charter*, till this explanatory Renewal of it, or rather till this supplemental Ingraftment on the great Charter; the Bounds of Liberty and Prerogative were so indistinctly mark'd out, and so indeterminately known, that the Names of *Liberty* and *Prerogative* were made use of both by *Prince* and *People*, just as Opportunity favour'd the arbitrary Views of the one, or the licentious Disposition of the other.

No body knew the just Degrees of either; Tyranny often wore the plausible Title of the one, and Rebellion as often took the specious Form of the other, according as Occasions offer'd, and as the Temper and Circumstances of the Times, gave handle and colour to favour the Schemes and Pretensions of one or the other of these Excesses . . .

The greatest Misfortune therefore that can happen to a Country that is under a mix'd Government like ours, is to have the Districts of the chief Parts of that Government so indistinctly known, that those who should be joint Administrators of the Good of the whole, are more concern'd about having the Power to administer it, than about the Good itself; and are striving for the one, when they should be promoting the other . . .

As therefore no Government can be free but a mix'd Government, and no mix'd Government peaceable, but where the particular Jurisdictions are allotted, and the Bounds of each Part fully known and settled; so I think one may with great Truth and Justice affirm, this Government was never on so free and so desirable a Foot, as after the *Bill of Rights* was pass'd, and when the farther Limitations on the Crown by the Act of Settlement took place.

Those therefore who say *our Government is founded on Resistance*, and from thence infer that *Resistance* and *Struggle* is the Situation in which the People in this Country, whether oppress'd or not, ought always to keep themselves in order to preserve their Liberties; are as great Enemies in my Opinion to this Constitution, at least to the Peace of it, as those who would advise the Crown, instead of maintaining its legal Prerogative, to be watching every favourable Opportunity to increase it; since the one must produce the other; and if that State of Contention between *King* and *People*, is the Point at which both these Doctrines must meet, it is pretty immaterial which End you begin at.

I desire not to be misunderstood in this Point, or misinterpreted; I am far from contending for that infamous, servile, and unnatural Doctrine of *Non-Resistance*; I know that every Blessing we now enjoy is owing to the exploding of that Doctrine, and to the acting contrary to its unreasonable Maxims and slavish Tenets. When the People are injur'd, when they are oppress'd, when their Rights are infring'd, their

Liberties invaded, and the Constitution hurt and wounded, let them resist; it is their Interest, and it is their Duty to resist; it is their Nature, it has been their Practice, and I hope ever will be so in that Case. But what I condemn is the general Doctrine of Resistance, now so industriously preach'd and inculcated; and I do affirm, that if without any Allegation of Injury suffer'd, or Wrong attempted, this general Doctrine is to keep the People for ever on the Brink of Insurrection and Rebellion; if it is at all Times to be preach'd to the People (tho' the Government be ever so duly administer'd) if it is to operate equally under the best and the worst King; I say it must tend to making the Prince and his People always act as natural and irreconcilable Enemies, who should always act as natural and inseparable Friends; it must make them look on each others Interest, which should always be mutually pursued, as opposite and incompatible Interests; it must sow the Seeds of eternal Discord where Union only should be cultivated; and *at this time* I am sure, if this general Way of Reasoning were to influence the Actions of the People, without any one just Pretence of Encroachment made by the Crown upon the People; it is opening a Gate to such Strife and such Confusion, as in my Opinion would temporarily weaken each of them, and must finally conclude in the absolute Ruin of one or the other; perhaps in the Ruin of both; by making way for *One*; who could have as little Chance otherwise to succeed in his long baffled Schemes and Pretensions, as the People would have for their Liberties if in such Confusion he ever should succeed.

2.2 JOSIAH TUCKER (1713–1799)

From *Four letters on important national subjects, addressed to the right honourable the Earl of Shelburne, His Majesty's first lord commissioner of the treasury*, London, 1783, pp. 96–102.

Tucker, who was a Rector in Bristol and Dean of Gloucester, wrote widely on theology, politics and economics. Tucker condemned what he judged to be the populist assumptions of Locke's political theory on a number of occasions. In *A treatise concerning civil government* (1781), for instance, he attributed the reforming zeal of eighteenth-century radicals to the 'Lockian Principle of the indefeasible Right of private Judgment', which, though sound as a basis for religious toleration, could only subvert the balanced constitution if extended into politics. Tucker renewed his offensive in the *Four letters*. Locke had directed his *Two treatises of government* against Sir Robert Filmer, whose *Patriarcha*

(1680) affirmed the divine right of absolute monarchy. In supposing that government could be safely entrusted to an uncontrolled King, Tucker suggested in the following extract, Filmer had ignored the imperfections of human nature. But Locke's belief in natural human equality, from which arguments for a more democratic suffrage were now derived, also rested upon a foolishly optimistic view of mankind.

In his Tract on Government, (the 2d Part of which is nothing more than the Resolves of the *Cromwellian* Levellers, worked up into a System) [Locke] maintains such Principles, as must necessarily destroy every Government upon Earth, without erecting, or establishing any. *His* Error, and Sir ROBERT FILMER'S, though seemingly arising from opposite Schemes, tend to the same Centre, and rest on the same Foundation; namely, A false Idea of the present (supposed) Perfections and Excellencies of Human Nature. Sir ROBERT'S System must suppose (whether he intended it, or not) that a moral Man, by being exalted into the highest Station of all, and invested with arbitrary Sway over his Fellow-Mortals, becomes so much the better, and wiser, and fitter to govern, than he was before: Whereas the very Reverse to this is nearer to the Truth. Mr LOCKE'S System is much alike; for it supposes, that Mankind, taken in their *aggregate* or *collective* Capacity, are so much the less positive and dogmatical in their Opinions, the less liable to be perverted in their Judgments, the more humane and candid in their Decisions, and the more discreet and dispassionate in their Resolves, than otherwise they would have been. Whereas every Tittle of this is false. In short, if Experience shall be allowed to decide this Question, it will almost universally tell us, that when a Multitude are invested with the Power of governing, they prove the very worst of Governors. They are rash and precipitate, giddy and inconstant, and ever the Dupes of designing Men, who lead them to commit the most atrocious Crimes, in order to make them subservient to their own Purposes. Besides, a democratic Government is despotic in its very Nature; because it supposes itself to be the only Fountain of Power, from which there can be no Appeal. Hence, therefore, it comes to pass, that this many headed Monster, an absolute Democracy, has all the Vices and Imperfections of its Brother-Tyrant, an absolute Monarchy, without any of the shining Qualities of the latter to hide its Deformity. And what is still worse, it feels no Remorse of Conscience; and it never blushes.

IF therefore both these Species of Government are generally so bad, that they ought to be avoided as much as possible; – perhaps your Lordship might here be apt to ask, 'Is there any that is good, according to your present Description? For Government of some Sort or other there must be, notwithstanding its manifold Imperfections.' To this I answer, that *that* Government may be denominated good, in this relative or comparative Sense, which grants sufficient Liberty both civil and religious, to the Governed to do what is right, agreeably to the Dictates of sound Reason; and yet retains Power and Authority enough to restrain the ill-intentioned, and to punish the wrong Doers. – Doubtless many Checks may be introduced into every Government, for preventing an Abuse of Power to a great Degree; – and many Expedients may be devised for giving Energy to a weak and impotent Constitution: – Yet, after all, I think it must be allowed, that the very best Form of Government for answering those good Purposes, seems to be the MIXT – so mixt, as to partake of the Firmness of a regal Form, and the Credit or Reputation of a popular one. For by such an happy Temperament, many of the Advantages of both may be obtained, and their chief Inconveniences be avoided. But in order to ensure this good End, and to make it permanent, by keeping a due Medium between both Extremes, the Regal and the Popular, a THIRD POWER should intervene: – A Power, whose peculiar Interest it is, to maintain the Balance even between the opposite and contending Parties, and to prevent either of them getting such an Ascendency, as would render the other useless or unnecessary. And such a Power can be no other than an *hereditary Nobility* invested with Privileges of a peculiar Nature, for *erecting a Counter-poise.* This Institution here in *England* is honourably distinguished by the Title of *Lords*; and is so constituted, as to partake of the Qualities both of the regal and of the popular State; because it would inevitably lose by the Loss or Destruction of either of the other two, and yet be no Gainer by its Exaltation. Therefore such a *Balancing Power* will of Course, – I might say, it will through *Necessity*, throw its Weight into the opposite Scale, if either of the other Powers should be found to preponderate too much.

AND, my Lord, it was this very Circumstance, and no other, which produced the glorious Revolution of 1688. King JAMES attempted to be arbitrary: His Designs of engrossing all Power to himself, were too apparent to be denied; and no Remonstrances, however full of duty and Respect, could stop his Proceedings. Then he was opposed, most justly opposed, – not by the People only, but by the Nobility also. Nay, I might add with the strictest Truth, that the Nobility were the *foremost*, because they led the Way in this Affair. For it cannot be denied, but that they had *originally* a much greater Share in bringing about this Event, than most Commoners, though afterwards they seemed rather tardy. – Many Proofs and Evidences might be adduced; but they are needless.

2.3 CHARLES JAMES FOX (1749–1806)

From 'Mr Fox's amendments to the address on the King's speech at the opening of the session' (1792), in Irene Cooper Willis (ed.), *The speeches of Charles James Fox: French revolutionary war period*, J. M. Dent: London and Toronto, 1924, pp. 8–11, 17, 18–19.

Whigs did not form a homogeneous group, and their tendency to split into factions was aggravated by failure to attain political office for several decades after 1784. This experience renewed among some Whigs the conviction that, as custodians of the balanced constitution, they had a particular responsibility to resist arbitrary executive power. Fox, who held office several times between 1770 and 1784, became the most illustrious of opposition Whigs. He did not share Edmund Burke's implacable hostility to the French Revolution. In their assault upon a tyrannical State and intolerant church, he believed, the revolutionaries were following in the footsteps of Englishmen a century earlier. Fox was concerned, however, to withstand the authoritarian backlash which the Revolution provoked in England, where the Government, on the pretext of quelling possible insurrection, proposed to introduce various draconian measures against people who professed democratic and republican beliefs. This proscription of civil liberties, in Fox's opinion, amounted to a conspiracy to undermine limited government.

Now this, Sir, is the crisis which I think so truly alarming. We are come to the moment when the question is whether we shall give to the king, that is, to the executive government, complete power over our thoughts: whether we are to resign the exercise of our natural faculties to the ministers for the time being, or whether we shall maintain that in England no man is criminal but by the commission of overt acts forbidden by the law. This I call more imminent and tremendous than any that the history of this country ever exhibited ...

I will act against the cry of the moment, in the confidence that the good sense and reflection of the people will bear me out. I know well that there are societies who have published opinions, and circulated pamphlets, containing doctrines tending, if you please, to subvert our establishments. I say that they have done nothing unlawful in this; for these pamphlets have not been suppressed by law. Show me the law that orders these books to be burnt, and I will acknowledge the illegality of their proceedings: but if there be no such law, you violate the law in acting without authority. You have taken upon you to do that for which you have no warrant; you have voted them to be guilty. What is the course prescribed by law? If any doctrines are published tending to subvert the constitution in church and state, you may take cognisance of the fact in a court of law. What have you done? Taken upon you by your own authority to suppress them – to erect every man, not merely into an inquisitor, but into a judge, a spy, an informer – to set father against father, brother against brother, and neighbour against neighbour, and in this way you expect to maintain the peace and tranquillity of the country! You have gone upon the principles of slavery in all your proceedings: you neglect in your conduct the foundation of all legitimate government, the rights of the people: and, setting up this bugbear, you spread a panic for the very purpose of sanctifying this infringement while, again, the very infringement engenders the evil which you dread. One extreme naturally leads to another. Those who dread republicanism fly for shelter to the crown. Those who desire reform and are calumniated are driven by despair to republicanism. And this is the evil that I dread!

These are the extremes into which these violent agitations hurry the people, to the gradual decrease of that middle order of men who shudder as much at republicanism on the one hand as they do at despotism on the other. That middle order of men who have hitherto preserved to this country all that is dear in life, I am sorry to say it, is daily lessening; but permit me to add that while my feeble voice continues it shall not be totally extinct; there shall at least be one man who will, in this ferment of extremes, preserve the centre point. I may be abused by one side, I may be libelled by the other; I may be branded at one and the same time with the terms of firebrand and lukewarm politician; but though I love popularity, and own that there is no external reward so dear to me as the good opinion and confidence of my fellow-citizens, yet no temptation whatever shall ever induce me to join any association that has for its object a change in the basis of our constitution, or an extension of that basis beyond the just proportion. I will stand in the gap, and oppose myself to all the wild projects of a newfangled theory, as much as against the monstrous iniquity of exploded doctrines. I conceive the latter to be more our present danger than the former. I see, not merely in the panic of the timorous, but in the acts of the designing, cause for alarm against the most abhorrent doctrines. The new associations have acted with little disguise. One of them, the association for preserving liberty and property against republicans and levellers, I must applaud for the sincerity of its practice. Mr Chairman Reeves says that they will not only *prosecute*, but they will *convince* men, and they recommend, among other publications, a hand-bill entitled *One Pennyworth of Truth from Thomas Bull to his brother John*, in which, among other odd things, it is said, 'Have you not read the Bible? Do you not know that it is there written that kings are the Lord's anointed? But whoever heard of an anointed republic?' Such is the manner in which these associations are to 'convince' the minds of men! In the course of the present century, their recommendation would have been prosecuted as high treason. In the years 1715 and 1745, the person who dared to say that kings derived their power from divine right would have been prosecuted for treason; and I ask if, even now, this is the way to inculcate the principles of genuine loyalty? No, Sir, thank God, the people of this country have a better ground of loyalty to the house of Brunswick than that of divine right, namely, that they are the sovereigns of their own election; that their right is not derived from superstition, but from the choice of the people themselves; that it originated in the only genuine fountain of all royal power, the will of the many; and that it has been strengthened and confirmed by the experience of the blessings they have enjoyed, because the house of Brunswick has remembered the principles upon which they received the crown ...

It may be asked, would I prosecute such papers? To this I answer very candidly, I would not. I never yet saw the seditious paper that I would have thought it necessary to prosecute: but this by no means implies that emergencies may not make it proper; but surely there is nothing so essential to the true check of sedition as impartiality in prosecution. If a government wishes to be respected, they must act with the strictest impartiality, and show that they are as determined to prevent the propagations of doctrines injurious to the rights of the people as of those which are hostile to the rights of the crown. If men are to be encouraged to rally round the one standard, you must not, you ought not to prevent volunteers from rallying round the other; unless you desire to stifle in the breasts of men the surest and most active principle of obedience, a belief in your impartiality ...

But, it may be asked, what would I propose to do in times of agitation like the present? I will answer openly. If there is a tendency in the dissenters to discontent, because they conceive themselves to be unjustly suspected and cruelly calumniated, what would I do? – I would instantly repeal the test and corporation acts, and take from them, by such a step, all cause of complaint. If there were any persons tinctured with a republican spirit, because they thought that the representative government was more perfect in a republic, I would endeavour to amend the representation of the Commons, and to show that the House of Commons, though not chosen by all, should have no other interest than to prove itself the representative of all. If there were men dissatisfied in Scotland or Ireland, or elsewhere, on account of disabilities and exemptions, of unjust prejudices, and of cruel restrictions, I would repeal the penal statutes, which are a disgrace to our law books. If there were other complaints of grievances, I would redress them where they were really proved; but above all I would constantly, cheerfully, patiently listen. I would make it known that if any man felt, or thought he felt, a grievance, he might come freely to the bar of this House and bring his proofs: and it should be made manifest to all the world that where they did exist they would be redressed; where they did not, that it should be made evident. If I were to issue a proclamation, this should be my proclamation: 'If any man has a grievance, let him bring it to the bar of the Commons' House of Parliament with the firm persuasion of having it honestly investigated.' These are the subsidies that I would grant to government. What, instead of this, is done? Suppress the complaint – check the circulation of knowledge – command that no man shall read; or that as no man under £100 a year can kill a partridge, so no man under £20 or £30 a year shall dare to read or to think! . . .

Sir, I love the constitution as it is established. It has grown up with me as a prejudice and a habit, as well as from conviction. I know that it is calculated for the happiness of man, and that its constituent branches of king, lords and commons could not be altered or impaired without entailing on this country the most dreadful miseries. It is the best adapted to England, because . . . the people of England think it the best; and the safest course is to consult the judgment and gratify the predilections of a country. Heartily convinced, however, as I am, that to secure the peace, strength and happiness of the country we must maintain the constitution against all innovation, yet I do not think so superstitiously of any human institution as to imagine that it is incapable of being perverted: on the contrary, I believe that it requires an increasing vigilance on the part of the people to prevent the decay and dilapidations to which every edifice is subject. I think, also, that we may be led asleep to our real danger by these perpetual alarms to loyalty, which, in my opinion, are daily sapping the constitution. Under the pretext of guarding it from the assaults of republicans and levellers, we run the hazard of leaving it open on the other and more feeble side. We are led insensibly to the opposite danger; that of increasing the power of the crown, and of degrading the influence of the Commons' House of Parliament. It is such moments as the present that the most dangerous, because unsuspected, attacks may be made on our dearest rights; for let us only look back to the whole course of the present administration, and we shall see that, from their outset to the present day, it has been their invariable object to degrade the House of Commons in the eyes of the people, and to diminish its power and influence in every possible way.

2.4 JOHN, LORD RUSSELL (1792–1878)

From *An essay on the history of the English government and constitution from the reign of Henry VII to the present time*, new edn, Longman: London, 1865, pp. xxxi–xxxii, xxxiv–xxxvi, xcvi–xcviii.

Russell, who entered Parliament in 1813, became Prime Minister twice – from 1846 to 1852 and from 1865 to 1866. Throughout the 1820s he spearheaded attempts to transfer parliamentary seats from corrupt boroughs to unenfranchized towns and eventually steered the passage of the 1832 Reform Bill through the Commons. Although a champion of reform, however, Russell shared the objections of other Whigs to adult male suffrage.

There were evidently two modes in which reform might be approached. The one was to consider the right of voting as a personal privilege possessed by every man of sound mind, and of years of discretion, as an inherent inalienable right, belonging to him as a member of a free country. According to this theory, the votes of the whole male adult population form the only basis of legitimate government.

Other political writers and eminent statesmen, while of opinion that a free and full representation of the people forms a necessary condition of free government, acknowledge no personal right of voting as inalienable and essential. They consider that the purpose to be attained is good government; the freedom of the people within the State, and their security from without; and that the best mode of attaining these ends is the problem to be solved.

It seemed to me that these last reasoners were in the right. A representation which should produce bad, hasty, passionate, unjust, and ignorant decisions could not conduce to that welfare of the people which is the supreme law. If it be said that no part of the property of the people ought to be levied in taxes by the Government, without the consent expressed or implied of the whole community, it may be answered that a man's life and liberty are as valuable to him as his property; yet no one contends that the judicial body and the jury in criminal trials should be selected by universal suffrage. On the contrary, the greatest care is taken to place on the judicial bench men qualified by learning and experience, and to form the list of the jury out of a portion of the community whose station in life affords some security for their average intelligence, information, and honesty ...

It seemed to me at least that it would be sufficient to lay down some such conditions as the following, as necessary qualifications for the body of electors.

1. That they should be of average intelligence.
2. That they should, upon the whole, form a security for stability of property.
3. That although bribery cannot be altogether excluded, the body of electors, as a mass, should not be tainted by corruption.
4. That the electoral body should be identified with the general sense of the community – in short with the public opinion of the time.

Such being the objects in view, there were two modes by which they were to be sought. One mode would be by the qualification of the franchise; the other by the distribution of the seats.

It appeared to me that the first mode alone would not be sufficient.

In large cities population would outweigh property. In large counties property would outweigh population.

There were required some seats where property could support the claims of an intelligence not popular with the masses, and not rich in land or funds ...

It was desirable, in short, as it appeared to me, while sweeping away gross abuses, to avail ourselves, as far as possible, of the existing frame and body of our institutions.

Thus, if the due weight and influence of property could be maintained by preserving the representation of a proportion of the small boroughs with an improved franchise, it was desirable rather to build on the old foundations than to indulge our fancy or our conceit in choosing a new site and erecting on new soil – perhaps on sand – an edifice entirely different from all which had hitherto existed ...

In considering whether the people of these islands would increase their political freedom and social happiness, by deliberately adopting or unconsciously gliding into a more democratic form of government, we should take care not to be misled by the notion that we should thereby be placing ourselves under the sway of pure reason. In North America, after the separation from England, monarchy, aristocracy and church establishments were impossible; but the wisest of the founders of the great Republic, such men as Washington and Hamilton, beheld with anxiety the absence of those barriers by which the stream of democracy might be somewhat restrained. They knew well that an attempt to form a government on pure reason was a pure delusion. Man may be rendered more humane by civilization, better informed by education, but to extirpate his passions, to prevent the aberrations of his will, is impossible ...

It is because man is a creature of passion and of imagination, as well as of reason, that in the constitution of a government by which he is to be ruled and directed, it is the concern of wisdom and of foresight to avail ourselves of all the influences which may give moderation, force, and sanctity to the supreme authority. Such may be, in a monarchy, the reverence paid to Royalty, the awe inspired by religion, the respect which grows around an ancient aristocracy, the attachment to long-established laws, the refinement of polished manners, and the social kindness which adorns and animates the domestic relations of a cultivated people. Let no one imagine that without such influences, or some of them at least, a political constitution can reach its highest perfection.

2.5 THOMAS BABINGTON, LORD MACAULAY (1800–1859)

From a review of Henry Hallam's *The constitutional history of England*, in the *Edinburgh Review*, vol. 48, September 1828, pp. 167–9.

Macaulay, famous for his *History of England*, was a regular contributor to the *Edinburgh Review* in the decade preceding the passage of the Reform Bill in 1832. It was the responsibility of Whigs, he argued, to occupy the middle ground between democrats who would subvert the balanced constitution and die-hards opposed to every innovation. The middle classes should be enfranchised, according to Macaulay, because history taught that revolution could be avoided by means of gradual constitutional adjustment to evolving social circumstances.

From the time of the Revolution the House of Commons has been gradually becoming what it now is, – a great council of state, containing many members chosen freely by the people, and many others anxious to acquire the favour of the people, but, on the whole, aristocratical in its temper and interest. It is very far from being an illiberal and stupid oligarchy; but it is equally far from being an express image of the general feeling. It is influenced by the opinion of the people, and influenced powerfully, but slowly and circuitously.

Instead of out-running the public mind, as before the Revolution it frequently did, it now follows with slow steps, and at a wide distance. It is therefore necessarily unpopular; and the more so, because the good which it produces is much less evident to common perception than the evil which it inflicts. It bears the blame of all the mischief which is done, or supposed to be done, by its authority or by its connivance. It does not get the credit, on the other hand, of having prevented those innumerable abuses, which do not exist solely because the House of Commons exists.

A large part of the nation is certainly desirous of a reform in the representative system. How large that part may be, and how strong its desires on the subject may be, it is difficult to say. It is only at intervals that the clamour on the subject is loud and vehement. But it seems to us that, during the remissions, the feeling gathers strength, and that every successive burst is more violent than that which preceded it ...

A great statesman might, by judicious and timely reformations, by reconciling the two great branches of the natural aristocracy, the capitalists and the landowners, by so widening the base of the government as to interest in its defence the whole of the middling class, that brave, honest, and sound-hearted class, which is as anxious for the maintenance of order, and the security of property, as it is hostile to corruption and oppression, succeed in averting a struggle to which no rational friend of liberty or of law can look forward without great apprehensions. There are those who will be contented with nothing but demolition; and there are those who shrink from all repair. There are innovators who long for a President and a National Convention; and there are bigots, who, while cities larger and richer than the capitals of many great kingdoms are calling out for representatives to watch over their interests, select some hackneyed jobber in boroughs, some peer of the narrowest and smallest mind, as the fittest depositary of a forfeited franchise. Between these extremes there lies a more excellent way. Time is bringing round another crisis analogous to that which occurred in the seventeenth century. We stand in a situation similar to that in which our ancestors stood under the reign of James the First. It will soon again be necessary to reform that we may preserve; to save the fundamental principles of the constitution by alterations in the subordinate parts. It will then be possible, as it was possible two hundred years ago, to protect vested rights, to secure every useful institution – every institution endeared by antiquity and noble associations; and, at the same time, to introduce into the system improvements harmonizing with the original plan. It remains to be seen whether two hundred years have made us wiser.

We know of no great revolution which might not have been prevented by compromise early and graciously made. Firmness is a great virtue in public affairs; but it has its proper sphere. Conspiracies and insurrections in which small minorities are engaged, the outbreakings of popular violence unconnected with any extensive project or any durable principle, are best repressed by vigour and decision. To shrink from them is to make them formidable. But no wise ruler will confound the pervading taint with the slight local irritation. No wise ruler will treat the deeply seated discontents of a great party, as he treats the conduct of a mob which destroys mills and powerlooms. The neglect of this distinction has been fatal even to governments strong in the power of the sword. The present time is indeed a time of peace and order. But it is at such a time that fools are most thoughtless and wise men most thoughtful. That the discontents which have agitated the country during the late and the present reign, and which, though not always noisy, are never wholly dormant, will again break forth with aggravated symptoms, is almost as certain as that the tides and seasons will follow their appointed course. But in all movements of the human mind which tend to great revolutions, there is a crisis at which moderate concession may amend, conciliate, and preserve. Happy will it be for England if, at that crisis, her interests be confided to men for whom history has not recorded the long series of human crimes and follies in vain.

Part three
FROM NATURAL TO DEMOCRATIC RIGHTS

3.1 JOHN TRENCHARD (1662–1723) AND THOMAS GORDON (d. 1750)

> From *Cato's letters; or, Essays on liberty, civil and religious, and other important subjects,* 3rd edn, London, 1733, vol. 2, pp. 16, 85, 88, 90, 244–52, 257–9.

Cato's letters originally appeared as weekly newspaper articles in the *London Journal* between 1720 and 1723. They were highly popular expressions of radical Whiggism. Trenchard, principal author of the *Letters,* had been a vehement opponent of standing armies during the reign of William III. Gordon, who was Trenchard's collaborator and scribe and who eventually married his widow, supervised the printing of the various collected editions of the *Letters.* Trenchard and Gordon used contractual arguments in order to counter what they considered to be a drift towards executive tyranny. They also emphasized the link between economic and political power and urged a wider distribution of property as a means of curbing arbitrary power. The following extracts are taken from *Letters* 35, 45, 62 and 63, which were originally printed in 1721.

As Liberty can never subsist without Equality, nor Equality be long preserved without an *Agrarian* Law, or something like it; so when Men's Riches are become immeasureably or surprizingly great, a People, who regard there own Security, ought to make a strict Enquiry how they came by them, and oblige them to take down their own Size, for fear of terrifying the Community, or mastering it. In every Country, and under every Government, particular Men may be too rich ...

But, will some say, is it a Crime to be rich? Yes, certainly, at the publick Expence, or to the Danger of the Publick. A Man may be too rich for a Subject; even the Revenues of Kings may be too large. It is one of the Effects of Arbitrary Power, that the Prince has too much, and the People too little; and such Inequality may be the Cause too of Arbitrary Power ...

MEN are naturally equal, and none ever rose above the rest but by Force or Consent: No Man was ever born above all the rest, nor below them all; and therefore there never was any Man in the World so good or so bad, so high or so low, but he had his Fellow. Nature is a kind and benevolent Parent; she constitutes no particular Favourites with Endowments and Privileges above the rest; but for the most part sends all her Offspring into the World furnished with the Elements of Understanding and Strength to provide for themselves: She gives them Heads to consult their own Security, and Hands to execute their own Counsels; and according to the Use that they make of their Faculties, and of the Opportunities that they find, Degrees of Power and Names of Distinction grow amongst them, and their natural Equality is lost.

Thus Nature, who is their Parent, deals with Men: But Fortune, who is their Nurse, is not so benevolent and impartial; she acts wantonly and capriciously, often cruelly; and counterplotting Justice as well as Nature, frequently sets the Fool above the wise Man, and the best below the worst ...

All the Arts and Endowments of Men to acquire Preheminence and Advantages over one another, are so many Proofs and Confessions that they have not such Preheminence and Advantages from Nature; and all their Pomp, Titles, and Wealth, are Means and Devices to make the World think that they who possess them are superior in Merit to those that want them. But it is not much to the Glory of the upper Part of Mankind, that their boasted and superior Merit is often the Work of Heralds, Artificers, and Money; and that many derive their whole stock of Fame from Ancestors, who lived an Age or many Ages ago ...

There is nothing moral in Blood, or in Title, or in Place: Actions only, and the Causes that produce them, are moral. He therefore is best that does best. Noble Blood prevents neither Folly, nor Lunacy, nor Crimes; but frequently begets or promotes them: And Noblemen, who act infamously, derive no Honour from virtuous Ancestors, whom they dishonour. A Man who does base Things, is not noble; nor great, if he do little Things: A sober Villager is a better Man than a debauched Lord; an honest Mechanick, than a Knavish Courtier ...

We cannot bring more natural Advantages into the World, than other Men do; but we can acquire more Virtue in it than we generally acquire. To be great, is not in every Man's Power; but to be good, is in the Power of all: Thus far every Man may be upon a Level with another, the lowest with the highest; and Men might thus come to be morally as well as naturally equal ...

By Liberty, I understand the Power which every Man has over his own Actions, and his Right to enjoy the Fruits of his Labour, Art and Industry, as far as by it he hurts not the Society, or any Members of it, by taking from any Member, or by hindering him from enjoying what he himself enjoys. The Fruits of a Man's honest Industry are the just Rewards of it, ascertained to him by natural and eternal Equity, as is his Title to use them in the Manner which he thinks fit: And thus, with the above Limitations, every Man is sole Lord and Arbiter of his own private Actions and Property–A Character of which no Man living can divest him but by Usurpation, or his own Consent.

The entering into political Society, is so far from a Departure from this natural Right, that to preserve it, was the sole Reason why Men did so; and mutual Protection and Assistance is the only reasonable Purpose of all reasonable Societies. To make such protection practicable, Magistracy was formed, with Power to defend the Innocent from Violence, and to punish those that offered it; nor can there be any other Pretence for Magistracy in the World. In order to this good End, the Magistrate is intrusted with conducting and applying the united Force of the Community; and with exacting such a Share of every Man's Property, as is necessary to preserve the Whole, and to defend every Man and his Property from foreign and domestick Injuries. These are Boundaries of the Power of the Magistrate, who deserts his Function whenever he breaks them. By the Laws of Society, he is more limited and restrained than any Man amongst them; since, while they are absolutely free in all their Actions, which purely concern themselves; all his Actions, as a public Person, being for the Sake of the Society, must refer to it, and answer the Ends of it.

It is a mistaken Notion in government, that Interest of the Majority is only to be consulted, since in Society every Man has a Right to every Man's Assistance in the Enjoyment and Defence of his private Property; otherwise the greater Number may sell the lesser, and divide their estates amongst themselves; and so, instead of a Society, where all peaceable Men are protected, become a Conspiracy of the Many against the Minority. With as much Equity may one Man wantonly dispose of all, and Violence may be sanctified by mere Power.

And it is as foolish to say, that Government is concerned to meddle with the private Thoughts and Actions of Men, while they injure neither the Society, or any of its Members. Every Man is, in Nature and Reason, the Judge and Disposer of his own domestick Affairs; and, according to the Rules of Religion and Equity, every Man must carry his own Conscience. So that neither has the Magistrate a Right to direct the private Behaviour of Men; nor has the Magistrate, or any Body else, any manner of Power to model People's Speculations, no more than their Dreams. Government being intended to protect Men from the Injuries of one another, and not to direct them in their own Affairs, in which no one is interested but themselves; it is plain, that their Thoughts and domestick Concerns are exempted intirely from its Jurisdiction: In Truth, Men's Thoughts are not subject to their own Jurisdiction.

Idiots and Lunaticks indeed, who cannot take Care of themselves, must be taken Care of by others: But whilst Men have their five Senses, I cannot see what the Magistrate has to do with Actions by which the Society cannot be affected; and where he meddles with such, he meddles impertinently or tyrannically. Must the Magistrate tye up every Man's Legs, because some Men fall into Ditches? Or, must he put out their Eyes, because with them they see lying Vanities? Or, would it become the Wisdom and Care of Governors to establish a travelling Society, to prevent People by a proper Confinement from throwing themselves into Wells, or over Precipices? Or to endow a Fraternity of Physicians and Surgeons all over the Nation, to take Care of their Subjects Health, without being consulted; and to vomit, bleed, purge, and scarify them at Pleasure, whether they would or no, just as these established Judges of Health should think fit? If this were the Case, what a Stir and Hubbub should we soon see kept about the established Potions and Lancets; every Man, Woman, and Child, though ever so healthy, must be a patient, or woe be to them! The best Diet and Medicines would soon grow pernicious from any other Hand; and their Pills alone, however ridiculous, insufficient, or distasteful, would be attended with a Blessing.

Let People alone, and they will take care of themselves, and do it best; and if they do not, a sufficient Punishment will follow their Neglect, without the Magistrate's Interposition and Penalties. It is plain that such busy Care and officious Intrusion into the personal Affairs, or private Actions, Thoughts and Imaginations of Men, has in it more Craft than Kindness; and is only a Device to mislead people, and pick their Pockets, under the false Pretence of the publick and their private Good. To quarrel with any Man for his Opinions, Humours, or the Fashion of his Cloaths, is an Offence taken without being given. What is it to a Magistrate how I wash my Hands, or cut my Corns, what Fashion or Colours I wear, or what Notions I entertain, or what Gestures I use, or what Words I pronounce, when they please me, and do him and my Neighbour no hurt? As well may he determine the Colour of my Hair, and controul my Shape and Features.

True and impartial Liberty is therefore the Right of every Man to pursue the natural, reasonable, and religious Dictates of his own Mind; to think what he will, and act as he thinks, provided he acts not to the Prejudice of another; to spend his own Money himself, and lay out the Produce of his Labour his own Way; and to labour for his own Pleasure and Profit, and not for others who are idle, and would live and riot by pillaging and oppressing him, and those that are like him.

So that Civil Government is only a partial Restraint put by the Laws of Agreement and Society upon natural and absolute Liberty, which might otherwise grow licentious: And Tyranny is an unlimited Restraint put upon natural Liberty, by the Will of one or a few. Magistracy, amongst a free People, is the Exercise of Power for the sake of the People; and Tyrants abuse the People, for the sake of Power. Free Government is the protecting the People in their Liberties by stated Rules; Tyranny is a brutish Struggle for unlimited Liberty to one or a few, who would rob all others of their Liberty, and act by no Rule but lawless Lust.

So much for an Idea of Civil Liberty. I will now add a Word or two, to shew how much it is the Delight and Passion of Mankind; and then shew its Advantages.

The Love of Liberty is an Appetite so strongly implanted in the Nature of all living Creatures, that even the Appetite of Self-preservation, which is allowed to be the strongest, seems to be contained in it; since by the Means of Liberty, they enjoy the Means of preserving themselves, and of satisfying their Desires in the Manner which they themselves chuse and like best ...

This passion for Liberty in Men, and their Possession of it, is of that efficacy and Importance, that it seems the Parent of all the Virtues: And therefore, in free Countries there seems to be another Species of Mankind, than is to be found under Tyrants ...

Education alters Nature, and becomes stronger. Slavery, while it continues, being a perpetual Awe upon the Spirits, depresses them, and sinks natural Courage; and Want and Fear, the Concomitants of Bondage, always produce Despondency and Baseness: Nor will Men in Bonds ever fight bravely, but to be free. Indeed, what else should they fight for; since every Victory that they gain for a Tyrant, makes them poorer and fewer, and, increasing his Pride, increases his Cruelty, with their own Misery and Chains?

Those, who from Terror and Delusion, the frequent Causes and certain Effects of Servitude, come to think their Governors greater than Men, as they find them worse, will be as apt to think themselves less: And when the Head and the Heart are thus both gone, the Hands will signify little. They who are used like Beasts, will be apt to degenerate into Beasts. But those, on the contrary, who by the Freedom of their Government and Education, are taught and accustomed to think freely of Men and Things, find, by comparing one Man with another, that all Men are naturally alike; and that their Governors, as they have the same Face, Constitution and Shape with themselves, and are subject to the same Sickness, accidents, and Death, with the meanest of their People; so they possess the same Passions and Faculties of the Mind which their Subjects possess, and not better. They therefore scorn to degrade and prostrate themselves, to adore those of their own Species, however covered with Titles, and disguised by Power: They consider them as their own Creatures; and, as far as they surmount themselves, the Work of their own Hands, and only the chief Servants of the State, who have no more Power to do Evil than one of themselves, and are void of every Privilege and Superiority, but to serve them and the State. They know it to be a Contradiction in Religion and Reason, for any Man to have a Right to do Evil; that not to resist any Man's Wickedness, is to encourage it; and that they have the least Reason to bear Evil and Oppression from their Governors, who of all Men are the most obliged to do them Good. They therefore detest Slavery, and despise or pity Slaves; and, adoring Liberty alone, as they who see its Beauty and feel its Advantages always will, it is no wonder that they are brave for it.

Indeed, Liberty is the divine Source of all human Happiness. To possess, in Security, the Effects of our Industry, is the most powerful and reasonable Incitement to be industrious: And to be able to provide for our Children, and leave them all that we have, is the best Motive to beget them. But where Property is precarious, Labour will languish. The Privileges of thinking, saying, and doing what we please, and of growing as rich as we can, without any other Restriction, than that by all this we hurt not the Publick, nor one another, are the glorious Privileges of Liberty; and its Effects, to live in Freedom, Plenty, and Safety.

These are Privileges that increase Mankind, and the Happiness of Mankind. And therefore Countries are generally peopled in Proportion as they are free, and are certainly happy in that Proportion: And upon the same Tract of Land that would maintain a Hundred Thousand Free-men in Plenty, Five Thousand Slaves would starve . . .

I Go on with my Considerations upon Liberty, to shew that all Civil Virtue and Happiness, every moral Excellency, all Politeness, all good Arts and Sciences, are produced by Liberty; and that all Wickedness, Baseness, and Misery, are immediately and necessarily produced by Tyranny; which being founded upon the Destruction of every thing that is valuable, desirable, and noble, must subsist upon Means suitable to its Nature, and remain in everlasting Enmity to all Goodness and every human Blessing.

By the Establishment of Liberty, a due Distribution of Property and an equal Distribution of Justice is established and secured. As Rapine is the Child of Oppression, Justice is the Offspring of Liberty, and her Hand-maid; it is the Guardian of Innocence, and the Terror of Vice: And when Fame, Honour, and Advantages are the Rewards of Virtue, she will be courted for the Dower which she brings; otherwise, like Beauty without Wealth, she may be praised, but more probably will be calumniated, envied, and very often persecuted; while Vice, when it is gainful, like rich Deformity and prosperous Folly, will be admired and pursued. Where Virtue is all her own Reward, she will be seldom thought any; and few will buy That for a great Price, which will sell for none. So that Virtue, to be followed, must be endowed, and her Credit is best secured by her Interest; that is, she must be strengthened and recommended by the publick Laws, and embellished by publick Encouragements, or else she will be slighted and shunned.

Now the Laws which encourage and encrease Virtue, are the fixed Laws of general and impartial Liberty; Laws, which being the Rule of every Man's Actions, and the Measure of every Man's Power, make Honesty and Equity their Interest. Where Liberty is thoroughly established, and its Laws equally executed, every man will find his Account in doing as he would be done unto, and no Man will take from another what he would not part with himself: Honour and Advantage will follow the Upright, Punishment overtake the Oppressor. The Property of the Poor will be as sacred as the Privileges of the Prince, and the Law will be the only Bulwark of both. Every Man's honest Industry and useful Talents, while they are employed for the Publick, will be employed for himself; and while he serves himself, he will serve the Publick: Publick and private Interest will secure each other; all will chearfully give a Part to secure the Whole, and be brave to defend it.

These certain Laws therefore are the only certain Beginnings and Causes of Honesty and Virtue amongst Men. There may be other Motives, I own; but such as only sway particular Men, few enough, God knows: And universal Experience has shewn us, that they are not generally prevailing, and never to be depended upon. Now these Laws are to be produced by Liberty alone, and only by such Laws can Liberty be secured and increased: And to make Laws certainly good, they must be made by mutual Agreement, and have for their End the general Interest.

3.2 JOSEPH PRIESTLEY (1733–1804)

From *An essay on the first principles of government; and on the Nature of political, civil, and religious liberty*, Dublin, 1768, pp. 13–14, 16–17, 19, 21–3, 53–61.

Priestley taught for a period at Warrington Academy for dissenters, and later ministered to congregations in Leeds and Birmingham. He is now remembered mainly for his scientific work, which included a *History of electricity* and the discovery of oxygen. But he also published widely on theology, philosophy, education and politics. Although Priestley defended religious freedom as a natural right, he nevertheless conceded that matters such as the proper extent of the franchise should be settled on empirical rather than deductive grounds.

(I)f I be asked what I mean by *liberty,* I should chuse for the sake of greater clearness, to divide it into two kinds, *political,* and *civil;* and the importance of having clear ideas on this subject will be my apology for the innovation. *Political liberty,* I would say, consists in the power, which the members of the state reserve to themselves, of arriving at the public offices, or at least of having votes in the nomination of those who fill them: and I would chuse to call *civil liberty* that power over their own actions, which the members of the state reserve to themselves, and which their officers must not infringe. Political liberty, therefore, is equivalent to the right of magistracy, being the claim that any member of the state hath, to have his private opinion or judgement become that of the public, and thereby control the actions of others; whereas civil liberty, extends no farther than to a man's own conduct, and signifies the right he has to be exempt from the control of the society, or its agents; that is, the power he has of providing for his own advantage and happiness. It is a man's civil liberty, which is originally in its full force, and part of which he sacrifices when he enters into a state of society; and political liberty is that which he may or may not acquire in the compensation he receives for it. For he may either stipulate to have a voice in the publick determinations, or, as far as the public determination doth take place, he may submit to be governed wholly by others. Of these two kinds of liberty, which it is of the greatest importance to distinguish, I shall treat in the order in which I have mentioned them ...

And since every man retains, and can never be deprived of his natural right (founded on a regard to the general good) of relieving himself from all oppression, that is, from every thing that has been imposed upon him without his own consent; this can be the only true and proper foundation of all governments subsisting in the world, and that to which the people who compose them have an unalienable right to bring them back.

It must necessarily be understood, therefore, whether it be expressed or not, that all people live in society for their mutual advantage; so that the good and happiness of the members, that is the majority of the members of any state, is the great standard by which every thing relating to that state must finally be determined. And though it may be supposed, that a body of people may be bound by a voluntary resignation of all their interests (which they have been so infatuated as to make) to a single person, or to a few, it can never be supposed that the resignation is obligatory to their posterity; because it is manifestly *contrary to the good of the whole that it should be so* ...

Let it be observed, in this place, that I by no means assert, that the good of mankind requires a state of the most perfect political liberty ...

In general, it should seem, that none but persons of considerable fortune should be capable of arriving at the highest offices in the government; not only because, all other circumstances being equal, such persons will generally have had the best education, and consequently be the best qualified to act for the public good; but also, as they will necessarily have the most property at stake, and will, therefore, be most interested in the fate of their country.

For the same reason, it may, perhaps, be more eligible, that those who are extremely dependent should not be allowed to have votes in the nomination of the chief magistrates; because this might in some instances, be only throwing more votes into the hands of those persons on whom they depend. But if, in every state of considerable extent, we suppose a gradation of elective offices, and if we likewise suppose the lowest classes of the people to have votes in the nomination of the lowest officers, and, as they increase in wealth and importance, to have a share in the choice of persons to fill the higher posts, till they themselves be admitted candidates for places of public trust: we shall, perhaps, form an idea of as much political liberty as is consistent with the state of mankind. And I think experience shews, that the highest offices of all, equivalent to that of king, ought to be in some measure hereditary, as in England; elective monarchies having generally been the theatre of cabals, confusion, and misery.

But though the exact medium of political liberty be not easily fixed, it is not of much consequence to do it; since a considerable degree of perfection in government will admit of great varieties in this respect . . .

IT is a matter of the greatest importance, that we carefully distinguish between the *form*, and the *extent of power* in a government; for many maxims in politics depend upon the one, which are too generally ascribed to the other.

It is comparatively of small consequence *who*, or *how many* be our governors, or *how long* their office continues, provided their power be the same while they are in office, and the administration be uniform and certain. All the difference which can arise to states from diversities, in the number or duration of governors, can only flow from the motives and opportunities, which those different circumstances may give their deputies, of extending, or making a bad use of their power. But whether a people enjoy more or fewer of their natural rights, under any form of government, is a matter of the last importance; and upon this depends, what, I should chuse to call the *civil liberty* of the state, as distinct from its political liberty.

If the power of government be very extensive, and the subjects of it have, consequently, little power over their own actions, that government is tyrannical, and oppressive; whether, with respect to its form, it be a monarchy, an aristocracy, or even a republic. For the government of the temporary magistrates of a democracy, or even the laws themselves may be as tyrannical as the maxims of the most despotic monarchy, and the administration of the government may be as destructive of private happiness. The only consolation that a democracy suggests in those circumstances is, that every member of the state has a chance of arriving at a share in the chief magistracy, and consequently of playing the tyrant in his turn; and as there is no government in the world so perfectly democratical, as that every member of the state, without exception, has a right of being admitted into the administration, great numbers will be in the same condition as if they had lived under the most absolute monarchy; and this is, in fact, almost universally the case with the poor in all governments.

For the same reason, if there were no fixed laws, but every thing was decided according to the will of the persons in power; who is there that would think it of much consequence, whether his life, his liberty, or his property were at the mercy of one, of a few, or of a great number of people, that is, of a mob, liable to the worst of influences. So far, therefore, we may safely say, with Mr. Pope, that *those governments which are best administered are best:*—that is, provided the power of government be moderate, and leave a man the most valuable of his private rights; provided the laws be certainly known to every one, and the administration of them be uniform, it is of no consequence how many, or how few persons are employed in the administration ...

Political and civil liberty, as before explained, though very different, have, however, a very near and manifest connection; and the former is the chief guard of the latter, and on that account, principally, is valuable, and worth contending for. If all the political power of this country were lodged in the hands of one person, and the government thereby changed into an absolute monarchy, the people would find no difference, provided the same laws and the same administration, which now subsist, were continued. But then, the people, having no political liberty, would have no security for the continuance of the same laws, and the same administration. They would have no guard for their civil liberty. The monarch, having it in his option, might not chuse to continue the same laws, and the same administration. He might fancy it to be for his own interest to alter them, and to abridge his subjects in their private rights; and in general, it may be depended upon, that governors will not consult the interest of the people, except it be their own interest too, because governors are but men. But while a number of the people have a share in the legislature, so as to be able to control the supreme magistrate, there is a great probability that things will continue in a good state. For the more political liberty the people have, the safer is their civil liberty.

Besides, political and civil liberty have many things in common, which indeed, is the reason why they have been so often confounded. A sense both of political and civil slavery makes a man think meanly of himself. The feeling of his insignificance debases his mind, checks every great and enterprising sentiment; and, in fact, renders him that poor abject creature, which he fancies himself to be. Having always some unknown evil to fear, tho' it should never come, he has no perfect enjoyment of himself, or of any of the blessings of life; and thus, his sentiments and his enjoyments being of a lower kind, the man sinks nearer to the state of the brute creation.

On the other hand, a sense of political and civil liberty, though there should be no great occasion to exert it in the course of a man's life, gives him a constant feeling of his own power and importance; and is the foundation of his indulging a free, bold, and manly turn of thinking, unrestrained by the most distant idea of control. Being free from all fear, he has the most perfect enjoyment of himself, and of all the blessings of life; and his sentiments and enjoyments, being raised, his very *being* is exalted, and the man makes nearer approaches to superior natures.

3.3 THOMAS PAINE (1737–1809)

From *Rights of man: being an answer to Mr Burke's attack on the French Revolution,* ed. Hypatia Bradlaugh Bonner, Watts: London, 1913, Pt. I (1791), pp. 27–30, 71–3; Pt. II (1792) pp. 93–6.

Paine, whose father was a Norfolk Quaker, emigrated to America in 1774. His *Common sense* (1776) was a widely read appeal for American independence from Britain. Paine later participated in the Revolution in France, where he became an elected representative but was subsequently imprisoned during the Terror. The *Rights of man,* which combined support for the French Revolution with a condemnation of British monarchy and aristocracy, was banned as seditious in England. Paine returned to America where he spent his final years in obscurity. The following extract illustrates how he used the doctrine of natural rights to undermine the hierarchical assumptions associated with the Whig defence of mixed government, and urged the implementation of a written constitution framed upon democratic and republican principles.

Man did not enter into society to become *worse* than he was before, nor to have fewer rights than he had before, but to have those rights better secured. His natural rights are the foundation of all his civil rights. But in order to pursue this distinction with more precision, it will be necessary to mark the different qualities of natural and civil rights.

A few words will explain this. Natural rights are those which appertain to man in right of his existence. Of this kind are all the intellectual rights, or rights of the mind, and also all those rights of acting as an individual for his own comfort and happiness, which are not injurious to the natural rights of others. Civil rights are those which appertain to man in right of his being a member of society. Every civil right has for its foundation some natural right pre-existing in the individual, but to the enjoyment of which his individual power is not, in all cases, sufficiently competent. Of this kind are all those which relate to security and protection.

From this short review it will be easy to distinguish between that class of natural rights which man retains after entering into society and those which he throws into the common stock as a member of society.

The natural rights which he retains are all those in which the *power* to execute is as perfect in the individual as the right itself. Among this class, as is before mentioned, are all the intellectual rights, or rights of the mind; consequently religion is one of those rights. The natural rights which are not retained, are all those in which, though the right is perfect in the individual, the power to execute them is defective. They answer not his purpose. A man, by natural right, has a right to judge in his own cause, and so far as the right of the mind is concerned, he never surrenders it. But what availeth it him to judge, if he has not power to redress? He therefore deposits this right in the common stock of society, and takes the arm of society, of which he is a part, in preference and in addition to his own. Society *grants* him nothing. Every man is a proprietor in society, and draws on the capital as a matter of right.

From these premises two or three certain conclusions will follow:

First, That every civil right grows out of a natural right; or, in other words, is a natural right exchanged.

Secondly, That civil power properly considered as such is made up of the aggregate of that class of the natural rights of man, which becomes defective in the individual in point of power, and answers not his purpose, but when collected to a focus becomes competent to the purpose of every one.

Thirdly, That the power produced from the aggregate of natural rights, imperfect in power in the individual, cannot be applied to invade the natural rights which are retained in the individual, and in which the power to execute it is as perfect as the right itself.

We have now, in a few words, traced man from a natural individual to a member of society, and shown, or endeavoured to show, the quality of the natural rights retained, and of those which are exchanged for civil rights. Let us now apply these principles to governments.

In casting our eyes over the world, it is extremely easy to distinguish the governments which have arisen out of society, or out of the social compact, from those which have not; but to place this in a clearer light than what a single glance may afford, it will be proper to take a review of the several sources from which governments have arisen and on which they have been founded.

They may be all comprehended under three heads. First, Superstition. Secondly, Power. Thirdly, The common interest of society and the common rights of man.

The first was a government of priestcraft, the second of conquerors, and the third of reason . . .

It has been thought a considerable advance towards establishing the principles of Freedom to say that government is a compact between those who govern and those who are governed; but this cannot be true, because it is putting the effect before the cause; for as man must have existed before governments existed, there necessarily was a time when governments did not exist, and consequently there could originally exist no governors to form such a compact with. The fact therefore must be that the *individuals themselves,* each in his own personal and sovereign right, *entered into a compact with each other* to produce a government: and this is the only mode in which governments have a right to arise, and the only principle on which they have a right to exist.

To possess ourselves of a clear idea of what government is, or ought to be, we must trace it to its origin. In doing this we shall easily discover that governments must have arisen either *out* of the people or *over* the people ...

But it will be first necessary to define what is meant by a *constitution.* It is not sufficient that we adopt the word; we must fix also a standard signification to it.

A constitution is not a thing in name only, but in fact. It has not an ideal, but a real existence; and wherever it cannot be produced in a visible form, there is none. A constitution is a thing *antecedent* to a government, and a government is only the creature of a constitution. The constitution of a country is not the act of its government, but of the people constituting its government. It is the body of elements, to which you can refer, and quote article by article; and which contains the principles on which the government shall be established, the manner in which it shall be organized, the powers it shall have, the mode of elections, the duration of parliaments, or by what other name such bodies may be called; the powers which the executive part of the government shall have; and in fine, everything that relates to the complete organization of a civil government, and the principles on which it shall act, and by which it shall be bound. A constitution, therefore, is to a government what the laws made afterwards by that government are to a court of judicature. The court of judicature does not make the laws, neither can it alter them; it only acts in conformity to the laws made: and the government is in like manner governed by the constitution. Can, then, Mr. Burke produce the English Constitution? If he cannot, we may fairly conclude that though it has been so much talked about, no such thing as a constitution exists, or ever did exist, and consequently that the people have yet a constitution to form.

Mr. Burke will not, I presume, deny the position I have already advanced–namely, that governments arise either *out* of the people or *over* the people. The English Government is one of those which arose out of a conquest, and not out of society, and consequently it arose over the people; and though it has been much modified from the opportunity of circumstances since the time of William the Conqueror, the country has never yet regenerated itself, and is therefore without a constitution ...

REASON and Ignorance, the opposite to each other, influence the great bulk of mankind. If either of these can be rendered sufficiently extensive in a country, the machinery of government goes easily on. Reason obeys itself; and Ignorance submits to whatever is dictated to it.

The two modes of government which prevail in the world, are, *first* government by election and representation; *secondly,* government by hereditary succession. The former is generally known by the name of republic; the latter by that of monarchy and aristocracy.

Those two distinct and opposite forms erect themselves on the two distinct and opposite bases of Reason and Ignorance. As the exercise of government requires talents and abilities, and as talents and abilities cannot have hereditary descent, it is evident that hereditary succession requires a belief from man to which his reason cannot subscribe, and which can only be established upon his ignorance; and the more ignorant any country is, the better it is fitted for this species of government.

On the contrary, government, in a well-constituted republic, requires no belief from man beyond what his reason can give. He sees the *rationale* of the whole system, its origin and its operation; and as it is best supported when best understood, the human faculties act with boldness, and acquire under this form of government a gigantic manliness.

As, therefore, each of those forms acts on a different base, the one moving freely by the aid of reason, the other by ignorance, we have next to consider, what it is that gives motion to that species of government which is called mixed government, or, as it is sometimes ludicrously stiled, a government of *this, that and t'other.*

The moving power in this species of government is of necessity corruption. However imperfect election and representation may be in mixed governments, they still give exercise to a greater portion of reason than is convenient to the hereditary part; and therefore it becomes necessary to buy the reason up. A mixed government is an imperfect everything, cementing and soldering the discordant parts together by corruption, to act as a whole. Mr. Burke appears highly disgusted that France, since she had resolved on a revolution, did not adopt what he calls *'A British Constitution';* and the regretful manner in which he expresses himself on this occasion, implies a suspicion that the British Constitution needed something to keep its defects in countenance.

In mixed governments there is no responsibility: the parts cover each other till responsibility is lost; and the corruption which moves the machine, contrives at the same time its own escape. When it is laid down as a maxim, that *a King can do no wrong,* it places him in a state of similar security with that of idiots and persons insane, and responsibility is out of the question with respect to himself. It then descends upon the minister, who shelters himself under a majority in parliament, which by places, pensions, and corruption, he can always command; and that majority justifies itself by the same authority with which it protects the minister. In this rotatory motion, responsibility is thrown off from the parts, and from the whole.

When there is part in a government which can do no wrong, it implies that it does nothing; and is only the machine of another power, by whose advice and direction it acts. What is supposed to be the King in the mixed governments, is the cabinet; and as the cabinet is always a part of the parliament, and the members justifying in one character what they advise and act in another, a mixed government becomes a continual enigma; entailing upon a country, by the quantity of corruption necessary to solder the parts, the expence of supporting all the forms of government at once, and finally resolving into a government by committee; in which the advisers, the actors, the approvers, the justifiers, the persons responsible, and the persons not responsible, are the same persons.

By this pantomimical contrivance, and change of scene and character, the parts help each other out in matters which neither of them singly would assume to act. When money is to be obtained, the mass of variety apparently dissolves, and a profusion of parliamentary praises passes between the parts. Each admires with astonishment, the wisdom, the liberality, and disinterestedness of the other; and all of them breathe a pitying sigh at the burdens of the nation.

But in a well-constituted republic, nothing of this soldering, praising, and pitying, can take place; the representation being equal throughout the country, and compleat in itself, however it may be arranged into legislative and executive, they have all one and the same natural source. The parts are not foreigners to each other, like democracy, aristocracy, and monarchy. As there are no discordant distinctions, there is nothing to corrupt by compromise, nor confound by contrivance. Public measures appeal of themselves to the understanding of the nation, and resting on their own merits, disown any flattering applications to vanity. The continual whine of lamenting the burden of taxes, however successfully it may be practised in mixed governments, is inconsistent with the sense and spirit of a republic. If taxes are necessary, they are of course advantageous, but if they require an apology, the apology itself implies an impeachment ...

From the revolutions of America and France, and the symptoms that have appeared in other countries, it is evident that the opinion of the world is changed with respect to systems of government, and that revolutions are not within the compass of political calculations. The progress of time and circumstances, which men assign to the accomplishment of great changes, is too mechanical to measure the force of the mind, and the rapidity of reflection, by which revolutions are generated: All the old governments have received a shock from those that already appear, and which were once more improbable, and are a greater subject of wonder, than a general revolution in Europe would be now.

When we survey the wretched condition of man, under the monarchical and hereditary systems of government, dragged from his home by one power, or driven by another, and impoverished by taxes more than by enemies, it becomes evident that those systems are bad, and that a general revolution in the principle and construction of governments is necessary.

What is government more than the management of the affairs of a nation? It is not, and from its nature cannot be, the property of any particular man or family, but of the whole community, at whose expence it is supported; and though by force and contrivance it has been usurped into an inheritance, the usurpation cannot alter the right of things. Sovereignty, as a matter of right, appertains to the nation only, and not to any individual; and a nation has at all times an inherent, indefeasible right to abolish any form of government it finds inconvenient, and to establish such as accords with its interest, disposition, and happiness. The romantic and barbarous distinction of men into Kings and subjects, though it may suit the conditions of courtiers, cannot that of citizens; and is exploded by the principle upon which governments are now founded. Every citizen is a member of the sovereignty, and, as such, can acknowledge no personal subjection: and his obedience can be only to the laws ...

Republican government is no other than government established and conducted for the interest of the public, as well individually as collectively. It is not necessarily connected with any particular form, but it most naturally associates with the representative form, as being best calculated to secure the end for which a nation is at the expence of supporting it ...

That which is called government or rather that which we ought to conceive government to be, is no more than some common centre, in which all the parts of society unite. This cannot be accomplished by any method so conducive to the various interests of the community as by the representative system ...

A nation is not a body, the figure of which is to be represented by the human body, but is like a body contained within a circle, having a common centre in which every radius meets; and that centre is formed by representation. To connect representation with what is called monarchy is eccentric government. Representation is of itself the delegated monarchy of a nation, and cannot debase itself by dividing it with another ...

In the representative system, the reason for everything must publicly appear. Every man is a proprietor in government, and considers it a necessary part of his business to understand. It concerns his interest, because it affects his property. He examines the cost, and compares it with the advantages; and above all, he does not adopt the slavish custom of following what in other governments are called LEADERS.

It can only be by blinding the understanding of man, and making him believe that government is some wonderful mysterious thing, that excessive revenues are obtained. Monarchy is well-calculated to ensure this end. It is the popery of government, a thing kept up to amuse the ignorant and quiet them into taxes.

3.4 EDWARD MIALL (1809–1881)

From *Reconciliation between the middle and labouring classes,*
B. Hudson: Birmingham, 1842, pp. 8–9, 13, 15, 18–20.

Miall, a Congregational minister in Leicester, moved to London in 1841 to establish and edit the *Nonconformist,* an organ of militant dissent which advocated the disestablishment and disendowment of the Church of England. Miall, who believed in political as well as religious equality, had links with the Complete Suffrage Union whose leader was Joseph Sturge, a Birmingham Quaker and corn merchant. The *Reconciliation between the middle and labouring classes,* which expressed the opinions of the Suffrage Union, consists of articles initially printed in the *Nonconformist.* Miall was elected to parliament in 1852 and remained an important figure in radical politics. The Liberation Society – which Miall had founded in 1844 under a different name, the Anti State Church Society – was an influential pressure group in mid-Victorian Britain. Its many local branches helped to consolidate the bond between Nonconformity and liberalism, especially after 1868 when the Society became formally tied to the Liberal Party. The following extract urges democratic reform as a matter of natural right, and also conveys the faith of middle-class radicals in the bourgeois potential of the lower classes.

The suffrage has been denied to be a right, otherwise than as that right is conferred upon subjects by legislation. The theory is to this effect. 'Organised society is the creature of conventional arrangement, in which natural rights are resigned in exchange for the advantage of protection. As a member of society, man can possess no rights but those with which society endows him. He has entered upon a new state. He comes under an entirely new set of conditions. His natural rights are left behind him when he quits a position of isolated independence, and the political rights which thenceforth he may enjoy, are conferred upon him by an understood mutual agreement, Government is *for* the people – and when we avail ourselves of its benefits, we give up all claim of independent right, and come under law to what is expedient. What is expedient for society becomes the proper measure of our privileges, and all questions affecting our political relations must be referred to that standard. Now the franchise is clearly a question of this sort – consequently no right to the franchise can be admitted, but such as society confers.' ...

When man enters into a conventional state, and gives up independence with a view to protection, a tacit compact, we take it, is effected between the several members of society considered in its collective capacity. He passes away from a state of unitude (if we may coin a word to express our meaning with precision) into a state of aggregation, as a means to an end–that end comprehending all the advantages arising from social order. Government is his creature, framed exclusively for his benefit, and invested with powers delegated by himself to answer purposes essential to his welfare. 'I give you authority that you may give me protection', is the true interpretation of the maxim, that 'the people are the only legitimate source of power.' Now a compact supposes that, whatever else we concede to the covenanting party, we do not, and cannot, part with the ultimate right to see that the conditions of the agreement are fulfilled. That must remain with us; for the very essence of a bargain resides in the right of each party to demand the fulfilment of its terms. To government it belongs to define allegiance; to us it belongs to define protection. We have clearly a right to demand that the thing for which we invest the state with power, be performed by the state – and of the fidelity of the state to its trust, we reserve to ourselves the right of exercising judgment. We reserve it – it is not bestowed upon us by government – it belongs to us irrespectively of all conventional law; for, without it, conventionalism is a mere contradiction; and the doctrine, that government is either *from* the people or *for* them, is a sheer absurdity.

Here, then, we have one right enjoyed by men in society, having its foundations deeper than society itself – the right of claiming from the state, that it accomplish the ends for which it was originally constituted, and of judging for themselves whether it has accomplished them or not. But this right infers another. It infers that they retain the power to give expression to that judgment, and that such expression becomes a component element of the influence by which government is ultimately controlled. When the right remains with us to demand, the right to enforce the demand is pre-supposed, and is checked only by the higher laws of morality and religion. But subject to such checks, there is but one conceivable method of giving to our judgment a practical authority – namely, that of allowing it a fair representation in the national councils. The right, consequently, to be part and parcel of the government which exists *for* us, and whose power is power delegated to it by ourselves; in other words, the right to enforce our view of its obligations by proxy – i.e. to have our voice in the election of those who are to determine upon what is, or what is not, protection, is evidently antecedent to all conventional arrangement, and must stand or fall with the maxim with which we started; 'that the people are the only legitimate source of power.' . . .

It is one thing to recognise a right; it is another and much more difficult one to give to that right a complete practical expression . . .

Political power and personal independence must stand or fall together. This is no new doctrine. Our forefathers recognised it. Feudal serfs they excluded from the franchise, and, practically, none but feudal serfs. This we may take some future occasion of proving. Meanwhile, every one must admit, that parties whose actions are under the legal control of others, who in the eye of law are not their own masters, free to choose their own occupation, and enjoy for themselves the proceeds of their own labour, can hardly be invested with the responsibility of the franchise. This limitation excludes all minors and paupers. Not until the age of twenty-one years does a man in this country attain to the station of an independent freeman; and when dependent upon the resources of society, so as to take from, instead of adding to, the general stock, as in the case of the recipients of parish relief, he may be regarded as foregoing his independence. A receiver of public money, for which no equivalent return is made, clearly has no right to a voice in the imposition of taxes. He pays nothing to the state. He is himself an incumbrance upon it. He cannot equitably claim, therefore, to have any control over its movements . . .

Only let the poor be taken politically by the hand – placed on a level with other classes – brought forward into association with these whose social position is above them – and the spirit within them will naturally awake to new life, and become sensible to wants before unknown. Education will not need then to be forced upon the poor. They will pant for education. Man soon accommodates himself to a new sphere, when once he is allowed to move in it – seldom qualifies himself for that sphere before he is called to occupy it. Raise the tone of his self-respect by raising his position, and you awaken in his bosom an honourable ambition to act his part with becoming dignity. The extension to the people of complete suffrage, so far from exciting insubordination, would, calculating upon the ordinary laws of human nature, give a mighty impulse to popular intelligence and morality; and in the course of a short time would secure an amount of education, order, and even religion, which no other means could possibly effect.

The great *desideratum* of society is that all classes should be guided in their conduct by systematic self-government, rather than by the external restraints of law. But men never care to obey, themselves, until they receive from others the respect to which they are entitled. Until then, apart from religion, with which human governments have nothing to do, the grand motive is wanting – the inner spring is sealed up – and men are what they are forced to be, rather than what they wish to be. The way to make them aspire is not to treat them as things of nought – to make them love order and revere law is not to refuse them the benefits of order, and turn law into an engine for their oppression. Place them where they are entitled to be, give them what they are entitled to have, and whilst you take away the main inducement to insubordination, you supply at the same time the main motive to industrious, sober, and peaceable behaviour ...

Can any thinking man doubt for a moment, that if the great body of the middle class were thus to hold out the hand of friendship to the unrepresented masses, and evince a sincere desire to put them in possession of the rights so long withheld from them, they might lead them almost whithersoever they please? Revolution! spoliation! Yes, if we compel the excluded millions to wrestle with us for their own, the very heat of passion generated by the conflict, may inflame them with the spirit of retaliation, in the frenzy of which nothing would be safe. But let us justly, kindly, cheerfully, restore them to political equality with ourselves, and we say there is nothing forbearing, nothing generous, nothing self-sacrificing to which they might not be led. Proudly do we bear our testimony to their susceptibility of gratitude. In all instances we have ever observed, that respect paid to them they are ready to repay tenfold. Kindness touches them more closely than it does us, for they are less familiar with it. If ignorant men can mislead them, it is only because intelligent men have seen fit to spurn them. Mere demagogues would lose both their influence and their trade, were men of character willing to deal justice to the poor. What they require in their leaders is a sincere recognition of their rights as free men – and this once obtained, sound advice and rational measures would avail to win their suffrage, to the full as readily as that of any other class.

On the whole, we have no manner of doubt that the moral effects to be anticipated from the adoption of complete suffrage would be even more valuable than those which are purely political. The bonds by which society is held together would be drawn more closely – party conflicts would soon cease – reason and rights would have fair play – education would be coveted – morals would improve – and religion itself would appeal with much greater probability of success to the myriads who now suspect it to be an instrument of oppression.

4.1 ADAM SMITH (1723–1790)

From *An inquiry into the nature and causes
of the wealth of nations* (1776), Nelson and Brown: Edinburgh, 1834, Bk
IV, ch. ix, pp. 285–6, Bk V, ch. 1, pp. 302, 327–30.

Smith, who taught at Glasgow University from 1751 to 1764, was the
founding father of political economy. The most effective guarantee of
wealth, he argued, was a free-market economy guided by the 'invisible
hand' of providence rather than by government. He nevertheless
acknowledged that an extensive division of labour, from which flowed
increased productivity, generated serious moral and political problems.
Hence, as this extract reveals, he urged government to take steps to
foster habits of citizenship among common people.

It is thus that every system which endeavours, either, by extraordinary
encouragements to draw towards a particular species of industry a
greater share of the capital of the society than what would naturally go
to it, or, by extraordinary restraints, to force from a particular species
of industry some share of the capital which would otherwise be
employed in it, is, in reality, subversive of the great purpose which it
means to promote. It retards, instead of accelerating the progress of
the society towards real wealth and greatness; and diminishes, instead
of increasing, the real value of the annual produce of its land and
labour.

All systems, either of preference or of restraint, therefore, being
thus completely taken away, the obvious and simple system of natural
liberty establishes itself of its own accord. Every man, as long as he
does not violate the laws of justice, is left perfectly free to pursue his
own interest his own way, and to bring both his industry and capital
into competition with those of any other man, or order of men. The
sovereign is completely discharged from a duty, in the attempting to

perform which he must always be exposed to innumerable delusions, and for the proper performance of which, no human wisdom or knowledge could ever be sufficient; the duty of superintending the industry of private people, and of directing it towards the employments most suitable to the interests of the society. According to the system of natural liberty, the sovereign has only three duties to attend to; three duties of great importance, indeed, but plain and intelligible to common understandings: first, the duty of protecting the society from the violence and invasion of other independent societies; secondly, the duty of protecting, as far as possible, every member of the society from the injustice or oppression of every other member of it, or the duty of establishing an exact administration of justice ...

The third and last duty of the sovereign or commonwealth, is that of erecting and maintaining those public institutions and those public works, which though they may be in the highest degree advantageous to a great society, are, however, of such a nature, that the profit could never repay the expense to any individual, or small number of individuals; and which it, therefore, cannot be expected that any individual, or small number of individuals, should erect or maintain. The performance of this duty requires, too, very different degrees of expense in the different periods of society.

After the public institutions and public works necessary for the defence of the society, and for the administration of justice, both of which have already been mentioned, the other works and institutions of this kind are chiefly for facilitating the commerce of the society, and those for promoting the instruction of the people. The institutions for instruction are of two kinds: those for the education of the youth, and those for the instruction of people of all ages ...

In some cases, the state of society necessarily places the greater part of individuals in such situations as naturally form in them, without any attention of government, almost all the abilities and virtues which that state requires, or perhaps can admit of. In other cases, the state of the society does not place the greater part of individuals in such situations; and some attention of government is necessary, in order to prevent the almost entire corruption and degeneracy of the great body of the people.

In the progress of the division of labour, the employment of the far greater part of those who live by labour, that is, of the great body of the people, comes to be confined to a few very simple operations; frequently to one or two. But the understandings of the greater part of men are necessarily formed by their ordinary employments. The man whose whole life is spent in performing a few simple operations, of which the effects, too, are perhaps always the same, or very nearly the same, has no occasion to exert his understanding, or to exercise his invention, in finding out expedients for removing difficulties which never occur. He naturally loses, therefore, the habit of such exertion, and generally becomes as stupid and ignorant as it is possible for a human creature to become. The torpor of his mind renders him not only incapable of relishing or bearing a part in any rational conversation, but of conceiving any generous, noble, or tender sentiment, and consequently of forming any just judgment concerning many even of the ordinary duties of private life. Of the great and extensive interests of his country he is altogether incapable of judging; and unless very particular pains have been taken to render him otherwise, he is equally incapable of defending his country in war. The uniformity of his stationary life naturally corrupts the courage of his mind, and makes him regard, with abhorrence, the irregular, uncertain, and adventurous life of a soldier. It corrupts even the activity of his body, and renders him incapable of exerting his strength with vigour and perseverance in any other employment, than that to which he has been bred. His dexterity at his own particular trade seems, in this manner, to be acquired at the expense of his intellectual, social, and martial virtues. But in every improved and civilized society, this is the state into which the labouring poor, that is, the great body of the people, must necessarily fall, unless government takes some pains to prevent it.

It is otherwise in the barbarous societies, as they are commonly called, of hunters, or shepherds, and even of husbandmen in that rude state of husbandry which precedes the improvement of manufactures, and the extension of foreign commerce. In such societies, the varied occupations of every man oblige every man to exert his capacity, and to invent expedience for removing difficulties which are continually occurring. Invention is kept alive, and the mind is not suffered to fall into that drowsy stupidity, which, in a civilized society, seems to benumb the understanding of almost all the inferior ranks of people . . .

The education of the common people requires, perhaps, in a civilized and commercial society, the attention of the public, more than that of people of some rank and fortune. People of some rank and fortune are generally eighteen or nineteen years of age, before they enter upon that particular business, profession or trade, by which they propose to distinguish themselves in the world. They have, before that, full time to acquire, or at least to fit themselves for afterwards acquiring, every accomplishment which can recommend them to the public esteem, or render them worthy of it. Their parents or guardians are generally sufficiently anxious that they should be so accomplished, and are, in most cases, willing enough to lay out the expense which is necessary for that purpose. If they are not always properly educated, it is seldom from the want of expense laid out upon their education, but from the improper application of that expense. It is seldom from the want of masters, but from the negligence and incapacity of the masters who are to be had, and from the difficulty, or rather from the impossibility, which there is, in the present state of things, of finding any better. The employments, too, in which people of some rank or fortune spend the greater part of their lives, are not, like those of the common people, simple and uniform. They are almost all of them extremely complicated, and such as exercise the head more than the hands. The understandings of those who are engaged in such employments, can seldom grow torpid for want of exercise. The employments of people of some rank and fortune, besides, are seldom such as harass them from morning to night. They generally have a good deal of leisure, during which they may perfect themselves in every branch, either of useful or ornamental knowledge, of which they may have laid the foundation, or for which they may have acquired some taste in the earlier part of life.

It is otherwise with the common people. They have little time to spare for education. Their parents can scarce afford to maintain them, even in infancy. As soon as they are able to work, they must apply to some trade, by which they can earn their subsistence. That trade, too, is generally so simple and uniform, as to give little exercise to the understanding; while, at the same time, their labour is both so constant and so severe, that it leaves them little leisure and less inclination to apply to, or even to think of any thing else.

But though the common people cannot, in any civilized society, be so well instructed as people of some rank and fortune; the most essential parts of education, however, to read, write, and account, can be acquired at so early a period of life, that the greater part, even of those who are to be bred to the lowest occupations, have time to acquire them before they can be employed in those occupations. For a very small expense, the public can facilitate, can encourage, and can even impose upon almost the whole body of the people, the necessity of acquiring those most essential parts of education.

The public can facilitate this acquisition, by establishing in every parish or district a little school, where children may be taught for a reward so moderate, that even a common labourer may afford it; the master being partly, but not wholly, paid by the public; because, if he was wholly, or even principally, paid by it, he would soon learn to neglect his business ...

Though the state was to derive no advantage from the instruction of the inferior ranks of people, it would still deserve its attention that they should not be altogether uninstructed. The state, however, derives no inconsiderable advantage from their instruction. The more they are instructed, the less liable they are to the delusions of enthusiasm and superstition, which, among ignorant nations, frequently occasion the most dreadful disorders. An instructed and intelligent people, besides, are always more decent and orderly than an ignorant and stupid one. They feel themselves, each individually, more respectable, and more likely to obtain the respect of their lawful superiors, and they are, therefore, more disposed to respect those superiors. They are more disposed to examine, and more capable of seeing through, the interested complaints of faction and sedition; and they are, upon that account, less apt to be misled into any wanton or unnecessary opposition to the measures of government. In free countries, where the safety of government depends very much upon the favourable judgment which the people may form of its conduct, it must surely be of the highest importance, that they should not be disposed to judge rashly or capriciously concerning it.

4.2 THOMAS ROBERT MALTHUS (1766–1834)

From *An essay on the principle of population; or, a view of its past and present effects on human happiness; with an inquiry into our prospects respecting the future removal or mitigation of the evils which it occasions* (1798), 6th edn, John Murray: London, 1826, vol. 2, pp. 427–9, 438–40.

Malthus was an Anglican priest who in 1805 became Professor of Modern History and Political Economy at Haileybury College. In the first edition of his *Essay on the principle of population,* published in 1798, Malthus suggested that an expanding population would always tend to outstrip the means of subsistence. In subsequent editions, however, he expressed greater confidence in the capacity of the poor to grasp simple economic truths. They would thereby become law-abiding citizens, and also improve their living standards by exercising prudence with regard to family size. This more optimistic version of the Malthusian theory of population, which is captured in the following extract, had an important influence upon nineteenth-century liberal thought.

It has been generally found that the middle parts of society are most favourable to virtuous and industrious habits, and to the growth of all kinds of talents. But it is evident that all cannot be in the middle. Superior and inferior parts are in the nature of things absolutely necessary; and not only necessary, but strikingly beneficial. If no man could hope to rise, or fear to fall in society; if industry did not bring with it its reward, and indolence its punishment; we could not expect to see that animated activity in bettering our condition, which now forms the master-spring of public prosperity. But in contemplating the different states of Europe, we observe a very considerable difference in the relative proportions of the superior, the middle and the inferior parts; and from the effect of these differences it seems probable, that our best-grounded expectations of an increase in the happiness of the mass of human society are founded in the prospect of an increase in the relative proportions of the middle parts. And if the lower classes of people had acquired the habit of proportioning the supplies of labour to a stationary or even decreasing demand, without an increase of misery and mortality, as at present, we might even venture to indulge a hope that at some future period the processes for abridging human labour, the progress of which has of late years been so rapid, might ultimately supply all the wants of the most wealthy society with less personal effort than at present; and if they did not diminish the severity of individual exertion, might, at least, diminish the number of those employed in severe toil. If the lowest classes of society were thus diminished, and the middle classes increased, each labourer might indulge a more rational hope of rising by diligence and exertion into a better station; the rewards of industry and virtue would be increased in number; the lottery of human society would appear to consist of fewer blanks and more prizes; and the sum of social happiness would be evidently augmented.

To indulge, however, in any distant views of this kind, un-accompanied by the evils usually attendant on a stationary or decreasing demand for labour, we must suppose the general prevalence of such prudential habits among the poor, as would prevent them from marrying, when the actual price of labour, joined to what they might have saved in their single state, would not give them the prospect of being able to support a wife and five or six children without assistance. And undoubtedly such a degree of prudential restraint would produce a very striking melioration in the condition of the lower classes of people ...

That the principal and most permanent cause of poverty has little or no *direct* relation to forms of government, or the unequal division of property; and that, as the rich do not in reality possess the *power* of finding employment and maintenance for the poor, the poor cannot, in the nature of things, possess the *right* to demand them; are important truths flowing from the principle of population, which, when properly explained, would by no means be above the most ordinary comprehensions. And it is evident that every man in the lower classes of society, who became acquainted with these truths, would be disposed to bear the distresses in which he might be involved with more patience; would feel less discontent and irritation at the government and the higher classes of society, on account of his poverty; would be on all occasions less disposed to insubordination and turbulence; and if he received assistance, either from any public institution or from the hand of private charity, he would receive it with more thankfulness, and more justly appreciate its value.

If these truths were by degrees more generally known, (which in the course of time does not seem to be improbable from the natural effects of the mutual interchange of opinions,) the lower classes of people, as a body, would become more peaceable and orderly, would be less inclined to tumultuous proceedings in seasons of scarcity, and would at all times be less influenced by inflammatory and seditious publications, from knowing how little the price of labour and the means of supporting a family depend upon a revolution. The mere knowledge of these truths, even if they did not operate sufficiently to produce any marked change in the prudential habits of the poor with regard to marriage, would still have a most beneficial effect on their conduct in a political light; and undoubtedly, one of the most valuable of these effects would be the power, that would result to the higher and middle classes of society, of gradually improving their governments, without the apprehension of those revolutionary excesses, the fear of which, at present, threatens to deprive Europe even of that degree of liberty, which she had before experienced to be practicable, and the salutary effects of which she had long enjoyed.

4.3 THOMAS CHALMERS (1780–1847)

From *The supreme importance of a right moral to a right economical state of the community* (1832), in *The works of Thomas Chalmers,* William Collins: Glasgow, 1836–42, vol. 20, pp. 220–1, 223–5.

Chalmers, a Scottish Presbyterian minister, was a great preacher and prolific writer who became Professor of Moral Philosophy at St Andrews, and later held the Chair of Theology at Edinburgh. On

moving to Glasgow in 1815, Chalmers sought to implement the
parochial system with which he had been familiar in rural Fife. Parishes
were divided into districts in which lay helpers ran day schools and
Sunday schools, administered poor relief, and encouraged such schemes
as popular savings banks. In these ways, Chalmers believed, an
enlightened middle class could fulfil its Christian duty by imparting to
the urban poor the Malthusian message of moral and educational
self-improvement.

What all economists admit to be of some importance, we pronounce to
be of supreme importance: That moral worth, which they regard as but
helpful, we regard as indispensable, to the economic well-being of the
people.

While we would leave the elevated parts of our social fabric
untouched, all our fondest wishes are on the side of the common
people. It is our belief, that through the medium, not of a political
change in the state, but of a moral and personal change upon
themselves, there is not one desirable amelioration which they might
not mount their way to... The condition to which they might
hopefully aspire – and it is the part of every honest and enlightened
philanthropist to help them forward to it – is that of less work and
higher wages; and this, not only that they might participate more
largely in the physical enjoyments of life, but that, in exemption from
oppressive toil, and with the command of dignified leisure, there
might be full opportunity and scope for the development of their
nobler faculties, in the prosecution of all the higher objects of a rational
and immortal existence. There is but one practicable opening, we hold,
to such an enlargement for the working classes, and which can be made
good by the strength of their own moral determination – when, after
the spectacle of cheerful and well-paid industry has been fully realized,
we shall at length behold them emancipated from their sore bondage,
and these brethren of our common nature transformed into lettered,
and humanized, and companionable men ...

To change the habit of a nation, must ever seem a Utopian
enterprise, so long as we measure the achievement by our own
individual strength. But this is not the work of one man, but of many
thousand men; and it is not Utopianism, but experience, to affirm
the possibility that each of those men shall, in his own territorial
vineyard, and among the people of his peculiar charge, realize the
union which obtains between the Christianity of a state, and those
blessings of a civil or temporal nature which follow in its train. Their
first concern is with the religion, the righteousness of the people; but
we are not to overlook the declaration, that when he who seeketh this

first also findeth it, all other things shall be added unto him. There is a most important connexion between the Christianity and the sound economic condition of our families; and while the lessons of political science, as they fall from the lips of philosophers, however just in principle, are wholly impotent in practice – we have long thought, that they are the clergymen of a land, who hold those master–springs, by a right impulse on which, they might speed forward, and at length achieve, all those objects, which are dearest to the heart, either of the philanthropist or of the patriot. More especially do we regard them as in occupation of the best vantage-ground, for combating all the difficulties which are felt or imagined in the problem of paupersm ... Believing, as we do, of that moral pestilence, that, in the deadly virus wherewith it is charged, there exist all the elements of misery and corruption – we cannot deem the question of parish economics unworthy of a place among the other cares and studies of a clergyman. Political economy is not theology; but political economy, as associated with the moral state and moral prospects of society, is that upon which even theology might deign to cast an eye. This science, celestial though it be, possesses a mighty ascendant over all terrestrial interests and affairs. Heaven is the ultimate landing-place of its contemplations – yet the history of earth has either been directed by its power, or deeply leavened by its presence. With its corruption stood palpably associated the darkness and despotism of the middle ages – and it is no less palpable, whether we look to the wider theatre of Europe, or to the struggles of piety and patriotism in our own land, that its Reformation was the harbinger of all the light and the liberty of our modern day. Now, let us hope there is reserved for it a more pacific, yet more glorious triumph – not on the arena of a stormy politics, but by its silent operation on the growth of popular intelligence and virtue throughout our parishes; thus providing the surest remedy for all the moral and political disorders to which a country is exposed.

4.4 RICHARD COBDEN (1804–1865)

From 'Free trade' (1844), in *Speeches on questions of public policy by Richard Cobden, M.P.,* ed. John Bright and James E. Thorold Rogers, 3rd edn, Fisher Unwin: London, 1908, vol. 1, pp. 62–3.

The mid-Victorian conflict about protection versus free-trade symbolized a cultural cleavage between the Tory–Anglican landed classes and the largely Nonconformist (although Cobden himself was an Anglican) manufacturing middle classes of the industrial North. Cobden, who led the anti-Corn Law campaign, was a Manchester calico printer who entered parliament in 1841 as Member for Stockport. Repeal of the Corn Laws, he argued, would generate prosperity throughout both industry and agriculture.

Now, let me be fully understood as to what Free Traders really do want. We do not want cheap corn merely in order that we may have low money prices. What we desire is plenty of corn, and we are utterly careless what its price is, provided we obtain it at the natural price. All we ask is this, that corn shall follow the same law which the monopolists in food admit that labour must follow; that 'it shall find its natural level in the markets of the world.'

And now, what would be the process of this equalisation of prices? I think I can give you the rationale of it. The effect of free trade in corn will be this: It would increase the demand for agricultural produce in Poland, Germany, and America. That increase in the demand for agricultural produce would give rise to an increased demand for labour in those countries, which would tend to raise the wages of the agricultural labourers. The effect of that would be to draw away labourers from manufactures in all those places. To pay for that corn, more manufactures would be required from this country; this would lead to an increased demand for labour in the manufacturing districts, which would necessarily be attended with a rise of wages, in order that the goods might be made for the purpose of exchanging for the corn brought from abroad. Whether prices would be equalised, according to the opinion expressed by my Lord Spencer, by a rise in the price of bread abroad to the level at which it is here, or whether it would be by a fall in the prices here to the level at which they now exist on the Continent, would not make the least earthly difference to the Free Traders; all they ask is, that they shall be put in the same position with others, and that there should be no bar or hindrance to the admission of food from any quarter into this country. I observe there are narrow-minded men in the agricultural districts, telling us, 'Oh, if you allow Free Trade, and bring in a quarter of corn from abroad, it is quite clear that you will sell one quarter less in England.' Those men, fellow-countrymen, who utter such nonsense as this, are a sample of the philosophers who are now governing this country. What! I would ask, if you can set more people to work at better wages – if you can clear your streets of those spectres which are now haunting your thoroughfares begging their daily bread – if you can depopulate your workhouses, and clear off the two millions of paupers which now exist in the land, and put them to work at productive industry – do you not think that they would consume some of the wheat as well as you; and may not they be, as we are now, consumers of wheaten bread by millions, instead of existing on their present miserable dietary? Mark me: these philosophical men, so profoundly ignorant of what is immediately around them, but who meet us at every turn with prophecies of what is going to happen in future, will tell us, forsooth, that Free Trade will throw their land out of cultivation, and deprive their labourers of employment ...

(S)o far from throwing land out of use or injuring the cultivation of the poorer soils, free trade in corn is the very way to increase the production at home, and stimulate the cultivation of the poorer soils by compelling the application of more capital and labour to them. We do not contemplate deriving one quarter less corn from the soil of this country; we do not anticipate having one pound less of butter or cheese, or one head less of cattle or sheep: we expect to have a great increase in production and consumption at home; but all we contend for is this, that when we, the people here, have purchased all that can be raised at home, we shall be allowed to go 3000 miles – to Poland, Russia, or America – for more; and that there shall be not let or hindrance put in the way of our getting this additional quantity.

4.5 JOHN BRIGHT (1811–1889)

From 'Foreign policy' (1858), in *Speeches on questions of public policy by the Right Honourable John Bright, M.P.*, ed. James E. Thorold Rogers, Macmillan: London, 1869, pp. 468, 470, 478.

Bright was born into a Quaker family which owned a cotton-spinning mill in Rochdale. A great orator, he became Cobden's 'speaking lieutenant' in the Anti–Corn Law League and entered Parliament in 1843. Following the League's success, however, Bright mounted a campaign to free foreign policy from aristocratic control. In the following speech, which was given to his Birmingham constituents, Bright attributed militarism to the effects of the Glorious Revolution.

Do not all statesmen know, as you know, that upon peace, and peace alone, can be based the successful industry of a nation, and that by successful industry alone can be created that wealth which, permeating all classes of the people, not confined to great proprietors, great merchants, and great speculators, not running in a stream merely down your principal streets, but fertilizing rivulets into every bye-lane and every alley, tends so powerfully to promote the comfort, happiness, and contentment of a nation? Do you not know that all progress comes from successful and peaceful industry, and that upon it is based your superstructure of education, of morals, of self-respect among your people, as well as every measure for extending and consolidating freedom in your public institutions? I am not afraid to acknowledge that I do oppose – that I do utterly condemn and denounce – a great part of the foreign policy which is practised and adhered to by the Government of this country.

You know, of course, that about 170 years ago there happened in this country what we have always been accustomed to call 'a Glorious Revolution' – a Revolution which had this effect: that it put a bit into the mouth of the monarch, so that he was not able of his own freewill to do, and he dared no longer attempt to do, the things which his predecessors had done without fear. But if at the Revolution the monarchy of England was bridled and bitted, at the same time the great territorial families of England were enthroned; and from that period, until the year 1831 or 1832 ... those territorial families reigned with an almost undisputed sway over the destinies and the industry of the people of these kingdoms. If you turn to the history of England, from the period of the Revolution to the present, you will find that an entirely new policy was adopted, and that while we had endeavoured in former times to keep ourselves free from European complications, we now began to act upon a system of constant entanglement in the affairs of foreign countries, as if there was neither property nor honours, nor anything worth striving for, to be acquired in any other field. The language coined and used then, has continued to our day. Lord Somers, in writing for William III, speaks of the endless and sanguinary wars of that period as wars 'to maintain the liberties of Europe.' There were wars 'to support the Protestant interest,' and there were many wars to preserve our old friend 'the balance of power.'

We have been at war since that time, I believe, with, for, and against every considerable nation in Europe ...

There is no actuary in existence who can calculate how much of the wealth, of the strength, of the supremacy of the territorial families of England has been derived from an unholy participation in the fruits of the industry of the people, which have been wrested from them by every device of taxation, and squandered in every conceivable crime of which a Government could possibly be guilty.

The more you examine this matter the more you will come to the conclusion which I have arrived at, that this foreign policy, this regard for 'the liberties of Europe,' this care at one time for 'the Protestant interests,' this excessive love for the 'balance of power,' is neither more nor less than a gigantic system of out-door relief for the aristocracy of Great Britain ...

I believe there is no permanent greatness to a nation except it be based upon morality. I do not care for military greatness or military renown. I care for the condition of the people among whom I live. There is no man in England who is less likely to speak irreverently of the Crown and Monarchy of England than I am; but crowns, coronets, mitres, military display, the pomp of war, wide colonies, and a huge empire, are, in my view, all trifles light as air, and not worth considering, unless with them you can have a fair share of comfort, contentment, and happiness among the great body of the people. Palaces, baronial castles, great halls, stately mansions, do not make a nation. The nation in every country dwells in the cottage; and unless the light of your Constitution can shine there, unless the beauty of your legislation and the excellence of your statesmanship are impressed there on the feelings and condition of the people, rely upon it you have yet to learn the duties of government.

I have not, as you have observed, pleaded that this country should remain without adequate and scientific means of defence. I acknowledge it to be the duty of your statesmen, acting upon the known opinions and principles of ninety-nine out of every hundred persons in the country, at all times, with all possible moderation, but with all possible efficiency, to take steps which shall preserve order within and on the confines of your kingdom. But I shall repudiate and denounce the expenditure of every shilling, the engagement of every man, the employment of every ship which has no object but intermeddling in the affairs of other countries, and endeavouring to extend the boundaries of an Empire which is already large enough to satisfy the greatest ambition, and I fear is much too large for the highest statesmanship to which any man has yet attained.

4.6 RICHARD COBDEN

From 'Free trade' (1843), in *Speeches on questions of public policy by Richard Cobden, M.P.,* ed. John Bright and James E. Thorold Rogers, 3rd edn, Fisher Unwin: London, 1908, vol. 1, p. 40.

Free Trade! What is it? Why, breaking down the barriers that separate nations; those barriers, behind which nestle the feelings of pride, revenge, hatred, and jealousy, which every now and then burst their bounds, and deluge whole countries with blood; those feelings which nourish the poison of war and conquest, which assert that without conquest we can have no trade, which foster that lust for conquest and dominion which sends forth your warrior chiefs to scatter devastation through other lands, and then calls them back that they may be enthroned securely in your passions, but only to harass and oppress you at home.

4.7 WILLIAM EWART GLADSTONE (1809–1898)

From 'Free trade', in the *North American Review*, vol. 150, January 1890, pp. 9–11, 25.

Born in Liverpool, Gladstone was educated at Eton and Christ Church, Oxford. In 1832 he entered Parliament as a High Church Tory, and was soon appointed a junior minister in Sir Robert Peel's administration, Gladstone gradually adopted more liberal opinions on such issues as free trade and religious dissent, and finally broke with the Tory Party in 1846 over the repeal of the Corn Laws. Gladstone was Liberal Prime Minister on three occasions between 1868 and 1894. The party which he led was initially an uneasy alliance of Whig grandees, Radicals and former Peelites who, like himself, had opposed the Tory defence of the Corn Laws. Although Gladstone failed to resolve all the tensions within the Liberal Party, he nevertheless consolidated its electoral support among Nonconformists and new working-class voters. Gladstone treated politics as a moral crusade; and his greatest passion was for peaceful co-existence between independent nations that were linked by policies of free trade.

With a view to presenting the argument for leaving trade to the operation of natural laws in the simplest manner, I shall begin with some postulates which I suppose to be incapable of dispute.

International commerce is based, not upon arbitrary or fanciful considerations, but upon the unequal distribution among men and regions of aptitudes to produce the several commodities which are necessary or useful for the sustenance, comfort, and advantage of human life.

If every country produced all commodities with exactly the same degree of facility or cheapness, it would be contrary to common-sense to incur the charge of sending them from one country to another.

But the inequalities are so great that (for example) region A can supply region B with many articles of food, and region B can in return supply region A with many articles of clothing, at such rates that, although in each case the charge of transmission has of necessity been added to the first cost, the respective articles can be sold after importation at a lower rate than if they were home-grown or home-manufactured in the one or the other country respectively.

The relative cost, in each case, of production and transmission, as compared with domestic production, supplies, while all remain untrammelled by state law, a rule, motive, or mainspring of distribution which may be termed natural.

The argument of the Free-Trader is that the legislator ought never to interfere, or only to interfere so far as imperative fiscal necessity may require it, with this natural law of distribution.

All interference with it by a government in order to encourage some dearer method of production at home, in preference to a cheaper method of production abroad, may fairly be termed artificial. And every such interference means simply a diminution of the national wealth. If region A grows corn at home for fifty shillings with which region B can supply it at forty, and region B manufactures cloth at twenty shillings with which region A can supply it at fifteen, the national wealth of each is diminished by the ten and the five shillings respectively.

And the capitalists and laborers in each of these countries have so much the less to divide into their respective shares, in that competition between capital and labor which determines the distribution between them of the price brought in the market by commodities.

In my view, and I may say for my countrymen in our view, protection, however dignified by the source from which it proceeds, is essentially an invitation to waste, promulgated with the authority of law. It may be more violent and prohibitory, or it may be less; but, up to the point to which it goes, it is a promise given to dear production to shield it against the competition of cheap production, or given to dearer production to hold it harmless against cheaper; to secure for it a market it could not otherwise hold, and to enable it to exact from the consumer a price which he would not otherwise pay.

Protection says to a producer, Grow this or manufacture that at a greater necessary outlay, though we might obtain it more cheaply from abroad, where it can be produced at a smaller necessary outlay. This is saying, in other words, waste a certain amount of labor and of capital; and do not be afraid, for the cost of your waste shall be laid on the shoulders of a nation which is well able to bear it . . .

(A)ll protection is morally as well as economically bad. This is a very different thing from saying that all Protectionists are bad. Many of them, without doubt, are good, nay, excellent, as were in this country many of the supporters of the Corn Law. It is of the tendencies of a system that I speak, which operate variously, upon most men unconsciously, upon some men not at all; and surely that system cannot be good which makes an individual, or a set of individuals, live on the resources of the community and causes him relatively to diminish that store which duty to his fellow-citizens and to their equal rights should teach him by his contributions to augment. The habit of mind thus engendered is not such as altogether befits a free country or harmonizes with an independent character. And the more the system of protection is discussed and contested, the more those whom it favors are driven to struggle for its maintenance, the farther they must insensibly deviate from the law of equal rights, and, perhaps, even from the tone of genuine personal independence.

In speaking thus, we speak greatly from our own experience. I have personally lived through the varied phases of that experience, since we began that battle between monopoly and freedom which cost us about a quarter of a century of the nation's life. I have seen and known, and had the opportunity of comparing, the temper and frame of mind engendered first by our protectionism, which we now look back upon as servitude, and then by the commercial freedom and equality which we have enjoyed for the last thirty or forty years. The one tended to harden into positive selfishness; the other has done much to foster a more liberal tone of mind.

Part five
UTILITARIANISM

5.1 JEREMY BENTHAM (1748–1832)

From 'Principles of the civil code', in *Theory of legislation,* trans. R. Hildreth, 8th edn, Kegan Paul: London, 1894, pp. 95–101, 109–13, 119–20, 122–3, 126–8, 130–3.

Bentham, who graduated from Oxford University at the age of sixteen, intended to practise law. Once he discovered the principle of utility in 1768, however, Bentham determined to become the Newton of the human world by providing the scientific foundations of widespread legislative and social reform. Intensive study for many hours each day yielded a mass of manuscripts which contained numerous schemes of social reconstruction. The following extract outlines the general responsibilities of government in its pursuit of utility. The *Theory of legislation* was originally published in French, in 1802, from manuscripts which Bentham had given to Etienne Dumont in 1788. As Hildreth translated freely from the French edition, in which Dumont had already compressed Bentham's ideas, the *Theory* may seem an odd choice from which to select an extract. The problem is that Bentham's style was horribly disjointed. 'The construction of his sentences is a curious frame-work with pegs and hooks to hang his thoughts upon, for his own use and guidance', wrote William Hazlitt in his essay on 'Jeremy Bentham' (1824), 'but almost out of the reach of everybody else.' Whatever the faults of editorial licence, it does in this case convey the drift of Bentham's thought more clearly than he managed to do himself.

The only object of government ought to be the greatest possible happiness of the community.

The happiness of an individual is increased in proportion as his sufferings are lighter and fewer, and his enjoyments greater and more numerous.

f his enjoyments ought to be left almost entirely to the
he principal function of government is to guard against

is object by creating rights, which it confers upon
individuals: rights of personal security, rights of protection for
honour, rights of property, rights of receiving aid in case of need. To
these rights correspond offences of different kinds. The law cannot
create rights except by creating corresponding obligations. It cannot
create rights and obligations without creating offences. It cannot
command nor forbid without restraining the liberty of individuals.

It appears, then, that the citizen cannot acquire rights except by
sacrificing a part of his liberty. But even under a bad government there
is no proportion between the acquisition and the sacrifice.
Government approaches to perfection in proportion as the sacrifice is
less and the acquisition more.

In the distribution of rights and obligations, the legislator, as we
have said, should have for his end the happiness of society.
Investigating more distinctly in what that happiness consists, we shall
find four subordinate ends:–

> Subsistence.
> Abundance.
> Equality.
> Security.

The more perfect enjoyment is in all these respects, the greater is the
sum of social happiness: and especially of that happiness which
depends upon the laws.

We may hence conclude that all the functions of law may be referred
to these four heads: – To provide subsistence; to produce abundance;
to favour equality, to maintain security ...

Some persons may be astonished to find that *Liberty* is not ranked
among the principal objects of law. But a clear idea of liberty will lead
us to regard it as a branch of security. Personal liberty is security
against a certain kind of injuries which affect the person. As to what is
called *political liberty,* it is another branch of security, – security
against injuries from the ministers of government. What concerns this
object belongs not to civil, but to constitutional law.

These four objects of law are very distinct in idea, but they are much
less so in practice. The same law may advance several of them; because
they are often united. That law, for example, which favours security,
favours, at the same time, subsistence and abundance.

But there are circumstances in which it is impossible to unite these objects. It will sometimes happen that a measure suggested by one of these principles will be condemned by another. Equality, for example, might require a distribution of property which would be incompatible with security.

When this contradiction exists between two of these ends, it is necessary to find some means of deciding the pre-eminence; otherwise these principles, instead of guiding us in our researches, will only serve to augment the confusion.

At the first glance we see subsistence and security arising together to the same level; abundance and equality are manifestly of inferior importance. In fact, without security, equality could not last a day; without subsistence, abundance could not exist at all. The two first objects are life itself; the two latter, the ornaments of life.

In legislation, the most important object is security. Though no laws were made directly for subsistence, it might easily be imagined that no one would neglect it. But unless the laws are made directly for security, it would be quite useless to make them for subsistence. You may order production; you may command cultivation; and you will have done nothing. But assure to the cultivator the fruits of his industry, and perhaps in that alone you will have done enough ...

Equality ought not to be favoured except in the cases in which it does not interfere with security; in which it does not thwart the expectations which the law itself has produced, in which it does not derange the order already established.

If all property were equally divided, at fixed periods, the sure and certain consequence would be, that presently there would be no property to divide. All would shortly be destroyed. Those whom it was intended to favour, would not suffer less from the division than those at whose expense it was made. If the lot of the industrious was not better than the lot of the idle, there would be no longer any motives for industry ...

What can the law do for subsistence? Nothing directly. All it can do is to create *motives,* that is, punishments or rewards, by the force of which men may be led to provide subsistence for themselves. But nature herself has created these motives, and has given them a sufficient energy. Before the idea of laws existed, *needs* and *enjoyments* had done in that respect all that the best concerted laws could do. Need, armed with pains of all kinds, even death itself, commanded labour, excited courage, inspired foresight, developed all the faculties of man. Enjoyment, the inseparable companion of every need satisfied, formed an inexhaustible fund of rewards for those who surmounted obstacles and fulfilled the end of nature. The force of the physical sanction being sufficient, the employment of the political sanction would be superfluous ...

But the laws provide for subsistence indirectly, by protecting men while they labour, and by making them sure of the fruits of their labour. *Security* for the labourer, *security* for the fruits of labour; such is the benefit of laws; and it is an inestimable benefit.

Shall laws be made directing individuals not to confine themselves to mere subsistence, but to seek abundance? No! That would be a very superfluous employment of artificial means, where natural means suffice. The attraction of pleasure; the succession of wants; the active desire of increasing happiness, will procure unceasingly, under the reign of security, new efforts towards new acquisitions. Wants, enjoyments, those universal agents of society, having begun with gathering the first sheaf of corn, proceed little by little, to build magazines of abundance, always increasing but never filled. Desires extend with means. The horizon elevates itself as we advance; and each new want, attended on the one hand by pain, on the other by pleasure, becomes a new principle of action. Opulence, which is only a comparative term, does not arrest this movement once begun. On the contrary, the greater our means, the greater the scale on which we labour; the greater is the recompense, and, consequently, the greater also the force of motive which animates to labour. Now what is the wealth of society, if not the sum of all individual wealth? And what more is necessary than the force of these natural motives, to carry wealth, by successive movements, to the highest possible point? ...

We come now to the principal object of law, – the care of security. That inestimable good, the distinctive index of civilization, is entirely the work of law. Without law there is no security; and, consequently, no abundance, and not even a certainty of subsistence; and the only equality which can exist in such a state of things is an equality of misery ...

To form a precise idea of the extent which ought to be given to the principle of security, we must consider that man is not like the animals, limited to the present, whether as respects suffering or enjoyment; but that he is susceptible of pains and pleasures by anticipation; and that it is not enough to secure him from actual loss, but it is necessary also to guarantee him, as far as possible, against future loss. It is necessary to prolong the idea of his security through all the perspective which his imagination is capable of measuring.

This presentment, which has so marked an influence upon the fate of man, is called *expectation*. It is hence that we have the power of forming a general plan of conduct; it is hence that the successive instants which compose the duration of life are not like isolated and independent points, but become continuous parts of a whole. *Expectation* is a chain which unites our present existence to our future existence, and which passes beyond us to the generation which is to follow. The sensibility of man extends through all the links of this chain.

The principle of security extends to the maintenance of all these expectations; it requires that events, so far as they depend upon laws, should conform to the expectations which law itself has created.

Every attack upon this sentiment produces a distinct and special evil, which may be called a *pain of disappointment* . . .

The better to understand the advantages of law, let us endeavour to form a clear idea of *property.* We shall see that there is no such thing as natural property, and that it is entirely the work of law.

Property is nothing but a basis of expectation; the expectation of deriving certain advantages from a thing which we are said to possess, in consequence of the relation in which we stand towards it . . .

Property and law are born together, and die together. Before laws were made there was no property; take away laws, and property ceases.

As regards property, security consists in receiving no check, no shock, no derangement to the expectation founded on the laws, of enjoying such and such a portion of good. The legislator owes the greatest respect to this expectation which he has himself produced. When he does not contradict it, he does what is essential to the happiness of society; when he disturbs it, he always produces a proportionate sum of evil . . .

In consulting the grand principle of security, what ought the legislator to decree respecting the mass of property already existing?

He ought to maintain the distribution as it is actually established. It is this which, under the name of *justice,* is regarded as his first duty. This is a general and simple rule, which applies itself to all states; and which adapts itself to all places, even those of the most opposite character . . .

When security and equality are in conflict, it will not do to hesitate a moment. Equality must yield. The first is the foundation of life; subsistence, abundance, happiness everything depends upon it. Equality produces only a certain portion of good. Besides, whatever we may do, it will never be perfect; it may exist a day; but the revolutions of the morrow will overturn it. The establishment of perfect equality is a chimera; all we can do is to diminish inequality.

If violent causes, such as a revolution of government, a division, or a conquest, should bring about an overturn of property, it would be a great calamity; but it would be transitory; it would diminish; it would repair itself in time. Industry is a vigorous plant which resists many amputations, and through which a nutritious sap begins to circulate with the first rays of returning summer. But if property should be overturned with the direct intention of establishing an equality of possessions, the evil would be irreparable. No more security, no more industry, no more abundance! Society would return to the savage state whence it emerged ...

Is it necessary that between these two rivals, *Security* and *Equality,* there should be an opposition, an eternal war? To a certain point they are incompatible: but with a little patience and address they may, in a great measure, be reconciled.

The only mediator between these contrary interests is time. Do you wish to follow the counsels of equality without contravening those of security? – await the natural epoch which puts an end to hopes and fears, the epoch of death.

When property by the death of the proprietor ceases to have an owner, the law can interfere in its distribution, either by limiting in certain respects the testamentary power, in order to prevent too great an accumulation of wealth in the hands of an individual; or by regulating the succession in favour of equality in cases where the deceased has left no consort, nor relation in the direct line, and has made no will. The question then relates to new acquirers who have formed no expectations; and equality may do what is best for all without disappointing any ...

It is worthy of remark that, in a nation prosperous in its agriculture, its manufactures, and its commerce, there is a continual progress towards equality. If the laws do nothing to combat it, if they do not maintain certain monopolies, if they put no shackles upon industry and trade, if they do not permit entails, we see great properties divided little by little, without effort, without revolution, without shock, and a much greater number of men coming to participate in the moderate favours of fortune. This is the natural result of the opposite habits which are formed in opulence and in poverty. The first, prodigal and vain, wishes only to enjoy without labour; the second, accustomed to obscurity and privations, finds pleasures even in labour and economy. Thence the change which has been made in Europe by the progress of arts and commerce, in spite of legal obstacles. We are at no great distance from those ages of feudality, when the world was divided into two classes: a few great proprietors, who were everything, and a multitude of serfs, who were nothing. These pyramidal heights have disappeared or have fallen; and from their ruins industrious men have formed those new establishments, the great number of which attests the comparative happiness of modern civilization. Thus we may conclude that *Security,* while preserving its place as the supreme principle, leads indirectly to *Equality;* while equality, if taken as the basis of the social arrangement, will destroy both itself and security at the same time ...

Ought we to reckon among those wants of the state which ought to be provided for by forced contributions, the care of the indigent? ...

In the highest state of social prosperity, the great mass of citizens will have no resource except their daily industry; and consequently will be always near indigence, always ready to be thrown into a state of destitution, by accidents, such as revolutions or commerce, natural calamities, and especially sickness. Infancy has no means of subsisting by its own strength; the feebleness of old age is equally destitute ...

There are only two means, independently of the laws, of making head against these evils, viz., *savings* and *voluntary contributions* ...

The resource of savings is insufficient. 1st, It evidently is so for those who do not gain enough to subsist upon; 2nd, It is equally so for those who gain a mere subsistence. As to the third class, which embraces all not included in the first two, savings are not naturally insufficient, but they become so through the deficiency of human prudence.

Let us now pass to the other resource – *voluntary contributions.* That, too, has many imperfections.

1st. Its uncertainty. It will experience daily vicissitudes, like the fortune and the liberality of the individuals on whom it depends. Is it insufficient? Such junctures are marked by misery and death. Is it superabundant? It will offer a reward to idleness and profusion.

2nd. The inequality of the burden. This supply for the wants of the poor is levied entirely at the expense of the more humane and the more virtuous, often without any proportion to their means; while the avaricious calumniate the poor, to cover their refusal with a varnish of system and of reason. Such an arrangment is a favour granted to selfishness, and a punishment to humanity, that first of virtues ...

3rd. The inconveniences of the distribution. If these contributions are abandoned to chance, as in the case of alms asked on the highway; if they are left to be paid, as occasion occurs, without any person intermediate between him who gives and him who asks, the uncertainty as to the sufficiency of these gifts is aggravated by another uncertainty. How appreciate in a multitude of cases the degree of want and of need? ...

In the division of voluntary contributions, the lot of the honest and virtuous poor is seldom equal to that of the impudent and obstreperous beggar . . .

It seems to me, after these observations, that we may lay it down as a general principle that the legislator ought to establish a regular contribution for the wants of indigence, it being understood that those only are to be regarded as indigent who are in want of what is absolutely necessary. From this definition of the indigent, it follows that their title as indigent is stronger than the title of the proprietor of superfluities as proprietor. For the pain of death, which would presently fall upon the starving poor, would be always a more serious evil than the pain of disappointment which falls upon the rich when a portion of his superfluity is taken from him.

In the amount of the legal contribution we ought not to go beyond what is simply necessary. To go beyond that would be taxing industry for the support of idleness. Those establishments which furnish more than is absolutely necessary are not good, except so far as they are supported at the expense of individuals, for individuals can make a discrimination in the distribution of these aids, and apply them to specific classes.

The details of the manner of assessing this contribution, and distributing its produce, belong to political economy, as also the inquiry into the means of encouraging a spirit of economy and foresight in the lower classes of society.

5.2 JOHN AUSTIN (1790–1859)

From *The province of jurisprudence determined,* John Murray: London, 1832, pp. 69–74, 76.

Austin, a member of the Benthamite circle, is today celebrated as pioneer of an empirical theory of law. *The province of jurisprudence determined* originated as lectures – at which student attendance was dismal – given at London University where Austin was Professor of Jurisprudence from 1827 to 1832. This extract conveys the optimistic utilitarian belief that familiarity with simple economic truths would transform the poor into solid citizens.

The broad or leading principles of the science of political economy, may be mastered, with moderate attention, in a short period. With these simple, but commanding principles, a number of important questions are easily resolved. And if the multitude (as they can and will) shall ever understand these principles, many pernicious prejudices will be extirped from the popular mind, and truths of ineffable moment planted in their stead.

For example, In many or all countries (the least uncivilized not excepted), the prevalent opinions and sentiments of the working people are certainly not consistent with the complete security of property. To the *ignorant* poor, the inequality which inevitably follows the beneficent institution of property is necessarily invidious ...

In the first place, this prejudice blinds the people to the cause of their sufferings, and to the only remedy or palliative which the case will admit.

Want and labour spring from the niggardliness of nature, and not from the inequality which is consequent on the institution of property. These evils are inseparable from the condition of man upon earth; and are lightened, not aggravated, by this useful, though invidious institution. Without *capital,* and the arts which depend upon capital, the reward of labour would be far scantier than it is; and capital, with the arts which depend upon it, are creatures of the institution of property. The institution is good for the many, as well as for the few. The poor are not stripped by it of the produce of their labour; but it gives them a part in the enjoyment of wealth which it calls into being. In effect, though not in law, the labourers are co-proprietors with the capitalists who hire their labour. The reward which they get for their labour is principally drawn from *capital;* and they are not less interested than the legal owners in protecting the fund from invasion.

It is certainly to be wished, that their reward were greater; and that they were relieved from the incessant drudgery to which they are now condemned. But the condition of the working people (whether their wages shall be high or low; their labour, moderate or extreme) depends upon their own will, and not upon the will of the rich. In the *true principle of population,* detected by the sagacity of Mr. Malthus, they must look for the cause and the remedy of their penury and excessive toil. There they may find the means which would give them comparative affluence; which would give them the degree of leisure necessary to knowledge and refinement; which would raise them to personal dignity and political influence, from grovelling and sordid subjection to the arbitrary rule of a few.

And these momentous truths are deducible from plain principles, by short and obvious inferences. Here, there is no need of large and careful research, or of subtle and sustained thinking. If the people understood distinctly a few indisputable propositions, and were capable of going correctly through an easy process of reasoning, their minds would be purged of the prejudice which blinds them to the cause of their sufferings, and they would see and apply the remedy which is suggested by the principle of population. Their repinings at the affluence of the rich, would be appeased. Their murmurs at the injustice of the rich, would be silenced. They would scarcely break machinery, or fire barns and corn ricks, to the end of raising wages, or the rate of parish relief. They would see that violations of property are mischievous to *themselves:* that such violations weaken the motives to accumulation, and, therefore, dimininish the fund which yields the labourer his subsistence. They would see that they are deeply interested in the security of property: that, if they adjusted their numbers to the demand for their labour, they would share abundantly, with their employers, in the blessings of that useful institution.

Another of the numerous evils which flow from the prejudice in question, is the frequency of crimes.

Nineteen offences out of twenty, are offences against property. And most offences against property may be imputed to the prejudice in question.

The authors of such offences are commonly of the poorer sort. For the most part, poverty is the incentive. And this prejudice perpetuates poverty amongst the great body of the people, by blinding them to the cause and the remedy.

And whilst it perpetuates the ordinary incentive to crime, it weakens the restraints.

As a check or deterring motive, as an inducement to abstain from crime, the fear of public disapprobation, with its countless train of evils, is scarcely less effectual than the fear of legal punishment. To the purpose of forming the moral character, of rooting in the soul a prompt aversion from crime, it is infinitely more effectual.

The help of the hangman and the gaoler would seldom be called for, if the *opinion* of the great body of the people were cleared of the prejudice in question, and, therefore, fell heavily upon all offenders against property. If the *general opinion* were thoroughly cleared of that prejudice, it would greatly weaken the temptations to crime, by its salutary influence on the moral character of the multitude: The motives which it would oppose to those temptations, would be scarcely less effectual than the motives which are presented by the law: and it would heighten the terrors, and strengthen the restraints of the law, by engaging a countless host of eager and active volunteers in the service of criminal justice. If the people saw distinctly the tendencies of offences against property; if the people saw distinctly the tendencies and the grounds of the punishments; and if they were, therefore, bent upon pursuing the criminals to justice; the laws which prohibit these offences would seldom be broken with impunity, and, by consequence, would seldom be broken. An enlightened people were a better auxiliary to the judge than an army of policemen ...

(N)othing but *the diffusion of knowledge through the great mass of the people* will go to the root of the evil. Nothing but this will cure or alleviate the poverty which is the ordinary incentive to crime. Nothing but this will extirpate their prejudices, and correct their moral sentiments: will lay them under the restraints which are imposed by enlightened opinion, and which operate so potently on the higher and more cultivated classes ...

And the multitude (in civilized communities) would soon apprehend these principles, and would soon acquire the talent of reasoning distinctly and justly, if one of the weightiest of the duties, which God has laid upon governments, were performed with fidelity and zeal. For, if we must construe those duties by the principle of general utility, it is not less incumbent on governments to forward the diffusion of knowledge, than to protect their subjects from one another by a due administration of justice, or to defend them by a military force from the attacks of external enemies. A small fraction of the sums which are squandered in needless war, would provide complete instruction for the working people: would give this important class that portion in the knowledge of the age, which consists with the nature of their callings, and with the necessity of toiling for a livelihood.

5.3 JEREMY BENTHAM

From 'Introduction' to *Plan of parliamentary reform, in the form of a catechism* (1817), in *The works of Jeremy Bentham*, ed. John Bowring, William Tait: Edinburgh, 1843, vol. 3, pp. 450–52, 459.

Although some commentators have suggested that Bentham was converted to democracy by the refusal of government to sponsor his model prison or panopticon, he had initially argued for an extended franchise at the time of the French Revolution. His *Plan of parliamentary reform*, with its condemnation of mixed government and of the sinister interests of a ruling minority, opened a fierce and lengthy debate between Benthamites and their Whig opponents.

Know ye not, that in a machine of any kind, when forces *balance* each other, the machine is at a stand? Well, and in the machine of government, immobility – the perpetual absence of all motion – is that the thing which is wanted? Know ye not that – since an emblem you must have – since you can neither talk, nor attempt to think but in hieroglyphics – know you not that, as in the case of the body *natural*, so in the case of the body *politic*, when motion ceases, the body dies?

So much for the *balance:* now the the *mixture* – the mixture to which, as such, such virtue is wont to be ascribed. Here is a form of government, in which the power is divided among three interests: – the interest of the great body of the people – of the *many:* – and two separate interests – the interest of the *one* and the interest of the *few* – both of which are adverse to it: – two separate and narrow interests, neither of which is kept on foot – but at the expense, to the loss, and by the sacrifice, of the broader interest. This form of government (say you) has its advantages. Its advantages? – compared with what? – compared with those forms of government, in which the people have no power at all, or in which, if they have any, they have not so much? Oh yes: with any such form of government for an object of comparison, its *excellence* is unquestionable. But, compare it with a form of government in which the interest of the people is the only interest that is looked to – in which neither a single man, with a separate and adverse interest of his own, nor a knot of men with a separate and adverse interest of their own, are to be found – where no interest is kept up at the expense, to the loss, by the sacrifice, of the universal interest to it, – where is *then* the *excellence?* . . .

A form of government, in which the interest of the whole is the only interest provided for – in which the only power is a power having for its object the support of that interest, – in this form of government behold the *simple* substance. To this simple substance add, separately or conjunctively, a power employed in the support of the interest of one *single* person, and a power employed in the support of the interest of a comparatively *small knot* of persons, – in either of these cases you have a *mixture:* – well: compared, then, with the simple substance, when and where can be advantages of this *mixture?* . . .

IMMEDIATE cause of the mischief – on the part of the men acting as representatives of the people, coupled with adequate *power* a sinister *interest,* productive of a constant sacrifice made of the interest of the people . . .

Here, in the above elements – here, in a nutshell, may be seen the mischief and its causes: – against this mischief, revolution apart, behold in *Parliamentary Reform* the name of the only possible remedy . . .

Take for the description of the *ultimate* end, *advancement of the universal interest.*

In the description of this end is included – *comprehension* of all distinguishable *particular interests:* viz, in such sort, that such of them, between which no repugnancy has place, may be provided for in conjunction, and *without defalcation:* – while, in regard to such of them, between which any such repugnancy has place, such defalcations, and such alone, shall be made, as, when taken all together, shall leave in the state of a *maximum* whatsoever residuum of comfort and security may be the result: – with exceptions to as *small* an extent as possible, interests *all* to be *advanced:* without *any* exception, all to be *considered.*

1. In the character of a means, in this same description is moreover included – if it be not rather the same thing in other words – *virtual universality of suffrage* ...

Now as to universal suffrage ... (I)n all eyes but those to which tyranny is the only endurable form of government, – what principle can be more impregnable?

1. Who is there, that is not susceptible of discomfort and comfort – of pain and pleasure?

2. Of what is human *happiness, felicity, well-being, welfare* – call it what you please – composed, but comfort and absence of discomfort – pleasure and exception from pain?

3. The happiness and unhappiness of any one member of the community – high or low, rich or poor – what greater or less part is it of the universal happiness and unhappiness, than that of any other?

4. Who is there, by whom unhappiness is not avoided – happiness pursued?

5. Who is there, by whom unhappiness ought not to be avoided – happiness ought not to be pursued?

6. Who is there, that, in avoidance of unhappiness, and pursuit of happiness, has not a course of conduct to maintain – which, in some way or other, he does maintain, – throughout life?

5.4 GEORGE GROTE (1794–1871)

From *Essentials of parliamentary reform* (1831), in *The minor works* of George Grote, ed. Alexander Bain, John Murray: London, 1873, pp. 14–26.

Grote is remembered today mainly as an historian of ancient Greece and a champion of Athenian democracy. A wealthy banker who entered Parliament in 1832 as member for the City of London, he persistently campaigned for secret ballots in order to eliminate bribery and corruption from elections. In 1821 he wrote a pamphlet, *Statement of the question of parliamentary reform*, which defended Bentham's *Plan of parliamentary reform* against a Whiggish attack by Sir James Mackintosh in the *Edinburgh Review*. In revising the pamphlet for publication as *Essentials of parliamentary reform*, however, Grote now stressed the desirability of a gradual extension of the franchise. The *Essentials*, in consequence, clearly expresses the conviction of some utilitarians that responsibility for the transition from aristocratic government to mass democracy ought to lie with an enlightened bourgeoisie.

So long as the House of Commons is chosen by a small fraction of the community, the community will derive from its existence no security which they would not have enjoyed equally well without it, from King and Peers only. Paucity of the real electors is the grand, the specific evil: multiplication of the real electors, until they cease to have a separate interest from the community, must be the vital, the effectual remedy ...

Among those doctrines, which divert the public eye from the real vices of our representation, there is none more current or more easily received than that of founding the Representative System on property – of making *property the basis of the elective franchise.* The sense put upon these words, indeed, is neither uniform nor well-defined: but all the fluctuations in their meaning appear reducible to two leading distinctions, which I propose successively to examine.

Some persons, when they affirm that property is the only suitable basis for representation, seem to intend that every man should be vested with an elective power proportioned to his fortune – that the weight of each in determining the members to be chosen should be measured by the amount of property which he possesses. Because (they maintain), the richer a man is, the greater the stake which he has in the country – the greater his interest in the preservation and augmentation of its wealth and power ...

But the reasoning, on which any such preference to great proprietors is founded, is altogether untenable and fallacious. Not only is it untrue that they have a greater interest than small proprietors, or non-proprietors, in good government, but it may be clearly shown that they have much less. Among all the obligations which a good government ought to discharge towards a body of citizens, there is none of which the omission will not be far more painfully felt by the small than by the great proprietor. Suppose the course of justice to be dilatory, expensive, or corrupt. By all these circumstances the small proprietor is ruinously aggrieved: the course of his industry is interrupted or cut off: that constant aggregation of petty savings, without which he cannot leave his family in the condition occupied by himself, is rendered impossible; and if he escapes loss or fraud in his own person, he is sure to be called on to rescue less fortunate friends or kinsmen. The great proprietor, on the other hand, is far less exposed to injury from such sources: he is embarrassed by no daily calling: his wealth attracts around him a host of private dependents, who conspire to protect him against the world without, and enable him almost to dispense with the shield of law: while he acquires a power, frightful indeed to society, but profitable to himself, of dealing out unredressed outrage to others ...

Take, again, the economy of the public revenue ... High taxation is to the rest of the community pure, uncompensated, sacrifice: to the great proprietor it is sacrifice on the one side, with the prospect of patronage on the other. In no case is he injured by this description of misgovernment so much as the small proprietor: frequently, he proves a considerable gainer by it.

But if the great proprietor is less interested than the small in the performance of the obvious duties of government, still more is this true with regard to the remote and exalted obligations. What member of the community has so little to gain by diffusing instruction among the poor, as a very rich man? He sees and hears less of them than any one else: and as he is always able to pay for the services of the choice few among them, his comfort is scarcely at all affected by the good or bad character of the mass. With respect, again, to the moral effect of the government – to its influence, so prodigious either to good or to evil on the minds and character of the citizens. Is the great proprietor more interested than others in so constructing all its machinery as to encourage probity, industry, and self-denial, and to discountenance fraud, rapacity, and improvidence? In this, as in the other cases, he will be found to have little or no interest in that salutary moral teaching which would be the first of all blessings to every other man in the community. To him the prevalence of such habits would be a loss of consequence, of ascendancy, of admiration. His position commands him to cherish far more unworthy and immoral dispositions among the community: to spread abroad that over-weening and prostrate veneration of wealth, which not only softens all scruples as to the mode of acquisition, but effaces true dignity of character, and renders men the pliant instruments of any one who can help them on in life: to plant in every one's bosom a passion for that show and ostentation, which none indeed can successfully exhibit except the rich themselves, but which every one may pant after and affect, until he loses both the relish for simple and accessible enjoyments, and the feeling of sympathy and brotherhood with men of inferior style. How lamentably such defects eat up the happiness and taint the springs of beneficence among the middling and the poor, is abundantly manifest: how they have been fostered in England under the baneful ascendancy of wealth in large masses, is matter of remark to all who compare it with the Continent.

It is then demonstrable, that the great proprietors are the precise persons in the nation to whom good government in all its branches is the least essential ...

But if there be no ground for privileging great proprietors on pretence of superior interest in good government, as little reason is there for doing so on the score of superior knowledge and intelligence ... The position and circumstances of a very rich man cut off all motive to mental labour: he is caressed and deified by his circle without any of those toils whereby others purchase an attentive hearing; and the purple, the fine linen, and the sumptuous fare every day, of Dives, are impediments to solid improvement, hardly less fatal than the sores and wretchedness of Lazarus ...

There is another sense in which some persons propose to make property *the basis of representation.* They are of opinion that no one who does not enjoy an income of a certain given amount, ought to exercise any political rights: to all above that minimum, they would award equal, not graduated, elective power; all below it they would disfranchise without exception. Some indeed are more indulgent, others more rigorous in determining the point of actual exclusion: but the principle of exclusion is the same with all.

The reasonings sometimes advanced on behalf of this opinion appear to imply that no person below the appointed minimum has any interest in preserving property: that property is an institution beneficial indeed to a fortunate minority, but injurious and oppressive to the remaining multitude; and that if the interest of the latter were consulted, not only existing possessions would be divided but the institution itself would be swept away. This theory of property, fatal as it would prove to the continuance of the institution, except in the most degraded state of the human intelligence, is not unfrequently resorted to by aristocratical advocates, when they wish to alarm the middling classes into uncomplaining submission.

It is fortunate that a just comprehension of the interests of all holds out brighter prospects. So far from being injured by the institution of property, the multitude have a deep and lasting interest in its continuance. No set of men, whether all poor, or all rich, or some poor and some rich, can possibly live together in society without some rules to define what shall be enjoyed by one and what by another. One man, by virtue of these rules, may acquire a greater amount of enjoyment than another, but the fixity and observance of the rules is as much necessary to the continuous sequence of smaller acquisitions as to the safe enjoyment of the greater. One man, in like manner, may turn the air and the sun to greater account than another; but these beneficent influences are alike indispensable to all. Here and there a being may be discovered so destitute and unhappy as to be inaccessible to any additional suffering: to have no enjoyment open to him, except that which he can find unappropriated, or that which he can snatch by force: to be, in other words, in the position to which all mankind would be reduced, if no laws of property were known or respected. But such cases are rare exceptions to the ordinary lot of the many, who derive a steady subsistence from the uninterrupted exercise of their industry. Scanty as this subsistence too frequently is, it would be intercepted altogether if the safety of property became a matter even of reasonable doubt: for it arises from the outlay of capitalists, made only under assured prospect of return, and ready to be withheld the moment future acquisitions can no longer be reckoned on. Deprived of all means of recruiting his little fund, the poor labourer passes from assured subsistence into absolute and irremediable starvation.

The disfranchisement of the body of the poor, then, cannot for a moment be sustained on the pretence that they have no interest in the maintenance of property. They have at least as great an interest in its stability as the rich: for even a temporary suspension of its laws would deprive them of existence, while the rich might stand some feeble chance of defending and reserving to themselves their pre-existing hoard.

But are the poor wise enough to recognise and act upon this interest? Many reasoners contend that they are not; and hence, in general, the reluctance to bestow on them political rights: though there are not wanting persons who, inconsistently enough, protest against universal suffrage, both on one ground and on the other; insisting on the one hand that the body of the poor have a real interest hostile to property, and reproaching the poor on the other for their brutish ignorance in not venerating so sacred and beneficent an institution.

The ignorance of the body of the people is a ground for their disfranchisement far more plausible than the former, because, to a certain extent, the fact is undeniable. No one can dispute that they ought to be, and might be, much more carefully educated than they are at present. Yet I feel well persuaded that their ignorance, comparatively to other classes, has been greatly over-stated, and in particular that no evidence can be adduced of unfriendly feelings, in the generality of them, towards the institution of property.

Is there any error or prejudice now current among the poorer classes, to which a parallel cannot be produced among the richer? If they are taunted with their hostility to machinery, may they not recriminate on the landlords by pointing to the Usury Laws and to the Corn Laws? If their misapprehension of the principle of population is cited as an evidence of stupidity, how will the squires and parsons, and the parochial chiefs in general, stand exonerated from the like imputation?

To me it appears that the poorer classes in general have an understanding sufficiently just, docile, and unprejudiced, to elect, and to submit to; the same legislators whom the middling classes themselves, if they voted apart and voted secretly, would single out. But assuming the contrary to be the fact, as so many sincere reformers believe and lament – admitting that the poor are at the present moment unprepared for the elective franchise – expedients may yet be found for allaying the apprehensions of the middling classes, without either degrading the lower by perpetual exclusion, or neglecting to provide for the duties of Government towards them.

Reasoning on this admission, we should of course acquiesce, under a certain modification, in the principle that property should at present form the basis of representation, – not under the belief that men of property had any superior interest in good government, but because, under the existing difficulties in obtaining, and carelessness in diffusing, knowledge, few persons below a certain amount of income could be presumed to have yet acquired mental aptitude for the elective function. It cannot with any pretence of reason be maintained, that a man of £100 annual income has not enjoyed full facilities instructing himself up to the requisite pitch. A pecuniary qualification, therefore, if fixed at £100 annual income, would embrace no one, as far as could be reasonably presumed, unworthy of the trust.

It has been stated that a qualification of £100 annual income would comprehend a million of electors: but if the conjecture were not confirmed by actual returns, I should think it requisite to lower the qualification until that number was attained. No number of voters falling much short of a million, could possibly put out of sight and out of apprehension that first of all evils, a separate interest from the community; and in order to purchase such a certainty, it would be well worth while to submit to such slight depression in the scale of instruction as might be incurred by introducing persons of an income the next degree below £100 per annum. Nor could any reasonable alarmist anticipate either hostility to property, or general unsoundness of views, from the richest million in the country. They might as soon be imagined to surrender England to a foreign enemy, or to plant in it the seeds of an epidemic disease, as to invade or unsettle the sanctity of property.

A representative system including one million of voters ... would purify the Government, thoroughly, at once and for ever, of that deep and inveterate oligarchical taint which now infects it in every branch. The Old Man of the Sea would be shaken from our backs, never more to resume his gripe. The interest and well-being of the middling classes would become the predominant object of solicitude, and would be followed out with earnest and single-hearted perseverance. Economy in the state expenditure; unremitting advance towards perfection in the law and in the administration of justice; entire abstinence from ambitious or unnecessary wars: all these great results would be ensured by such a legislature as completely as the most ardent patriot could desire. Nor would it fail to operate a wholesome change in the public sentiment, and to root out or mitigate many of our wide-spread national vices. It would suppress that avidity for patronage which now renders so many fathers of families petitioners at the doors of the neighbouring great: it would lower the value of the rich man's nod, and teach men to earn advance in the world, not by clinging to his skirts, but by their own industry and their own frugality; and it would eradicate the proneness to local jobbing which the imperfect constitution of parishes and corporate bodies so fatally implants and so abundantly remunerates. Legislators so chosen must be men of first-rate intelligence, whose discussions would rectify and elevate the tone of political reasoning throughout the whole country – men in whom the accident of birth and connection would be eclipsed by the splendour of their personal qualities – identified in heart and spirit with the happiness of the middling classes – and no less qualified, by laborious completion of their own mental training, to serve as an example and an incentive to aspiring youth ...

There needs but one addition to render such an electoral system every thing which the widest philanthropy could aim at. A provision should be annexed to it, gradually lowering the qualification at the end of certain fixed periods, so as to introduce successively fresh voters, and after a certain period to render the suffrage nearly co-extensive with the community. The interval might be employed in improving and extending education, so as to remove the only valid ground which is now supposed to command the disfranchisement of the poor.

This very deficiency in the poor, on which the necessity of their present exclusion is founded, demonstrates the vast importance of impressing on the Government peculiar motives to enlighten them. What portrait shall we draw of a government, under which four-fifths of the male adults are so degraded in understanding, as to be incapable of forming any opinion on the laws to which their obedience is exacted, and to be destitute therefore, of that rational attachment towards them which assists and seconds so materially the operations of justice? If their stupidity be really so deplorable, as to leave them ignorant whether they owe gratitude or execration to their laws and their legislators, it is impossible to make exertions too speedy or too strenous to amend it. Under a government faithful and energetic in the performance of all its duties, such mental darkness would be rapidly dispelled, and the reason for continued disfranchisement would disappear along with it.

6.1

From *On liberty* (1859), Longmans, Green, and Co: London, 1901, ch.
i, pp. 6–7, ch. iii, pp. 33–4, 37–40.

On liberty was published in the year following Mill's retirement from
the East India Company, where he had been employed since 1823. The
book was immediately recognized as a classic defence of individual
freedom. It nevertheless sparked a controversy, which rages perhaps
even more fiercely today, as to the precise message Mill intended to
convey in arguing that liberty is a condition both of self–development
and of social progress. Mill made such an absolute of liberty, it is
contended, that he ignored the need for freedom to be exercised
responsibly within a framework of communal traditions and values – cf.
Gertrude Himmelfarb, *On liberty and liberalism: the case of John
Stuart Mill,* Alfred Knopf: New York, 1974. It is argued, by contrast,
that Mill's concern to safeguard an enlightened minority from collective
mediocrity signifies an authoritarian impulse to subject common people
to the control of a moral and intellectual elite – cf. Maurice Cowling,
Mill and liberalism, Cambridge: CUP, 1963. In fact, as the following
extract reveals, Mill believed that responsible citizenship stems from the
cultivation of individuality; and, whereas he wanted the majority to be
guided by a minority in whom individuality was pronounced, he did not
advocate the establishment of a privileged group with powers of
compulsion.

The object of this Essay is to assert one very simple principle, as
entitled to govern absolutely the dealings of society with the individual
in the way of compulsion and control, whether the means used be
physical force in the form of legal penalties, or the moral coercion of
public opinion. That principle is, that the sole end for which mankind
are warranted, individually or collectively, in interfering with the
liberty of action of any of their number, is self-protection. That the

only purpose for which power can be rightfully exercised over any member of a civilized community, against his will, is to prevent harm to others. His own good, either physical or moral, is not a sufficient warrant. He cannot rightfully be compelled to do or forbear because it will be better for him to do so, because it will make him happier, because, in the opinions of others, to do so would be wise, or even right. These are good reasons for remonstrating with him, or reasoning with him, or persuading him, or entreating him, but not for compelling him, or visiting him with any evil in case he do otherwise. To justify that, the conduct from which it is desired to deter him, must be calculated to produce evil to some one else. The only part of the conduct of any one, for which he is amenable to society, is that which concerns others. In the part which merely concerns himself, his independence is, of right, absolute. Over himself, over his own body and mind, the individual is sovereign ...

I regard utility as the ultimate appeal on all ethical questions; but it must be utility in the largest sense, grounded on the permanent interests of a man as a progressive being. Those interests, I contend, authorize the subjection of individual spontaneity to external control, only in respect to those actions of each, which concern the interest of other people. If any one does an act hurtful to others, there is a *prima facie* case for punishing him, by law, or, where legal penalties are not safely applicable, by general disapprobation ...

But there is a sphere of action in which society, as distinguished from the individual, has, if any, only an indirect interest; comprehending all that portion of a person's life and conduct which affects only himself, or if it also affects others, only with their free, voluntary, and undeceived consent and participation. When I say only himself, I mean directly, and in the first instance: for whatever affects himself, may affect others through himself; and the objection which may be grounded on this contingency, will receive consideration in the sequel. This, then, is the appropriate region of human liberty. It comprises, first, the inward domain of consciousness; demanding liberty of conscience, in the most comprehensive sense; liberty of thought and feeling; absolute freedom of opinion and sentiment on all subjects, practical or speculative, scientific, moral, or theological. The liberty of expressing and publishing opinions may seem to fall under a different principle, since it belongs to that part of the conduct of an individual which concerns other people; but, being almost of as much importance as the liberty of thought itself, and resting in great part on the same reasons, is practically inseparable from it. Secondly, the principle requires liberty of tastes and pursuits; of framing the plan of our life to suit our own character; of doing as we like, subject to such consequences as may follow: without impediment from our fellow-creatures, so long as what we do does not harm them, even though they should think our conduct foolish, perverse, or wrong. Thirdly, from this liberty of each individual, follows the liberty, within the same limits, of combination among individuals; freedom to unite, for any purpose not involving harm to others: the persons combining being supposed to be of full age, and not forced or deceived ...

It is desirable, in short, that in things which do not primarily concern others, individuality should assert itself. Where, not the person's own character, but the traditions or customs of other people are the rule of conduct, there is wanting one of the principal ingredients of human happiness, and quite the chief ingredient of individual and social progress ...

But the evil is, that individual spontaneity is hardly recognised by the common modes of thinking, as having any intrinsic worth, or deserving any regard on its own account. The majority, being satisfied with the ways of mankind as they now are (for it is they who make them what they are), cannot comprehend why those ways should not be good enough for everybody; and what is more, spontaneity forms no part of the ideal of the majority of moral and social reformers, but is rather looked on with jealousy, as a troublesome and perhaps rebellious obstruction to the general acceptance of what these reformers, in their own judgment, think would be best for mankind. Few persons, out of Germany, even comprehend the meaning of the doctrine which Wilhelm von Humboldt, so eminent both as a *savant* and as a politician, made the text of a treatise – that 'the end of man, or that which is prescribed by the eternal or immutable dictates of reason, and not suggested by vague and transient desires, is the highest and most harmonious development of his powers to a complete and consistent whole;' that, therefore, the object 'towards which every human being must ceaselessly direct his efforts, and on which especially those who design to influence their fellow-men must ever keep their eyes, is the individuality of power and development;' that for this there are two requisites, 'freedom, and variety of situations;' and that from the union of these arise 'individual vigour and manifold diversity,' which combine themselves in 'originality.'* ...

He who does anything because it is the custom, makes no choice. He gains no practice either in discerning or in desiring what is best. The

---

* *The sphere and duties of government,* from the German of Baron Wilhelm von Humboldt, pp. 11-13.

mental and moral, like the muscular powers, are improved only by being used. The faculties are called into no exercise by doing a thing merely because others do it, no more than by believing a thing only because others believe it ...

He who lets the world, or his own portion of it, choose his plan of life for him, has no need of any other faculty than the ape-like one of imitation. He who chooses his plan for himself, employs all his faculties. He must use observation to see, reasoning and judgment to foresee, activity to gather materials for decision, discrimination to decide, and when he has decided, firmness and self-control to hold to his deliberate decision. And these qualities he requires and exercises exactly in proportion as the part of his conduct which he determines according to his own judgment and feelings is a large one ... Human nature is not a machine to be built after a model, and set to do exactly the work prescribed for it, but a tree, which requires to grow and develop itself on all sides, according to the tendency of the inward forces which make it a living thing ...

Having said that Individuality is the same thing with development, and that it is only the cultivation of individuality which produces, or can produce, well-developed human beings, I might here close the argument: for what more or better can be said of any condition of human affairs, than that it brings human beings themselves nearer to the best thing they can be? or what worse can be said of any obstruction to good, than that it prevents this? Doubtless, however, these considerations will not suffice to convince those who most need convincing; and it is necessary further to show, that these developed human beings are of some use to the underdeveloped – to point out to those who do not desire liberty, and would not avail themselves of it, that they may be in some intelligible manner rewarded for allowing other people to make use of it without hindrance.

In the first place, then, I would suggest that they might possibly learn something from them. It will not be denied by anybody, that originality is a valuable element in human affairs. There is always need of persons not only to discover new truths, and point out when what were once truths are true no longer, but also to commence new practices, and set the example of more enlightened conduct, and better taste and sense in human life. This cannot well be gainsaid by anybody who does not believe that the world has already attained perfection in all its ways and practices. It is true that this benefit is not capable of being rendered by everybody alike: there are but few persons, in comparison with the whole of mankind, whose experiments, if adopted by others, would be likely to be any improvement on established practice. But these few are the salt of the earth; without them, human life would become a stagnant pool. Not only is it they who introduce good things which did not before exist; it is they who keep the life in those which already exist. If there were nothing new to be done, would human intellect cease to be necessary? Would it be a reason why those who do the old things should forget why they are done, and do them like cattle, not like human beings? There is only too great a tendency in the best beliefs and practices to degenerate into the mechanical; and unless there were a succession of persons whose ever-recurring originality prevents the grounds of those beliefs and practices from becoming merely traditional, such dead matter would not resist the smallest shock from anything really alive, and there would be no reason why civilization should not die out, as in the Byzantine Empire. Persons of genius, it is true, are, and are always likely to be, a small minority; but in order to have them it is necessary to preserve the soil in which they grow. Genius can only breathe freely in an atmosphere of freedom ...

At present individuals are lost in the crowd. In politics it is almost a triviality to say that public opinion now rules the world. The only power deserving the name is that of masses, and of governments while they make themselves the organ of the tendencies and instincts of masses. This is as true in the moral and social relations of private life as in public transactions. Those whose opinions go by the name of public opinion, are not always the same sort of public: in America they are the whole white population; in England, chiefly the middle class. But they are always a mass, that is to say, collective mediocrity. And what is a still greater novelty, the mass do not now take their opinions from dignitaries in Church or State, from ostensible leaders, or from books. Their thinking is done for them by men much like themselves, addressing them or speaking in their name, on the spur of the moment, through the newspapers. I am not complaining of all this. I do not assert that anything better is compatible, as a general rule, with the present low state of the human mind. But that does not hinder the government of mediocrity from being mediocre government. No government by a democracy or a numerous aristocracy, either in its political acts or in the opinions, qualities, and tone of mind which it fosters, ever did or could rise above mediocrity, except in so far as the sovereign Many have let themselves be guided (which in their best times they always have done) by the counsels and influence of a more highly gifted and instructed One or Few. The initiation of all wise or noble things, comes and must come from individuals; generally at first from some one individual. The honour and glory of the average man is that he is capable of following that initiative; that he can respond internally to wise and noble things, and be led to them with his eyes open. I am not countenancing the sort of 'hero-worship' which applauds the strong man of genius for forcibly seizing on the government of the world and making it do his bidding in spite of itself. All he can claim is, freedom to point out the way. The power of compelling others into it, is not only inconsistent with the freedom and development of all the rest, but corrupting to the strong man himself. It does seem, however, that when the opinions of masses of merely average men are everywhere become or becoming the dominant power, the counterpoise and corrective to that tendency would be, the more and more pronounced individuality of those who stand on the higher eminences of thought. It is in these circumstances most especially, that exceptional individuals, instead of being deterred, should be encouraged in acting differently from the mass. In other times there was no advantage in their doing so, unless they acted not only differently, but better. In this age, the mere example of non-conformity, the mere refusal to bend the knee to custom, is itself a service. Precisely because the tyranny of opinion is such as to make eccentricity a reproach, it is desirable, in order to break through that tyranny, that people should be eccentric. Eccentricity has always abounded when and where strength of character has abounded; and the amount of eccentricity in a society has generally been proportional to the amount of genius, mental vigour, and moral courage it contained. That so few now dare to be eccentric, marks the chief danger of the time.

I have said that it is important to give the freest scope possible to uncustomary things, in order that it may in time appear which of these are fit to be converted into customs. But independence of action, and disregard of custom, are not solely deserving of encouragement for the chance they afford that better modes of action, and customs more worthy of general adoption, may be struck out; nor is it only persons of decided mental superiority who have a just claim to carry on their lives in their own way. There is no reason that all human existence should be constructed on some one or some small number of patterns. If a person possesses any tolerable amount of common sense and experience, his own mode of laying out his existence is the best, not because it is the best in itself, but because it is his own mode. Human beings are not like sheep; and even sheep are not undistinguishably alike. A man cannot get a coat or a pair of boots to fit him, unless they are either made to his measure, or he has a whole warehouseful to choose from: and is it easier to fit him with a life than with a coat, or are human beings more like one another in their whole physical and spiritual conformation than in the shape of their feet? If it were only that people have diversities of taste, that is reason enough for not attempting to shape them all after one model. But different persons also require different conditions for their spiritual development; and can no more exist healthily in the same moral, than all the variety of plants can in the same physical, atmosphere and climate. The same things which are helps to one person towards the cultivation of his higher nature, are hindrances to another. The same mode of life is a healthy excitement to one, keeping all his faculties of action and enjoyment in their best order, while to another it is a distracting burthen, which suspends or crushes all internal life. Such are the differences among human beings in their sources of pleasure, their susceptibilities of pain, and the operation on them of different physical and moral agencies, that unless there is a corresponding diversity in their modes of life, they neither obtain their fair share of happiness, nor grow up to the mental, moral, and aesthetic stature of which their nature is capable. Why then should tolerance, as far as the public sentiment is concerned, extend only to tastes and modes of life which extort acquiescence by the multitude of their adherents?

6.2

From *Thoughts on parliamentary reform* (1859), in *Dissertations and discussions political, philosophical, and historical reprinted chiefly from the Edinburgh and Westminster Reviews,* Longmans, Green, Reader and Dyer: London, 1868, vol. 3, pp. 17-18, 20-2, 26-7.

The system of plural voting outlined in this extract was only one of the devices recommended by Mill in order to stimulate a sense of responsible citizenship and also to counteract the tendency of the majority to enact ignorant policies. He also favoured, for example, a complicated scheme of proportional representation as a means of giving minorities a voice in parliament.

It is important that every one of the governed should have a voice in the government, because it can hardly be expected that those who have no voice will be unjustly postponed to those who have. It is still more important as one of the means of national education. A person who is excluded from all participation in political business is not a citizen. He has not the feelings of a citizen. To take an active interest in politics is, in modern times, the first thing which elevates the mind to large interests and contemplations; the first step out of the narrow bounds of individual and family selfishness, the first opening in the contracted round of daily occupations. The person who in any free country takes no interest in politics, unless from having been taught that he ought not to do so, must be too ill-informed, too stupid, or too selfish, to be interested in them; and we may rely on it that he cares as little for anything else, which does not directly concern himself or his personal connexions. Whoever is capable of feeling any common interest with his kind, or with his country, or with his city, is interested in politics; and to be interested in them, and not wish for a voice in them, is an impossibility. The possession and the exercise of political, and among others of electoral, rights, is one of the chief instruments both of moral and of intellectual training for the popular mind; and all governments must be regarded as extremely imperfect, until every one who is required to obey the laws, has a voice, or the prospect of a voice, in their enactment and administration.

But ought every one to have an *equal* voice? This is a totally different proposition; and in my judgment as palpably false, as the other is true and important. Here it is that I part company, on the question of principle, with the democratic reformers ...

There is no one who, in any matter which concerns himself, would not rather have his affairs managed by a person of greater knowledge and intelligence, than by one of less. There is no one who, if he was obliged to confide his interest jointly to both, would not desire to give a more potential voice to the more educated and more cultivated of the two.

This is no justification for making the less educated the slave, or serf, or mere dependent of the other. The subjection of any one individual or class to another, is always and necessarily disastrous in its effects on both. That power should be exercised over any portion of mankind without any obligation of consulting them, is only tolerable while they are in an infantile, or a semi-barbarous state. In any civilized condition, power ought never to be exempt from the necessity of appealing to the reason, and recommending itself by motives which justify it to the conscience and feelings, of the governed. In the present state of society, and under representative institutions, there is no mode of imposing this necessity on the ruling classes, as towards all other persons in the community, except by giving to every one a vote. But there is a wide interval between refusing votes to the great majority, and acknowledging in each individual among them a right to have his vote counted for exactly as much as the vote of the most highly educated person in the community; with the further addition that, under the name of equality, it would in reality count for vastly more, as long as the uneducated so greatly outnumber the educated. There is no such thing in morals as a *right* to power over others; and the electoral suffrage is that power. When all have votes, it will be both just in principle and necessary in fact, that some mode be adopted of giving greater weight to the suffrage of the more educated voter; some means by which the more intrinsically valuable member of society, the one who is more capable, more competent for the general affairs of life, and possessed more of the knowledge applicable to the management of the affairs of the community, should, as far as practicable, be singled out, and allowed a superiority of influence proportioned to his higher qualifications.

The most direct mode of effecting this, would be to establish plurality of votes, in favour of those who could afford a reasonable presumption of superior knowledge and cultivation. If every ordinary unskilled labourer had one vote, a skilled labourer, whose occupation requires an exercised mind and a knowledge of some of the laws of external nature, ought to have two. A foreman, or superintendent of labour, whose occupation requires something more of general culture, and some moral as well as intellectual qualities, should perhaps have three. A farmer, manufacturer, or trader, who requires a still larger range of ideas and knowledge, and the power of guiding and attending to a great number of various operations at once, should have three or four. A member of any profession requiring a long, accurate, and systematic mental cultivation, – a lawyer, a physician or surgeon, a clergyman of any denomination, a literary man, an artist, a public functionary (or, at all events, a member of every intellectual profession at the threshold of which there is a satisfactory examination test) ought to have five or six. A graduate of any university, or a person freely elected a member of any learned society, is entitled to at least as many. A certificate of having passed through a complete course of instruction at any place of education publicly recognised as one where the higher branches of knowledge are taught, should confer a plurality of votes; and there ought to be an organization of voluntary examinations throughout the country (agreeably to the precedent set by the middle-class examinations so wisely and virtuously instituted by the University of Oxford) at which any person whatever might present himself, and obtain, from impartial examiners, a certificate of his possessing the acquirements which would entitle him to any number of votes, up to the largest allowed to one individual. The presumption of superior instruction derived from mere pecuniary qualification is, in the system of arrangements we are now considering, inadmissible. It is a presumption which often fails, and to those against whom it operates, it is always invidious. What it is important to ascertain is education; and education can be tested directly, or by much stronger presumptive evidence than is afforded by income, or payment of taxes, or the quality of the house which a person inhabits.

The perfection, then, of an electoral system would be, that every person should have one vote, but that every well-educated person in the community should have more than one, on a scale corresponding as far as practicable to their amount of education . . . .

To make a participation in political rights the reward of mental improvement, would have many inestimable effects besides the obvious one. It would do more than merely admit the best and exclude the worst of the working classes; it would do more than make an honourable distinction in favour of the educated, and create an additional motive for seeking education. It would cause the electoral suffrage to be in time regarded in a totally different light. It would make it be thought of, not as now, in the light of a possession to be used by the voter for his own interest or pleasure, but as a trust for the public good. It would stamp the exercise of the suffrage as a matter of judgment, not of inclination; as a public function, the right to which is conferred by fitness for the intelligent performance of it.

Nobody will pretend that these effects would be completely produced by so low an educational qualification as reading, writing, and arithmetic; but it would be a considerable step towards them. The very novelty of the requirement – the excitement and discussion which it would produce in the class chiefly affected by it – would be the best sort of education; would make an opening in their minds that would let in light – would set them thinking in a perfectly new manner respecting political rights and responsibilities.

6.3

From *Considerations on representative government* (1861), George Routledge & Sons: London, 1905, ch. viii, pp. 175–7.

Mill attributed most of his progressive ideas to the influence of Mrs Harriet Taylor, whom he met in 1830 and eventually married in 1851. She certainly influenced *On liberty*, as well as *The subjection of women* in which Mill condemned the legal disabilities suffered by Victorian women. From 1865 to 1868 Mill was a Radical Member of Parliament, where he spoke on behalf of women's suffrage. In advocating female emancipation, however, Mill was far in advance of popular thinking; *The subjection of women* was his only book that did not become a commercial success. The following extract is a succinct expression of his arguments on behalf of equal political rights for men and women.

In the preceding argument for universal, but graduated suffrage, I have taken no account of difference of sex. I consider it to be as entirely irrelevant to political rights, as difference in height, or in the colour of the hair. All human beings have the same interest in good government; the welfare of all is alike affected by it, and they have equal need of a voice in it to secure their share of its benefits. If there be any difference, women require it more than men, since, being physically weaker, they are more dependent on law and society for protection. Mankind have long since abandoned the only premisses which will support the conclusion that women ought not to have votes. No one now holds that women should be in personal servitude; that they should have no thought, wish, or occupation, but to be the domestic drudges of husbands, fathers, or brothers . . .

Were it as right, as it is wrong, that they should be a subordinate class, confined to domestic occupations and subject to domestic authority, they would not the less require the protection of the suffrage to secure them from the abuse of that authority. Men, as well as women, do not need political rights in order that they may govern, but in order that they may not be misgoverned. The majority of the male sex are, and will be all their lives, nothing else than labourers in corn-fields or manufactories; but this does not render the suffrage less desirable for them, nor their claim to it less irresistible, when not likely to make a bad use of it. Nobody pretends to think that women would make a bad use of the suffrage. The worst that is said is, that they would vote as mere dependants, at the bidding of their male relations. If it be so, so let it be. If they think for themselves, great good will be done, and if they do not, no harm. It is a benefit to human beings to take off their fetters, even if they do not desire to walk. It would already be a great improvement in the moral position of women, to be no longer declared by law incapable of an opinion, and not entitled to a preference, respecting the most important concerns of humanity. There would be some benefit to them individually in having something to bestow which their male relatives cannot exact, and are yet desirous to have. It would also be no small matter that the husband would necessarily discuss the matter with his wife, and, that the vote would not be his exclusive affair, but a joint concern. People do not sufficiently consider how markedly the fact, that she is able to have some action on the outward world independently of him, raises her dignity and value in a vulgar man's eyes, and makes her the object of a respect which no personal qualities would ever obtain for one whose social existence he can entirely appropriate.

6.4

From *Principles of political economy with some of their applications to social philosophy* (1848), Longmans, Green, and Co: London, 1892, Bk. IV, ch. vi, pp. 453–5; Bk. IV, ch. vii, pp. 455–8, 460–1, 465, 474–7.

The *Principles* was widely used as an economics textbook and also appealed to thinkers anxious to solve the problems of an expanding industrial society. The chapters on the 'Stationary state' and the 'Probable futurity of the labouring classes', from which the following extract is taken, form the least orthodox section of the book.

I cannot ... regard the stationary state of capital and wealth with the unaffected aversion so generally manifested towards it by political economists of the old school. I am inclined to believe that it would be, on the whole, a very considerable improvement on our present condition. I confess I am not charmed with the ideal of life held out by those who think that the normal state of human beings is that of struggling to get on; that the trampling, crushing, elbowing, and treading on each other's heels, which form the existing type of social life, are the most desirable lot of human kind, or anything but the disagreeable symptoms of one of the phases of industrial progress ...

It is only in the backward countries of the world that increased production is still an important object: in those most advanced, what is economically needed is a better distribution, of which one indispensable means is a stricter restraint on population. Levelling institutions, either of a just or of an unjust kind, cannot alone accomplish it; they may lower the heights of society, but they cannot, of themselves, permanently raise the depths.

On the other hand, we may suppose this better distribution of property attained, by the joint effect of the prudence and frugality of individuals, and of a system of legislation favouring equality of fortunes, so far as is consistent with the just claim of the individual to the fruits, whether great or small, of his or her own industry. We may suppose, for instance ... a limitation of the sum which any one person may acquire by gift or inheritance, to the amount sufficient to constitute a moderate independence. Under this twofold influence, society would exhibit these leading features: a well-paid and affluent body of labourers; no enormous fortunes, except what were earned and accumulated during a single lifetime; but a much larger body of persons than at present, not only exempt from the coarser toils, but with sufficient leisure, both physical and mental, from mechanical details, to cultivate freely the graces of life, and afford examples of them to the classes less favourably circumstanced for their growth. This condition of society, so greatly preferable to the present, is not only perfectly compatible with the stationary state, but, it would seem, more naturally allied with that state than with any other ...

It is scarcely necessary to remark that a stationary condition of capital and population implies no stationary state of human improvement. There would be as much scope as ever for all kinds of mental culture, and moral and social progress; as much room for improving the Art of Living, and much more likelihood of its being improved, when minds ceased to be engrossed by the art of getting on. Even the industrial arts might be as earnestly and as successfully cultivated, with this sole difference, that instead of serving no purpose but the increase of wealth, industrial improvements would produce their legitimate effect, that of abridging labour. Hitherto it is questionable if all the mechanical inventions yet made had lightened the day's toil of any human being. They have enabled a greater population to live the same life of drudgery and imprisonment, and an increased number of manufacturers and others to make fortunes. They have increased the comforts of the middle classes. But they have not yet begun to effect those great changes in human destiny, which it is in their nature and in their futurity to accomplish. Only when, in addition to just institutions, the increase of mankind shall be under the deliberate guidance of judicious foresight, can the conquests made from the powers of nature by the intellect and energy of scientific discoverers, become the common property of the species, and the means of improving and elevating the universal lot ...

Considered in its moral and social aspect, the state of the labouring people has latterly been a subject of much more speculation and discussion than formerly; and the opinion, that it is now what it ought to be, has become very general. The suggestions which have been promulgated, and the controversies which have been excited, on detached points rather than on the foundations of the subject, have put in evidence the existence of two conflicting theories, respecting the social position desirable for manual labourers. The one may be called the theory of dependence and protection, the other that of self-dependence.

According to the former theory, the lot of the poor, in all things which affect them collectively, should be regulated *for* them, not *by* them. They should not be required or encouraged to think for themselves, or give to their own reflection or forecast an influential voice in the determination of their destiny. It is supposed to be the duty of the higher classes to think for them, and to take the responsibility of their lot, as the commander and officers of an army take that of the soldiers composing it ...

Of the working men, at least in the more advanced countries of Europe, it may be pronounced certain, that the patriarchal or paternal system of government is one to which they will not again be subject. That question was decided, when they were taught to read, and allowed access to newspapers and political tracts; when dissenting preachers were suffered to go among them, and appeal to their faculties and feelings in opposition to the creeds professed and countenanced by their superiors; when they were brought together in numbers, to work socially under the same roof; when railways enabled them to shift from place to place, and change their patrons and employers as easily as their coats; when they were encouraged to seek a share in the government, by means of the electoral franchise. The working classes have taken their interests into their own hands, and are perpetually showing that they think the interests of their employers not identical with their own, but opposite to them ...

The poor have come out of leading-strings, and cannot any longer be governed or treated like children. To their own qualities must now be commended the care of their destiny ... Whatever advice, exhortation, or guidance is held out to the labouring classes, must henceforth be tendered to them as equals, and accepted by them with their eyes open. The prospect of the future depends on the degree in which they can be made rational beings ...

In the present stage of human progress, when ideas of equality are daily spreading more widely among the poorer classes, and can no longer be checked by anything short of the entire suppression of printed discussion and even of freedom of speech, it is not to be expected that the division of the human race into two hereditary classes, employers and employed, can be permanently maintained. The relation is nearly as unsatisfactory to the payer of wages as to the receiver. If the rich regard the poor as, by a kind of natural law, their servants and dependents, the rich in their turn are regarded as a mere prey and pasture for the poor; the subject of demands and expectations wholly indefinite, increasing in extent with every concession made to them. The total absence of regard for justice or fairness in the relations between the two, is as marked on the side of the employed as on that of the employers. We look in vain among the working classes in general for the just pride which will choose to give good work for good wages: for the most part, their sole endeavour is to receive as much, and return as little in the shape of service, as possible. It will sooner or later become insupportable to the employing classes to live in close and hourly contact with persons whose interests and feelings are in hostility to them. Capitalists are almost as much interested as labourers, in placing the operations of industry on such a footing, that those who labour for them may feel the same interest in the work, which is felt by those who labour on their own account . . .

Hitherto there has been no alternative for those who lived by their labour, but that of labouring either each for himself alone, or for a master. But the civilizing and improving influences of association, and the efficiency and economy of production on a large scale, may be obtained without dividing the producers into two parties with hostile interests and feelings, the many who do the work being mere servants under the command of the one who supplies the funds, and having no interest of their own in the enterprise except to earn their wages with as little labour as possible. The speculations and discussions of the last fifty years, and the events of the last twenty, are abundantly conclusive on this point. If the improvement which even triumphant military despotism has only retarded, not stopped, shall continue its course, there can be little doubt that the *status* of hired-labourers will gradually tend to confine itself to the description of workpeople whose low moral qualities render them unfit for anything more independent: and that the relation of masters and workpeople will be gradually superseded by partnership, in one of two forms: in some cases, association of the labourers with the capitalist; in others, and perhaps finally in all, association of labourers among themselves.

The first of these forms of association has long been practised, not indeed as a rule, but as an exception. In several departments of industry there are already cases in which every one who contributes to the work, either by labour or by pecuniary resources, has a partner's interest in it, proportional to the value of his contribution. It is already a common practice to remunerate those in whom peculiar trust is reposed, by means of a percentage on the profits: and cases exist in which the principle is, with excellent success, carried down to the class of mere manual labourers . . .

The form of association, however, which if mankind continue to improve, must be expected in the end to predominate, is not that which can exist between a capitalist as chief, and workpeople without a voice in the management, but the association of the labourers themselves on terms of equality, collectively owning the capital with which they carry on their operations, and working under managers elected and removable by themselves ...

From the progressive advance of the co-operative movement, a great increase may be looked for even in the aggregate productiveness of industry. The sources of the increase are two-fold. In the first place, the class of mere distributors, who are not producers but auxiliaries of production, and whose inordinate numbers, far more than the gains of capitalists, are the cause why so great a portion of the wealth produced does not reach the producers – will be reduced to more modest dimensions ...

The other mode in which co-operation tends, still more efficaciously, to increase the productiveness of labour, consists in the vast stimulus given to productive energies, by placing the labourers, as a mass, in a relation to their work which would make it their principle and their interest – at present it is neither – to do the utmost instead of the least possible in exchange for their remuneration. It is scarcely possible to rate too highly this material benefit, which yet is as nothing compared with the moral revolution in society that would accompany it: the healing of the standing feud between capital and labour; the transformation of human life, from a conflict of classes struggling for opposite interests, to a friendly rivalry in the pursuit of a good common to all; the elevation of the dignity of labour, a new sense of security and independence in the labouring class, and the conversion of each human being's daily occupation into a school of the social sympathies and the practical intelligence ...

Eventually, and in perhaps a less remote future than may be supposed, we may, through the co-operative principle, see our way to a change in society, which would combine the freedom and independence of the individual, with the moral, intellectual, and economical advantages of aggregate production; and which, without violence or spoliation, or even any sudden disturbance of existing habits and expectations, would realise, at least in the industrial department, the best aspirations of the democratic spirit, by putting an end to the division of society into the industrious and the idle, and effacing all social distinctions but those fairly earned by personal services and exertions. Associations like those which we have described, by the very process of their success, are a course of education in those moral and active qualities by which alone success can be either deserved or attained. As associations multiplied, they would tend more and more to absorb all workpeople, except those who have too little understanding, or too little virtue, to be capable of learning to act on any other system than that of narrow selfishness. As this change proceeded, owners of capital would gradually find it to their advantage, instead of maintaining the struggle of the old system with workpeople of only the worst description, to lend their capital to the associations; to do this at a diminishing rate of interest, and at last, perhaps, even to exchange their capital for terminable annuities. In this or some such mode, the existing accumulations of capital might honestly, and by a kind of spontaneous process, become in the end the joint property of all who participate in their productive employment: a transformation which, thus effected, (and assuming of course that both sexes participate equally in the rights and in the government of the association) would be the nearest approach to social justice, and the most beneficial ordering of industrial affairs for the universal good, which it is possible at present to foresee.

I agree, then, with the Socialist writers in their conception of the form which industrial operations tend to assume in the advance of improvement; and I entirely share their opinion that the time is ripe for commencing this transformation, and that it should by all just and effectual means be aided and encouraged. But while I agree and sympathize with Socialists in this practical portion of their aims, I utterly dissent from the most conspicuous and vehement part of their teaching, their declamations against competition. With moral conceptions in many respects far ahead of the existing arrangements of society, they have in general very confused and erroneous notions of its actual working; and one of their greatest errors, as I conceive, is to charge upon competition all the economical evils which at present exist. They forget that wherever competition is not, monopoly is; and that monopoly, in all its forms, is the taxation of the industrious for the support of indolence, if not of plunder. They forget, too, that with the exception of competition among labourers, all other competition is for the benefit of the labourers, by cheapening the articles they consume; that competition even in the labour market is a source not of low but of high wages, wherever the competition *for* labour exceeds the competition *of* labour, as in America, in the colonies, and in the skilled trades; and never could be a cause of low wages, save by the overstocking of the labour market through the too great numbers of the labourers' families; while, if the supply of labourers is excessive, not even Socialism can prevent their remuneration from being low. Besides, if association were universal, there would be no competition between labourer and labourer; and that between association and association would be for the benefit of the consumers, that is, of the associations; of the industrious classes generally.

7.1 ALFRED MARSHALL (1842–1924)

From 'The Future of the working classes' (1873), in *Memorials of Alfred Marshall*, ed. A. C. Pigou, Macmillan: London, 1925, pp. 102–6, 109–15, 117.

Marshall, who in 1885 became Professor of Political Economy at Cambridge, was instrumental in transforming economics into a respectable academic discipline. Although essentially cautious and sceptical about the possibilities of radical social reform, he nevertheless tended to indulge in Victorian pieties which, according to J. M. Keynes, emanated from a desire 'to do good'. His penchant for moralizing emerges in this extract, taken from a youthful essay, where Marshall expresses faith in the benevolent potential of capitalism to secure J. S. Mill's ideal of a society in which poverty had been abolished and where common people were eager to improve themselves.

I propose to sketch in rough outline a portion of the ground that must be worked over if we would rightly examine whether the amelioration of the working classes has limits beyond which it cannot pass; whether it be true that the resources of the world will not suffice for giving to more than a small portion of its inhabitants an education in youth and an occupation in after-life, similar to those which we are now wont to consider proper to gentlemen ...

The question is not whether all men will ultimately be equal – that they certainly will not – but whether progress may not go on steadily if slowly, till the official distinction between working man and gentleman has passed away; till, by occupation at least, every man is a gentleman. I hold that it may, and that it will ...

Is it not true that when we say a man belongs to the working classes we are thinking of the effect that his work produces on him rather than of the effect that he produces on his work? If a man's daily task tends to give culture and refinement to his character, do we not, however coarse the individual man may happen to be, say that his occupation is that of a gentleman? If a man's daily task tends to keep his character rude and coarse, do we not, however truly refined the individual man may happen to be, say that he belongs to the working classes?

It is needful to examine more closely the characteristics of those occupations which directly promote culture and refinement of character. They demand powers and activities of mind of various kinds. They demand the faculty of maintaining social intercourse with a large number of persons; they demand, in appearance at least, the kindly habit of promptly anticipating the feelings of others on minor points, of ready watchfulness to avoid each trivial word or deed that may pain or annoy. These qualities are required for success, and they are therefore prepared in youth by a careful and a long continued education. Throughout life they are fostered and improved by exercise and by contact with persons who have similar qualities and require them of their associates. A man's sympathies thus become broad because he knows much of life, and is adapted for taking interest in what he knows. He has a wide range of pleasures; each intellectual energy, each artistic perception, each fellow-feeling with men far off and near, gives him a new capacity of enjoyment, removes from him more and more the desire for coarse delights. Wealth is not indispensable; but it frequently gives its aid ... Wealth, in general, implies a liberal education in youth, and throughout life broad interests and refined associations; and it is to these effects on character that the chief attractiveness of wealth is due ...

At what point, then, in the scale do we first meet the working man? It is an important and a hopeful fact that we cannot say where – that the chain is absolutely continuous and unbroken. There is a tendency to regard somewhat slightingly the distinction between skilled and unskilled labour. But the fact remains that artisans whose manual labour is not heavy, who are paid chiefly for their skill and the work of their brains, are as conscious of the superiority of their lot over that of their poorer brethren as is the highest nobleman of the land. And they are right; for their lot does just offer them the opportunity of being gentlemen in spirit and in truth; and, to the great honour of the age be it said, many of them are steadily becoming gentlemen. They are steadily striving upwards; steadily aiming at a higher and more liberal preparation in youth; steadily learning to value time and leisure for themselves, learning to care more for this than for mere increase of wages and material comforts; steadily developing independence and a manly respect for themselves, and, therefore, a courteous respect for others; they are steadily accepting the private and public duties of a citizen; steadily increasing their grasp of the truth that they are men, and not producing machines. They are steadily becoming gentlemen. Steadily: we hope to be able ere long to say 'steadily and rapidly'; but even now the picture is not altogether a gloomy one.

But let us turn our eyes on that darker scene which the lot of unskilled labour presents. Let us look at those vast masses of men who, after long hours of hard and unintellectual toil, are wont to return to their narrow homes with bodies exhausted and with minds dull and sluggish. That men do habitually sustain hard corporeal work for eight, ten or twelve hours a day, is a fact so familiar to us that we scarcely realize the extent to which it governs the moral and mental history of the world; we scarcely realize how subtle, all-pervading and powerful may be the effect of the work of man's body in dwarfing the growth of the man ...

Let us venture to picture to ourselves the state of a country from which such circumstances have been excluded. We shall have made much progress on our way, when we have seen that such a country would contain within it no seeds of the ruin of its material or moral prosperity; that it would be vigorous and full of healthy life ...

We know then pretty clearly what are the conditions under which our fancied country is to start; and we may formulate them as follows. It is to have a fair share of wealth, and not an abnormally large population. Everyone is to have in youth an education which is thorough while it lasts, and which lasts long. No one is to do in the day so much manual work as will leave him little time or little aptitude for intellectual and artistic enjoyment in the evening. Since there will be nothing tending to render the individual coarse and unrefined, there will be nothing tending to render society coarse and unrefined ... This, then, is the condition in which our fancied country is to be when we first consider it. We have to inquire whether this condition can be maintained. Let us examine such obstacles to its maintenance as may be supposed to exist.

First, it may be argued that a great diminution of the hours of manual labour below their present amount would prevent the industry of the country from meeting its requirements, so that the wealth of the country could not be sustained. This objection is an instance of the difficulty with which we perceive things that are familiar. We all know that the progress of science and invention has multiplied enormously the efficiency of labour within the last century ... But, further, the only labour excluded from our new society is that which is so conducted as to stunt the mental growth, preventing people from rising out of old narrow grooves of thought and feeling, from obtaining increased knowledge, higher tastes, and more comprehensive interests. Now it is to such stunting almost alone that indolence is due. Remove it, and work rightly applied, the vigorous exercise of faculties would be the main aim of every man. The total work done per head of the population would be greater than now. Less of it would be devoted directly to the increase of material wealth, but far more would be indirectly efficient for this end. Knowledge is power; and man would have knowledge. Inventions would increase, and they would be readily applied. All labour would be skilled, and there would be no premium on setting men to tasks that required no skill. The work which man directs the forces of nature to perform for him, would thus be incomparably greater than now ...

But, secondly, it might be argued that short hours of work might ruin the foreign trade of the country. Such a doctrine might derive support from the language of some of our public men, even in recent times. But it is a fallacy. It contradicts a proposition which no one who had thought on the subject would dream of deliberately denying; one which is as well established and as rigorously proved as any in Euclid. This proposition is, that low wages, if common to all occupations, cannot enable one country to undersell another. A high rate of wages, or short hours of work, if common to all industries, cannot cause a country to be undersold: though, if they were confined to some industries, they might of course cause these particular industries to be undersold.

A danger, however, might be incurred by high wages or short hours of work. If the rate of profits were reduced thereby, capital would be tempted to migrate. But the country we are picturing to ourselves would be specially defended against such a danger. To begin with, its labourers would be highly skilled. And the history of the progress of manufactures in England and throughout the world proves that, if the number of hours' work per day be given, the capitalist can afford to pay almost any rate of wages in order to secure highly skilled labour. But such labour, partly as a cause and partly as a consequence of its skill, has in general not very many hours in its working-day; and for every hour, during which his untiring machinery is lying idle, the capitalist suffers loss. In our society the hours of labour are to be very short, but it does not follow that the hours of work of the machinery would be short too. The obstacles that now exist to the general adoption of the system of working in 'shifts' are due partly to the unenlightened selfishness of workmen, partly to their careless and dishonest maltreatment of machinery, but mainly to the fact that, with the present number of hours' work done by each shift, one shift would have to commence work very early and the other to end work very late. But in our new society none of these obstacles would exist. A man would not in general perform manual work for more than six hours a day. Thus one set would work perhaps from 6 to 9.30 a.m. and from 2 to 4.30 p.m.; the other set from 10 a.m. to 1.30 p.m. and from 5 to 7.30 p.m. In heavy work three sets of men might each work a shift of four hours. For we must not suppose that an educated man would consent for any pay whatever to continue exhausting physical work so far as to cause the stupefaction of his intellect. For his severe work he would be highly paid; and, if necessary, he might add to his income by a few hours of lighter work.

But there is another special reason why capital should not leave our fancied country. All industries might be partly conducted by capitalists with labourers working for hire under them. But in many industries production would be mainly carried on, as Mr. and Mrs. Mill have prophesied, by 'the association of labourers among themselves on terms of equality, collectively owning the capital with which they carry on their operations, and working under managers elected and removable by themselves.' It will be said that such associations have been tried, and have seldom succeeded. They have not been tried. What have been tried are associations among, comparatively speaking, uneducated men, men who are unable to follow even the financial calculations that are required for an extensive and complicated business. What have to be tried are associations among men as highly educated as are manufacturers now. Such associations could not but succeed; and the capital that belonged to them would run no risk of being separated from them.

Again, it might be objected that it would be impossible to maintain that high standard of education which we have throughout assumed. Some parents, it might be said, would neglect their duty to their children. A class of unskilled labourers might again grow up, competing for hard toil, ready to sacrifice the means of their own culture to increased wages and physical indulgences. This class would marry improvidently: an increased population would press on the means of subsistence, the difficulty of imparting a high education would increase, and society would retrograde until it had arrived at a position similar to that which it now occupies – a position in which man, to a great extent, ignores his duty of anticipating, before he marries, the requirements of the bodily and mental nurture of his children; and thereby compels Nature, with her sorrowful but stern hands, to thin out the young lives before they grow up to misery. This is the danger most to be dreaded. But even this danger is not so great as it appears. An educated man would not only have a high conception of his duty to his children; he would be deeply sensitive to the social degradation which he and they would incur if he failed in it. Society would be keenly alive to the peril to itself of such failure, and would punish it as a form of treason against the State. Education would be unfailingly maintained. Every man, before he married, would prepare for the expense of properly educating his family; since he could not, even if he would, shirk this expense. The population would, therefore, be retained within due limits. Thus every single condition would be fulfilled which was requisite for the continued and progressive prosperity of the country which we have pictured. It would grow in wealth – material and mental. Vigorous mental faculties imply continual activity. Work, in its best sense, the healthy energetic exercise of faculties, is the aim of life, is life itself; and in this sense every one would be a worker more completely than now. But men would have ceased to carry on mere physical work to such an extent as to dull their higher energies. In the bad sense, in which work crushes a man's life, it would be regarded as a wrong. The active vigour of the people would continually increase; and in each successive generation it would be more completely true that every man was by occupation a gentleman.

Such a state of society in a country would then, if once attained, be ever maintained. Such a country would have in it the conditions of vitality more fully satisfied than any other country would. Is it not, then, a reasonable thing to believe that every movement towards the attainment of such conditions has vitality also? And, if we look around us, do we not find that we are steadily, if slowly, moving towards that attainment? All ranks of society are rising; on the whole they are better and more cultivated than their forefathers were; they are no less eager to do, and they are much more powerful greatly to bear, and greatly to forbear. Read of the ignorant crime that accompanied popular outbreaks even a generation ago, and then look at the orderly meetings by which the people now expresses its will. In the broad backbone of moral strength our people have never been wanting; but now, by the aid of education, their moral strength is gaining new life . . .

And what is society bound to do? It is bound to see that no child grows up in ignorance, able only to be a producing machine, unable to be a man; himself low and limited in his thoughts, his tastes, his feelings, his interests and his aims, to some extent probably low and limited in his virtues, and in every way lowering and limiting his neighbours. It is bound to compel children, and to help them, to take the first step upwards; and it is bound to help them to make, if they will, many steps upwards. If the growth of a man's mind, if his spiritual cultivation be the end of life; and material wealth, houses and horses, carpets and French cookery merely means; what temporary pecuniary loss can we set against the education of the nation? It is abundantly clear that, unless we can compel children into the schools, we cannot enable multitudes of them to escape from a life of ignorance so complete that they cannot fail to be brutish and degraded.

7.2 THOMAS HILL GREEN (1836–1882)

From 'Lecture on liberal legislation and freedom of contract' (1881), in *The works of Thomas Hill Green,* ed. R. L. Nettleship, Longmans, Green, and Co: London, 1888, vol. 3, pp. 370–4.

Green, son of an Anglican clergyman, became a Fellow of Balliol College, Oxford, in 1861, and was appointed Professor of Moral Philosophy in 1878. A Liberal Party activist, he was particularly concerned to promote education and temperance as means of elevating the working class. Although Green did not advocate an extensive programme of political reform, the ideas expressed in the following extract helped to shape the new liberalism of the late nineteenth century. Green's concept of positive freedom, as well as his suggestion that government should remove hindrances to the capacity of citizens to contribute to the common good, influenced many liberals who wished to extend the frontiers of the State.

We shall probably all agree that freedom, rightly understood, is the greatest of blessings; that its attainment is the true end of all our effort as citizens. But when we thus speak of freedom, we should consider carefully what we mean by it. We do not mean merely freedom from restraint or compulsion. We do not mean merely freedom to do as we like irrespective of what it is that we like. We do not mean a freedom that can be enjoyed by one man or one set of men at the cost of a loss of freedom to others. When we speak of freedom as something to be so highly prized, we mean a positive power or capacity of doing or enjoying something worth doing or enjoying, and that, too, something that we do or enjoy in common with others. We mean by it a power which each man exercises through the help or security given him by his fellow-men, and which he in turn helps to secure for them. When we measure the progress of a society by its growth in freedom, we measure it by the increasing development and exercise on the whole of those powers of contributing to social good with which we believe the members of the society to be endowed; in short, by the greater power on the part of the citizens as a body to make the most and best of themselves. Thus, though of course there can be no freedom among men who act not willingly but under compulsion, yet on the other hand the mere removal of compulsion, the mere enabling a man to do as he likes, is in itself no contribution to true freedom ...

If I have given a true account of that freedom which forms the goal of social effort, we shall see that freedom of contract, freedom in all the forms of doing what one will with one's own, is valuable only as a means to an end. That end is what I call freedom in the positive sense: in other words, the liberation of the powers of all men equally for contributions to a common good. No one has a right to do what he will with his own in such a way as to contravene this end. It is only through the guarantee which society gives him that he has property at all, or, strictly speaking, any right to his possessions. This guarantee is founded on a sense of common interest. Every one has an interest in securing to every one else the free use and enjoyment and disposal of his possessions, so long as that freedom on the part of one does not interfere with a like freedom on the part of others, because such freedom contributes to that equal development of the faculties of all which is the highest good for all. This is the true and the only justification of rights of property. Rights of property, however, have been and are claimed which cannot be thus justified. We are all now agreed that men cannot rightly be the property of men. The institution of property being only justifiable as a means to the free exercise of the social capabilities of all, there can be no true right to property of a kind which debars one class of men from such free exercise altogether. We condemn slavery no less when it arises out of a voluntary agreement on the part of the enslaved person. A contract by which any one agreed for a certain consideration to become the slave of another we should reckon a void contract. Here, then, is a limitation upon freedom of contract which we all recognise as rightful. No contract is valid in which human persons, willingly or unwillingly, are dealt with as commodities, because such contracts of necessity defeat the end for which alone society enforces contracts at all.

Are there no other contracts which, less obviously perhaps but really, are open to the same objection? In the first place, let us consider contracts affecting labour. Labour, the economist tells us, is a commodity exchangeable like other commodities. This is in a certain sense true, but it is a commodity which attaches in a peculiar manner to the person of man. Hence restrictions may need to be placed on the sale of this commodity which would be unnecessary in other cases, in order to prevent labour from being sold under conditions which make it impossible for the person selling it ever to become a free contributor to social good in any form. This is most plainly the case when a man bargains to work under conditions fatal to health, e.g. in an unventilated factory. Every injury to the health of the individual is, so far as it goes, a public injury. It is an impediment to the general freedom; so much deduction from our power, as members of society, to make the best of ourselves. Society is, therefore, plainly within its right when it limits freedom of contract for the sale of labour, so far as is done by our laws for the sanitary regulations of factories, workshops, and mines. It is equally within its right in prohibiting the labour of women and young persons beyond certain hours. If they work beyond those hours, the result is demonstrably physical deterioration; which, as demonstrably, carries with it a lowering of the moral forces of society. For the sake of that general freedom of its members to make the best of themselves, which it is the object of civil society to secure, a prohibition should be put by law, which is the deliberate voice of society, on all such contracts of service as in a general way yield such a result. The purchase or hire of unwholesome dwellings is properly forbidden on the same principle. Its application to compulsory education may not be quite so obvious, but it will appear on a little reflection. Without a command of certain elementary arts and knowledge, the individual in modern society is as effectually crippled as by the loss of a limb or a broken constitution. He is not free to develop his faculties. With a view to securing such freedom among its members it is as certainly within the province of the state to prevent children from growing up in that kind of ignorance which practically excludes them from a free career in life, as it is within its province to require the sort of building and drainage necessary for public health.

Our modern legislation then with reference to labour, and education, and health, involving as it does manifold interference with freedom of contract, is justified on the ground that it is the business of the state, not indeed directly to promote moral goodness, for that, from the very nature of moral goodness, it cannot do, but to maintain the conditions without which a free exercise of the human faculties is impossible.

7.3 THOMAS HILL GREEN

From *Lectures on the principles of political obligation*, new impression, Longmans, Green, and Co: London, 1907, pp. 225–9.

In this extract from his *Lectures*, published posthumously, Green revealed his attachment to some traditional liberal assumptions. Yet many liberals shared his conviction that a legacy of aristocratic power was primarily responsible for the defects of industrial society.

It is true that the accumulation of capital naturally leads to the employment of large masses of hired labourers. But there is nothing in the nature of the case to keep these labourers in the condition of living from hand to mouth, to exclude them from that education of the sense of responsibility which depends on the possibility of permanent ownership. There is nothing in the fact that their labour is hired in great masses by great capitalists to prevent them from being on a small scale capitalists themselves ... In fact, as we know, in the well-paid industries of England the better sort of labourers do become capitalists, to the extent often of owning their houses and a good deal of furniture, of having an interest in stores, and of belonging to benefit-societies through which they make provision for the future. It is not then to the accumulation of capital, but to the condition, due to antecedent circumstances unconnected with that accumulation, of the men with whom the capitalist deals and whose labour he buys on the cheapest terms, that we must ascribe the multiplication in recent times of an impoverished and reckless proletariate.

It is difficult to summarise the influences to which is due the fact that in all the chief seats of population in Europe the labour-market is constantly thronged with men who are too badly reared and fed to be efficient labourers; who for this reason, and from the competition for employment with each other, have to sell their labour very cheap; who have thus seldom the means to save, and whose standard of living and social expectation is so low that, if they have the opportunity of saving, they do not use it, and keep bringing children into the world at a rate which perpetuates the evil. It is certain, however, that these influences have no necessary connection with the maintenance of the right of individual property and consequent unlimited accumulation of capital, though they no doubt are connected with that régime of force and conquest by which existing governments have been established, – governments which do not indeed create the rights of individual property, any more than other rights, but which serve to maintain them. It must always be borne in mind that the appropriation of land by individuals has in most countries – probably in all where it approaches completeness – been originally effected, not by the expenditure of labour or the results of labour on the land, but by force. The original landlords have been conquerors.

This has affected the condition of the industrial classes in at least two ways: (1) When the application of accumulated capital to any work in the way of mining or manufacture has created a demand for labour, the supply has been forthcoming from men whose ancestors, if not themselves, were trained in habits of serfdom; men whose life has been one of virtually forced labour, relieved by church-charities or the poor law (which in part took the place of these charities); who were thus in no condition to contract freely for the sale of their labour, and had nothing of that sense of family-responsibility which might have made them insist on having the chance of saving. Landless countrymen, whose ancestors were serfs, are the parents of the proletariate of great towns. (2) Rights have been allowed to landlords, incompatible with the true principle on which rights of property rest, and tending to interfere with the development of the proprietorial capacity in others. The right to freedom in unlimited acquisition of wealth, by means of labour and by means of the saving and successful application of the results of labour, does not imply the right of anyone to do as he likes with those gifts of nature, without which there would be nothing to spend labour upon. The earth is just as much an original natural material necessary to productive industry, as are air, light, and water, but while the latter from the nature of the case cannot be appropriated, the earth can be and has been. The only justification for this appropriation, as for any other, is that it contributes on the whole to social well-being; that the earth as appropriated by individuals under certain conditions becomes more serviceable to society as a whole, including those who are not proprietors of the soil, than if it were held in common. The justification disappears if these conditions are not observed; and from government having been chiefly in the hands of appropriators of the soil, they have not been duly observed. Landlords have been allowed to 'do what they would with their own,' as if land were merely like so much capital, admitting of indefinite extension. The capital gained by one is not taken from another, but one man cannot acquire more land without others having less; and though a growing reduction in the number of landlords is not necessarily a social evil, if it is compensated by the acquisition of other wealth on the part of those extruded from the soil, it is only not an evil if the landlord is prevented from so using his land as to make it unserviceable to the wants of men (e.g. by turning fertile land into a forest), and from taking liberties with it incompatible with the conditions of general freedom and health; e.g. by clearing out a village and leaving the people to pick up house-room as they can elsewhere (a practice common under the old poor-law, when the distinction between close and open villages grew up), or, on the other hand, by building houses in unhealthy places or of unhealthy structure, by stopping up means of communication, or forbidding the erection of dissenting chapels. In fact the restraints which the public interest requires to be placed on the use of land if individual property in it is to be allowed at all, have been pretty much ignored, while on the other hand, that full development of its resources, which individual ownership would naturally favour, has been interfered with by laws or customs which, in securing estates to certain families, have taken away the interest, and tied the hands, of the nominal owner – the tenant for life – in making the most of his property.

Thus the whole history of the ownership of land in Europe has been of a kind to lead to the agglomeration of a proletariate, neither holding nor seeking property, wherever a sudden demand has arisen for labour in mines or manufactures. This at any rate was the case down to the epoch of the French Revolution; and this, which brought to other countries deliverance from feudalism, left England, where feudalism had previously passed into unrestrained landlordism, almost untouched. And while those influences of feudalism and landlordism which tend to throw a shiftless population upon the centres of industry have been left unchecked, nothing till quite lately was done to give such a population a chance of bettering itself, when it had been brought together. Their health, housing, and schooling were unprovided for. They were left to be freely victimised by deleterious employments, foul air, and consequent craving for deleterious drinks. When we consider all this, we shall see the unfairness of laying on capitalism or the free development of individual wealth the blame which is really due to the arbitrary and violent manner in which rights over land have been acquired and exercised, and to the failure of the state to fulfil those functions which under a system of unlimited private ownership are necessary to maintain the conditions of a free life.

Whether, when those functions have been more fully recognised and executed, and when the needful control has been established in the public interest over the liberties which landlords may take in the use of their land, it would still be advisable to limit the right of bequest in regard to land, and establish a system of something like equal inheritance, is a question which cannot be answered on any absolute principle. It depends on circumstances. Probably the question should be answered differently in a country like France or Ireland, where the most important industries are connected directly with the soil, and in one like England where they are not so. The reasons must be cogent which could justify that interference with the control of the parent over his family, which seems to be implied in the limitation of the power of bequeathing land when the parent's wealth lies solely in land,

and which arises, be it remembered, in a still more mischievous way from the present English practice of settling estates. But it is important to bear in mind that the question in regard to land stands on a different footing from that in regard to wealth generally, owing to the fact that land is a particular commodity limited in extent, from which alone can be derived the materials necessary to any industry whatever, on which men must find house-room if they are to find it at all, and over which they must pass in communicating with each other, however much water or even air may be used for that purpose. These are indeed not reasons for preventing private property in land or even free bequest of land, but they necessitate a special control over the exercise of rights of property in land, and it remains to be seen whether that control can be sufficiently established in a country where the power of great estates has not first been broken, as in France, by a law of equal inheritance.

7.4 DAVID LLOYD GEORGE (1863–1945)

From 'Poverty' (1906), in *Slings and arrows: sayings chosen from the speeches of the Rt. Hon. David Lloyd George,* ed. Philip Guedalla, Cassell: London, 1929, pp. 6–9.

Lloyd George was the last Liberal Prime Minister, holding office from 1916 to 1922. As Chancellor of the Exchequer from 1908 he taxed landed wealth in order to finance old-age pensions, national health insurance and other aspects of an embryonic welfare state. He is therefore associated with the reforming zeal of progressive liberalism. But Lloyd George had been reared in Caernarvonshire by his uncle, a Baptist shoemaker, and his political outlook was shaped by the conflict in rural Wales between tenants, who were largely liberal and nonconformist, and Tory-Anglican landowners; and, as the extract from this speech given at Penrhyndeudraeth illustrates, he had little grasp of the class conflicts endemic to an industrial society. 'Feudalism is the enemy', he proclaimed on another occasion, 'and we must deal with it' by reforming the system of land tenure in both countryside and new urban areas.

There are ten millions in this country enduring year after year the torture of living while lacking a sufficiency of the bare necessaries of life; and all this exists amid a splendid plenty, which pours into a land so wealthy that it can afford to lend, out of its spare riches, thousands of millions to less well endowed lands in other parts of the world.

What are some of the direct causes of poverty? There is the fact that a man's earnings are not adequate to maintain himself and his family;

there is the inability to obtain employment for economic reasons; and there is the inability of men to pursue their avocation owing to sickness, old age, or inherent lack of physical stamina or vitality. Then there is the most fertile cause of all – a man's own improvident habits, such as drinking and gambling. That is supposed to account for sixty per cent of the poverty in the land; it is indirectly responsible for more. Drink not only impoverishes the individual, but it indirectly contributes to unemployment by diverting earnings from necessaries of life, the manufacture of which would give three times as much employment as the production of drink ...

Drink is by no means alone responsible for the poverty in the United Kingdom. There are many thousands of sober, clean–living men and women in this country who to-day suffer the privations of unmerited poverty. There is more wealth per head of the population here than in any other land in the world. Shame upon rich Britain that she should tolerate so much poverty among her people! ... There is plenty of wealth in this country to provide for all and to spare. What is wanted is a fairer distribution ...

I do not suggest that there should be a compulsory equal distribution of the wealth of this country among its inhabitants, but I do say that the law which protects those men in the enjoyment of their great possessions should, first of all, see that those whose labour alone produces that wealth are amply protected with their families from actual need, where they are unable to purchase necessaries owing to circumstances over which they have no control. By that I mean not that they should be referred to the scanty and humiliating fare of the pauper, but that the spare wealth of the country should, as a condition of its enjoyment by its possessors, be forced to contribute first towards the honourable maintenance of those who have ceased to be able to maintain themselves.

Then there is our absurdly unjust land system. Drink and the land laws between them are responsible for nine-tenths of the slumminess of our towns, and our system of land ownership is responsible for labour conditions in the country which drive men in thousands from the villages into the towns. Who can expect anything else? Most of the landlords of Wales extort annually as much for the mere licence to till the land as the man who actually does the work obtains for his labour and his thought upon it the whole year round. Even then from year to year the man is subject to the caprice of the landlord. How long do you think that will last? It has broken down hopelessly in Ireland; if Britain had not been an exceptionally prosperous country, it would long ago have ended in revolution here.

7.5 HERBERT HENRY ASQUITH (1852–1928)

From 'Introduction' to Herbert Samuel, *Liberalism: an attempt to state the principles and proposals of contemporary liberalism in England*, Grant Richards: London, 1902, pp. vii, ix–x.

Asquith, who was Liberal Prime Minister from 1908 to 1916, had been tutored by T. H. Green at Balliol College, Oxford, in the early 1870s. The following extract, in which Asquith used the concept of positive liberty to advocate social reform, is pure Green.

A political party with great traditions and a venerable past carries with it a load of splendid but sometimes embarrassing memories. Its past records can always be made to furnish more or less effective ammunition to critics with a deficient sense of historical perspective. If it has within it a spring of real vitality, it must be constantly refashioning its weapons and shifting its camp. The process is generally gradual, sometimes so slow as to be for a long time almost imperceptible. But when the change at last becomes apparent even to the dullest witted, nothing is so natural to a certain class of opponents as to assail the new position with a fusillade of great names and old watchwords. What would Mr. Fox have said? What would have been the attitude of Mr Cobden? What about the principles of 1832 or 1880? And so on ...

It may seem a truism to say that the Liberal party inscribes among its permanent watchwords the name of Liberty. That this should sound like a commonplace is another illustration of the penalties of success. Freedom of speech, freedom of the press, freedom of association and combination, which we in these latter days have come to look upon as standing in the same category as the natural right to light and air, were in point of fact privileges long denied, slowly attained, and hardly won. But Liberty itself, like so many of the rallying cries in the secular struggle of parties, is a term which grows by what it feeds on, and acquires in each generation a new and larger content. To the early reformers it was a symbol of antagonism and almost of negation; it meant the removal of fetters, the emancipation both of individuals and of the community from legal and constitutional disabilities. The abolition of religious tests, the opening up of municipal corporations and the magistracy, the recognition of the legal status of Trade Unions (to take only a few illustrations) were all steps on the road to the peaceful obliteration of feudal and mediaeval privileges, which, elsewhere, have been violently submerged beneath the irresistible and often devastating influx of a revolutionary tide.

These things no longer admit of argument, but with the growth of experience a more matured opinion has come to recognize that Liberty (in a political sense) is not only a negative but a positive conception. Freedom cannot be predicated, in its true meaning, either of a man or of a society, merely because they are no longer under the compulsion of restraints which have the sanction of positive law. To be really free, they must be able to make the best use of faculty, opportunity, energy, life. It is in this fuller view of the true significance of Liberty that we find the governing impulse in the later developments of Liberalism in the direction of education, temperance, better dwellings, an improved social and industrial environment; everything, in short, that tends to national, communal, and personal efficiency.

7.6 HERBERT LOUIS SAMUEL (1870–1963)

From *Liberalism: an attempt to state the principles and proposals of contemporary liberalism in England*, Grant Richards: London, 1902, pp. 17, 19–21, 23–7, 29–31.

Samuel, like Asquith, was educated at Balliol College, Oxford. He was among the Radicals who founded the *Progressive Review* in 1896, and became leader of the Liberal Party for a brief period during the early 1930s. *Liberalism* detailed the kind of political programme favoured by progressive liberals at the turn of the century. Hence Samuel's concern to refute Social Darwinists and other advocates of *laissez-faire*.

Granted the need of further progress, to help the inferior types at the expense of the superior is not, it is said, the way to achieve it. Not by such means has man risen from the beasts and ascended step by step the path of civilization, but through a world process of evolution, which, cruel perhaps in its methods, yet most merciful in its results, unsparingly eliminates the weak in order that the race as a whole may advance. 'Their carnivorous enemies not only remove from the herbivorous herds the individuals past their prime,' says Herbert Spencer, the chief exponent of this doctrine, 'but also weed out the sickly, the malformed, and the least fleet or powerful ... The well-being of existing humanity, and the unfolding of it into ... ultimate perfection, are both secured by the same beneficent, though severe discipline, to which the animate creation at large is subject; a felicity-pursuing law which never swerves for the avoidance of partial and temporary suffering. The poverty of the incapable, the distresses that come upon the imprudent, the starvation of the idle, and those shoulderings aside of the weak by the strong, which leave so many in shallows and in miseries, are the decree of a large, far-seeing benevolence.'* To lighten the burdens of poverty would be blindly to counteract the great process by which Nature left to herself would ensure the progress of mankind.

There is 'little doubt that this argument, applied to politics, furnishes an intellectual basis for much of the opposition to social reform.

It implies three things. It implies that the poor are necessarily the unfit; they are the incapable, the imprudent, the idle, the weak. It implies that hard social conditions will crush out the unfit. And it implies that only through such hardship can unfitness be removed ...

Like those parents who 'first whipped their children till they cried and then went on whipping them to make them stop crying,' these political Darwinians would first degrade numbers of the people by bad social conditions, and then preserve the bad conditions on the ground that they are the proper punishment for degradation.

And to leave unregulated the 'natural struggle for existence' is not the only means – if it be a means – by which unfitness can be eradicated. Civilization supplies an alternative for the policy which civilization forbids. Among animals the incapable can only be removed by destruction. Among men the incapable can be removed by curing or preventing incapacity. Penalties no doubt there must be. The workhouse for the idle and drunken, the prison for the criminal, are recognized to be necessary. No one but a communist would suggest that competition should be destroyed, social grades abolished, and all men enjoy an equal comfort regardless of their character and their value to society. But the penalties may be accompanied by help. To extend education, to bring powerful moral influences to bear, to make surroundings better, to remove the causes that lower the physical type, to give a stimulus to self-improvement by making it easy for men to rise, these, experience proves, are the most powerful means for raising the standard of life and character. That such methods are possible makes the Spencerian policy as unnecessary as it is cruel.

When men say, therefore, that we need not vex our minds too much at the sight of the evils that fester at the base of society, for after all the fittest must survive and the unfit go to the wall, reformers answer that you are driving against the wall many who are not unfit, but only unfortunate; that the unfit are not by these means removed, they still survive as well as the fittest; that you are taking the surest means of producing fresh generations of weak and incapable; and that progress

* Herbert Spencer, *Social statics*, pp. 322–5 (edition of 1851).

can be made by methods more humane, by using the powerful agencies within our reach that tend not to kill but to cure, not to destroy but to raise, that would enlarge the opportunities for becoming fit rather than overwhelm with penalties those who fail. It is not the evolutionary argument which need stay the hand of reform.

The State, it is said, lastly, is incompetent to touch these grievances. State interference always fails. Leave men alone and they will find their own way out of their difficulties. Your policy of social reform will weaken self-reliance and cause more evils than it cures.

This was the view in the main of the older school of Liberals. Recent years have brought a striking change.

To many among the fathers of modern Liberalism, government action was anathema. They held, as we hold, that the first and final object of the State is to develop the capacities and raise the standard of living of its citizens; but they held also that the best means towards this object was the self-effacement of the State. Liberty is of supreme importance, and legal regulation is the opposite of liberty. Let governments abstain from war, let them practise economy, let them provide proper protection against violence and fraud, let them repeal restrictive laws, and then the free enterprise of commerce will bring prosperity to all classes, while their natural ambitions on the one hand, the pressure of need on the other, will stimulate the hindmost to seek and to attain their own well-being: such was their doctrine. The economics of Adam Smith and the philosophy of Bentham united to found a creed of non-interference which has inspired in large measure the politics of a century. Liberalism became a negative policy, opposing foreign enterprises and entanglements, attacking the laws regulating trade, opinion, combination, land tenure, which had been inherited from a previous generation; its positive proposals were constitutional, aiming at a democratic State structure, and they were constitutional only ...

We naturally seek the causes of the change, and in finding them we shall find also the answer to those who object to it.

In the first place, the State itself has become more competent. Its recent work inspires confidence instead of mistrust. The early Liberals lived under a constitution whose powers had been drawn by means of corruption into the hands of a limited class, and used in defiance of justice to serve the interest of that class. Industry lay at the mercy of a Parliament ignorant of the first laws of political economy, and of a Civil Service and magistracy inefficient for their duties. The State itself unrepresentative, selfish and unintelligent, had fallen into contempt and had become the aversion of thoughtful men.

Now democracy has been substituted for aristocracy as the root principle of the constitution. Court influence and the grosser kinds of corruption have disappeared. Efficient local authorities and an expert Civil Service have been created. The whole machinery of government has been vastly changed and improved. A new system has been called into being – mainly through the efforts of the early Liberals themselves – and the State of to-day is held worthy to be the agent of the community in many affairs for which the State of yesterday was clearly incompetent.

The machinery of government is different, and the difference is seen in its products. That generation had before it as an object lesson a whole series of unwise laws, some of them purposely hostile to the interests of the people, others well-meant but equally injurious. Seventy or eighty years ago, the nation was still oppressed by the Navigation and Corn Laws and the whole system of Protection; by the laws against workmen's combination; by the old Poor Law with its pauperizing doles from the rates in aid of wages; by the heavy penalties laid on religious Nonconformity and on the expression of certain forms of political opinion. Commerce was burdened with heavy taxation for wasteful purposes, and hampered by a multitude of well-intentioned but disastrous restrictions. The supreme need of the hour was a policy of repeal. The struggle to enforce it promised to be severe. The men were few who could look beyond its accomplishment. Now, however, the repeal has been for the most part won; these proofs of what follies a class legislature can commit have been forgotten, and in their place we have the experience of a great code of wise laws, the outcome of democracy, proving that State action can be beneficent in the highest degree. If one of the Philosophic Radicals, who had been a contemporary of Hume and Grote and James Mill, could reappear to observe our politics, he would be as deeply impressed by the contrast between the statute-book of to-day and that with which he had been familiar as by the contrast between the constitution of that day and of this. The laws against which he had fought he would not find; in their room he would see Factory and Workshop Acts, Mines Regulation Acts, Merchant Shipping Acts, Truck Acts, the great education and sanitary codes – a hundred effective safeguards against danger to health and mind, life and limb, a hundred successful defences against industrial oppression. He would observe the admirable work of the local authorities. And he would find that this system of regulation had not been accompanied by indirect effects for harm, but that with its growth, the productiveness, trade and wealth of the nation had grown also, and to a remarkable extent; that the self-reliance and capacity of the mass of citizens, in the general affairs of life, had visibly increased. He would not wonder that, with this change before them in the character of legislation, men had formed a new opinion of the capabilities of the State.

In the second place, while these experiments in legislation were modifying opinion by their success, the social conscience was becoming more fully awake to the urgent need of improvement, and the inability of the *laissez faire* policy to bring it about was gradually becoming more plain ...

The widespread eagerness for social progress which was so marked a feature of the nineteenth century, and particularly of the latter half of it, rebelled against the slow and doubtful methods of *laissez faire*. The restrictive laws, which the individualists declared to be the chief barriers to improvement, had been repealed. But the condition of the poorer classes seemed in many respects to be hardly at all the better. A stern experience was fast convincing the people that 'the free play of enlightened self-interest,' on which the Manchester School wholly relied to bring progress, was a force insufficient for the needs of the case; that the 'self-reliance and enterprise' of the working-classes were faced by barriers too formidable to be conquered without help. Inefficiency and distress, bad conditions of work, a low standard of living, were still obvious on every hand. The nation would not be induced by the distant promises of the theorists to allow further generations to be sacrificed in the attempt to cure these maladies by leaving them alone.

Another influence was also at work. So far as questions of labour regulation were concerned, there was arising a new doctrine of the true meaning and the best guarantees of liberty. It was urged that legal restrictions might after all be made to extend rather than to limit freedom, and would often stop more compulsion than they imposed.

Because the law does not interfere with his actions a man is not necessarily free. There is economic restriction as well as legal restriction. If the tramway conductor agrees to serve twelve hours a day for thirteen days out of fourteen, we cannot say that, because no law compels him, he does this of his own choice. The industrial system irresistibly bends to its will all who form part of it; the workman must submit to the customs of his trade and workshop under penalty of dismissal; liberty to 'go elsewhere' is an empty privilege when the conditions are everywhere the same; and the individual finds that he is hardly more free to decide, as an individual, the conditions of his own employment than a passenger is able to leave a train running at full speed or to alter its pace.

Even trade unionism, it was said, fails to establish a true freedom of contract in industry. Its area is limited. The lower grades of labour seem incapable of forming stable and effective organizations. Membership in a union may often entail sacrifices that average men are not prepared to make. Mutual distrust destroys many combinations. Moreover, where they are strongest, the unions are often too weak to cope with the concentrated force of capital, and in set battles find themselves out-matched again and again. And finally they are frequently unable to secure the redress of minor grievances – bad sanitation in the workshop, dangerous machinery, and so forth – because the strike is the sole weapon which their armoury contains, and only great questions justify the use of an instrument as destructive to the workers as it is injurious to the trades. In spite of their great achievements, trade unions have been found inadequate to safeguard the freedom of the working-classes against the overwhelming force of economic pressure.

Therefore, it was argued, the State must intervene in the interest of liberty itself. As the law prohibiting duelling provided the only means of escape from an oppressive social custom and enlarged freedom by means of restriction, so labour legislation is often the only means of rescue for those who are subject to oppresssive industrial customs.

Such was seen to be its results in practice. The Act, for example, which limited to ten in the day the number of hours to be worked by women in factories was in form rigidly restrictive. But in effect it was liberating; it freed the women from the compulsion to which they were unwillingly subject, and from which they could not otherwise escape, of working twelve hours or fourteen. Not State interference, but State assistance, is the true name for such legislation . . .

While Liberals hold that the State can do much, they are far from supposing, however, that the State can do all. Government may be more able to ensure progress than was formerly supposed, but its powers are not unlimited.

Of the social problems that face use, some are too vast for laws to be able to solve, some are too subtle and intangible, some depend too much on moral causes. Legislation dealing with industry can be so framed, indeed, that it will not injure liberty and self-reliance; but if it be pushed beyond a certain point it undoubtedly will injure liberty and self-reliance. Moderate reforms may help commerce and increase prosperity; extreme reforms would destroy commercial confidence, stop the investment of capital and destroy prosperity. There are boundaries beyond which State action cannot go . . .

Only in extreme cases, such as the case of the unhealthy trades, may the State use coercion except as a means of directly enlarging liberty. The law should not do for the individual that which he might do for himself without undue delay or an undue expenditure of energy; for otherwise self-reliance would be weakened. Distress must not be relieved in such a way as to encourage thriftlessness and burden the industrious for the benefit of the wilfully idle or vicious. If industry is touched it must be with a cautious hand, and so as not to lessen the volume of national trade. The laws must not discriminate between individuals. They must be such as can be practically enforced. They must not be of a kind to cause revolutionary disturbance. Examine the various measures which are now advocated by Liberals, and it will be found that it is these common-place rules that chiefly decide their character. These vaguely fix the practical limits of State interference.

7.7 LEONARD TRELAWNY HOBHOUSE (1864–1929)

From 'The ethical basis of collectivism', *International Journal of Ethics*, vol. 8, January 1898, pp, 144–5, 152–5.

Hobhouse, son an an Anglican clergyman in Cornwall, was elected to a Fellowship at Corpus Christi College, Oxford, in 1894. In 1897 he left Oxford to become a leader writer for the *Guardian* newspaper, and in 1907 went to London University as the first Professor of Sociology in Britain. He attempted, in numerous articles and books, to fashion a science of society that stood Herbert Spencer's evolutionary theory on its head. Hobhouse was to become a leading exponent of progressive liberalism. But in the 1890s, influenced by Fabian socialists, he believed that liberalism had become ossified by the kind of individualist perspective which Spencer endorsed. Although citing Green with approval in 'The ethical basis of collectivism', therefore, Hobhouse nevertheless identified socialism as the ideological expression of an evolving organic community.

It has been the mistake of many modern Evolutionists to eliminate love from consideration, and to leave hate, rivalry, competition as the sole spring of movement in organic life. The truth is rather that hate, and war, and the struggle for self belong essentially to the inorganic sphere. It is precisely so far as divergent claims are not adjusted, as individuals are not organized into association, as mutual dependence is not realized, that rivalry remains the principal means of subsistence and success. But from the lowest stages of organic life upward to civilized man there is an advance of integration which is constantly replacing the struggle of isolated atoms by the harmonious concurrence of interdependent parts. The lowest kind of compound animal is, I suppose, the cell colony, in which the association of parts is so loose that any component cell can emigrate when it chooses and live its own independent life. The loss of a limb matters little to the starfish and not as much as might be supposed to the limb. Even in the lower vertebrates, like the frog, the lower nerve centres retain a considerable degree of independence. But always as we mount the animal scale we come to a closer organization, in which, as between the myriads of living units which constitute the body, competition is reduced to very narrow limits, the health of the whole is essential to the life of each, and the cells secure their own maintenance by co-operating in the support of the entire body. In the relations of animals and of human beings to one another a somewhat similar development can be traced. Social life at any stage is a more or less organized structure as the case may be, and progress consists in the development of organization. At every stage competition is the law of unorganized, co-operation of organised, life.

I can perhaps best explain this by making clear what I do not mean. I do not mean that the best state is that in which liberty is subordinated to order and progress left to take care of itself. I do not mean that the higher the social state the more complete is the sacrifice of the individual to common ends. On the contrary, such a constitution of society, though it may be necessary in a state of siege, is just the negation of the organic idea as I would wish it to be conceived. A mechanical unity is as much opposed to organic co-operation as is anarchy itself, which is, indeed, its natural correlative. The true conception of an organic society is one in which the best life of each man is and is felt to be bound up with the best life of his fellow-citizens ...

Natural selection, as operating on individuals, has probably had little to do with the advance of civilization; but the success of one family, one tribe, one city, or one nation in the struggle with another has been a potent and constant influence. Now within certain groups rivalry is and always has been replaced in the main by co-operation. The family is by so much the most conspicuous example of what I mean that I will consider it alone. Imperfect, like other things human, it is nevertheless a striking and widespread example of the ethical spirit which I have tried to describe, – that is to say, it is a little society where the common welfare lies very close to the heart of each member, where self-sacrifice is cheerfully recognized as an honourable duty, and where the good of each is so much an object of real anxiety that more thought is taken for the weak than for the strong, and the deficiencies of any member are matter of honest regret rather than of secret satisfaction. If we pass outside the family to the relations of the average man to his immediate circle, we still find, if we are not prejudiced by cynicism, a good deal of the same spirit; at least, there is much genuine kindliness and good-will, and a tolerably high standard of honour in mutual dealings. Now moral progress, so far as there has been any, has consisted primarily in levelling up the standard of conduct towards mankind in general to something like the level commonly realized in the narrower relationships which we have mentioned. The process has been described by Green, in a well-known chapter, as the extension of the area of the common good. From the evolutionist point of view, it is the substitution of co-operation for competition, of the inclusive for the exclusive method of maintaining life and achieving progress ...

We take it, then, that the distinctly ethical consciousness, with its principle of mutual aid and its spirit of love and good-will, is a widespread force acting on nearly all men, but operative in a narrow sphere. And moral progress consists in directly or indirectly widening its influence. Not that it supersedes the reign of brute force, but rather that it qualifies it by some tincture of the human spirit. We continue to play a game against one another, but the rules of the game are gradually modified to the interests of humanity. Every such limitation of war and competition is a gain, and in the economic sphere such limitations as are imposed by Factory Acts, sanitary regulations, and even perhaps poor laws, have long been admitted as the most important applications of the Collectivist principle in modern legislation. They run parallel with the abolition of explosive bullets and the protection of the wounded and other regulations of war by the Geneva Convention. When all the world is one family, the millennium will have been reached.

7.8 LEONARD TRELAWNY HOBHOUSE

From *Liberalism*, Williams and Norgate: London, 1911, pp. 157–66, 189–92, 194, 202, 204–12.

Although 'The ethical basis of collectivism' was written from a socialist viewpoint, Hobhouse soon became disenchanted with a creed which he considered to be hidebound by notions of class conflict. He now sought to inject a socialist element into liberalism. *Liberalism*, which appeared in the Home University Library of Modern Knowledge Series, was perhaps intended by the publishers to be a detached account of the history and philosophy of the doctrine. It is, in fact, a plea for a liberal programme of radical reform to consolidate the evolution of society towards a more collectivist stage of human development.

On all sides we find the State making active provision for the poorer classes and not by any means for the destitute alone. We find it educating the children, providing medical inspection, authorizing the feeding of the necessitous at the expense of the ratepayers, helping them to obtain employment through free Labour Exchanges, seeking to organize the labour market with a view to the mitigation of unemployment, and providing old age pensions for all whose incomes fall below thirteen shillings a week, without exacting any contribution. Now, in all this, we may well ask, is the State going forward blindly on the paths of broad and generous but unconsidered charity? Is it and can it remain indifferent to the effect on individual initiative and personal or parental responsibility? Or may we suppose that the wiser heads are well aware of what they are about, have looked at the matter on all sides, and are guided by a reasonable conception of the duty of the State and the responsibilities of the individual? Are we, in fact – for this is really the question – seeking charity or justice?

We said above that it was the function of the State to secure the conditions upon which mind and character may develop themselves. Similarly we may say now that the function of the State is to secure conditions upon which its citizens are able to win by their own efforts all that is necessary to a full civic efficiency. It is not for the State to feed, house, or clothe them. It is for the State to take care that the economic conditions are such that the normal man who is not defective in mind or body or will can by useful labour feed, house, and clothe himself and his family. The 'right to work' and the right to a 'living wage' are just as valid as the rights of person or property. That is to say, they are integral conditions of a good social order. A society in which a single honest man of normal capacity is definitely unable to find the means of maintaining himself by useful work is to that extent suffering from malorganization. There is somewhere a defect in the social system, a hitch in the economic machine. Now, the individual workman cannot put the machine straight. He is the last person to have any say in the control of the market. It is not his fault if there is over-production in his industry, or if a new and cheaper process has been introduced which makes his particular skill, perhaps the product of years of application, a drug in the market. He does not direct or regulate industry. He is not responsible for its ups and downs, but he has to pay for them. That is why it is not charity but justice for which he is asking. Now, it may be infinitely difficult to meet his demand. To do so may involve a far-reaching economic reconstruction. The industrial questions involved may be so little understood that we may easily make matters worse in the attempt to make them better. All this shows the difficulty in finding means of meeting this particular claim of justice, but it does not shake its position as a claim of justice. A right is a right none the less though the means of securing it be imperfectly known; and the workman who is unemployed or underpaid through economic malorganization will remain a reproach not to the charity but to the justice of society as long as he is to be seen in the land.

If this view of the duty of the State and the right of the workman is coming to prevail, it is owing partly to an enhanced sense of common responsibility, and partly to the teaching of experience. In the earlier days of the Free Trade era, it was permissible to hope that self-help would be an adequate solvent, and that with cheap food and expanding commerce the average workman would be able by the exercise of prudence and thrift not only to maintain himself in good times, but to lay by for sickness, unemployment, and old age. The actual course of events has in large measure disappointed these hopes. It is true that the standard of living in England has progressively advanced throughout the nineteenth century. It is true, in particular, that, since the disastrous period that preceded the Repeal of the Corn Laws and the passing of the Ten Hours' Act, social improvement has been real and marked. Trade Unionism and co-operation have grown, wages upon the whole have increased, the cost of living has diminished, housing and sanitation have improved, the death rate has fallen from about twenty-two to less than fifteen per thousand. But with all this improvement the prospect of a complete and lifelong economic independence for the average workman upon the lines of individual competition, even when supplemented and guarded by the collective bargaining of the Trade Union, appears exceedingly remote. The increase of wages does not appear to be by any means proportionate to the general growth of wealth. The whole standard of living has risen; the very provision of education has brought with it new needs and has almost compelled a higher standard of life in order to satisfy them. As a whole, the working classes of England, though less thrifty than those of some Continental countries, cannot be accused of undue negligence with regard to the future. The accumulation of savings in Friendly Societies, Trade Unions, Co-operative Societies, and Savings Banks shows an increase which has more than kept pace with the rise in the level of wages; yet there appears no likelihood that the average manual worker will attain the goal of that full independence, covering all the risks of life for self and family, which can alone render the competitive system really adequate to the demands of a civilized conscience ... That system holds out no hope of an improvement which shall bring the means of such a healthy and independent existence as should be the birthright of every citizen of a free state within the grasp of the mass of the people of the United Kingdom. It is this belief slowly penetrating the public mind which has turned it to new thoughts of social regeneration. The sum and substance of the changes that I have mentioned may be expressed in the principle that the individual cannot stand alone, but that between him and the State there is a reciprocal obligation. He owes the State the duty of industriously working for himself and his family. He is not to exploit the labour of his young children, but to submit to the public requirements for their education, health, cleanliness and general well-being. On the other side society owes to him the means of maintaining a civilized standard of life, and this debt is not adequately discharged by leaving him to secure such wages as he can in the higgling of the market.

This view of social obligation lays increased stress on public but by no means ignores private responsibility. It is a simple principle of applied ethics that responsibility should be commensurate with power. Now, given the opportunity of adequately remunerated work, a man has the power to earn his living. It is his right and his duty to make the best use of his opportunity, and if he fails he may fairly suffer the penalty of being treated as a pauper or even, in an extreme case, as a criminal. But the opportunity itself he cannot command with the same freedom. It is only within narrow limits that it comes within the sphere of his control. The opportunities of work and the remuneration for work are determined by a complex mass of social forces which no individual, certainly no individual workman, can shape. They can be controlled, if at all, by the organized action of the community, and therefore, by a just apportionment of responsibility, it is for the community to deal with them.

But this, it will be said, is not Liberalism but Socialism. Pursuing the economic rights of the individual we have been led to contemplate a Socialistic organization of industry. But a word like Socialism has many meanings, and it is possible that there should be a Liberal Socialism, as well as a Socialism that is illiberal. Let us, then, without sticking at a word, seek to follow out the liberal view of the State in the sphere of economics. Let us try to determine in very general terms what is involved in realizing those primary conditions of industrial well-being which have been laid down, and how they consort with the rights of property and the claims of free industrial enterprise ...

The basis of property is social, and that in two senses. On the one hand, it is the organized force of society that maintains the rights of owners by protecting them against thieves and depredators. In spite of all criticism many people still seem to speak of the rights of property as though they were conferred by Nature or by Providence upon certain fortunate individuals, and as though these individuals had an unlimited right to command the State, as their servant, to secure them by the free use of the machinery of law in the undisturbed enjoyment of their possessions. They forget that without the organized force of society their rights are not worth a week's purchase. They do not ask themselves where they would be without the judge and the policeman and the settled order which society maintains. The prosperous business man who thinks that he has made his fortune entirely by self help does not pause to consider what single step he could have taken on the road to his success but for the ordered tranquillity which has made commercial development possible, the security by road, and rail, and sea, the masses of skilled labour, and the sum of intelligence which civilization has placed at his disposal, the very demand for the goods which he produces which the general progresses of the world has created, the inventions which he uses as a matter of course and which have been built up by the collective effort of generations of men of science and organizers of industry. If he dug to the foundations of his fortune he would recognize that, as it is society that maintains and guarantees his possessions, so also it is society which is an indispensable partner in its original creation.

This brings us to the second sense in which property is social. There is a social element in value and a social element in production. In modern industry there is very little that the individual can do by his unaided efforts. Labour is minutely divided; and in proportion as it is divided it is forced to be co-operative. Men produce goods to sell, and the rate of exchange, that is, price, is fixed by relations of demand and supply the rates of which are determined by complex social forces. In the methods of production every man makes use, to the best of his ability, of the whole available means of civilization, of the machinery which the brains of other men have devised, of the human apparatus which is the gift of acquired civilization. Society thus provides conditions or opportunities of which one man will make much better use than another, and the use to which they are put is the individual or personal element in production which is the basis of the personal claim to reward. To maintain and stimulate this personal effort is a necessity of good economic organization, and without asking here whether any particular conception of Socialism would or would not meet this need we may lay down with confidence that no form of Socialism which should ignore it could possibly enjoy enduring success. On the other hand, an individualism which ignores the social factor in wealth will deplete the national resources, deprive the community of its just share in the fruits of industry and so result in a one-sided and inequitable distribution of wealth. Economic justice is to render what is due not only to each individual but to each function, social or personal, that is engaged in the performance of useful service, and this due is measured by the amount necessary to stimulate and maintain the efficient exercise of that useful function. This equation between function and sustenance is the true meaning of economic equality ...

If we are right in considering that a great part of the wealth produced from year to year is of social origin, it would follow that, after the assignment of this remuneration, there would remain a surplus, and this would fall to the coffers of the community and be available for public purposes, for national defence, public works, education, charity, and the furtherance of civilized life ...

The true function of taxation is to secure to society the element in wealth that is of social origin, or, more broadly, all that does not owe its origin to the efforts of living individuals ...

(I)f we grant, in accordance with the idea with which we have been working all along, that it is demanded of all sane adult men and women that they should live as civilized beings, as industrious workers, as good parents, as orderly and efficient citizens, it is, on the other side, the function of the economic organization of society to secure them the material means of living such a life, and the immediate duty of society is to mark the points at which such means fail and to make good the deficiency. Thus the conditions of social efficiency mark the minimum of industrial remuneration, and if they are not secured without the deliberate action of the State they must be secured by means of the deliberate action of the State. If it is the business of good economic organization to secure the equation between function and maintenance, the first and greatest application of this principle is to the primary needs. These fix the minimum standard of remuneration beyond which we require detailed experiment to tell us at what rate increased value of service rendered necessitates corresponding increase of reward ...

The real question that may be raised by a critic is whether the considerable proportion of the working class whose earnings actually fall short, as we should contend, of the minimum, could in point of fact earn that minimum. Their actual value, he may urge, is measured by the wage which they do in fact command in the competitive market, and if their wage falls short of the standard society may make good the deficiency if it will and can, but must not shut its eyes to the fact that in doing so it is performing, not an act of economic justice, but of charity. To this the reply is that the price which naked labour without property can command in bargaining with employers who possess property is no measure at all of the addition which such labour can actually make to wealth. The bargain is unequal, and low remuneration is itself a cause of low efficiency which in turn tends to react unfavourably on remuneration. Conversely, a general improvement in the conditions of life reacts favourably on the productivity of labour. Real wages have risen considerably in the last half century, but the income–tax returns indicate that the wealth of the business and professional man has increased even more rapidly. Up to the efficiency minimum there is, then, every reason to think that a general increase of wages would positively increase the available surplus whether that surplus goes to individuals as profits or to the State as national revenue. The material improvement of working-class conditions will more than pay its way regarded purely as an economic investment on behalf of society ...

The central point of Liberal economics, then, is the equation of social service and reward. This is the principle that every function of social value requires such remuneration as serves to stimulate and maintain its effective performance; that every one who performs such a function has the right, in the strict ethical sense of that term, to such remuneration and to no more; that the residue of existing wealth should be at the disposal of the community for social purposes. Further, it is the right, in the same sense, of every person capable of performing some useful social function that he should have the opportunity of so doing, and it is his right that the remuneration that he receives for it should be his property, i.e. that it should stand at his free disposal enabling him to direct his personal concerns according to his own preferences. These are rights in the sense that they are conditions of the welfare of its members which a well-ordered State will seek by every means to fulfil. But it is not suggested that the way of such fulfilment is plain, or that it could be achieved at a stroke by a revolutionary change in the tenure of property or the system of industry. It is, indeed, implied that the State is vested with a certain overlordship over property in general and a supervisory power over industry in general, and this principle of economic sovereignty may be set side by side with that of economic justice as a no less fundamental conception of economic Liberalism. For here, as elsewhere, liberty implies control. But the manner in which the State is to exercise its controlling power is to be learnt by experience and even in large measure by cautious experiment ...

By keeping to the conception of harmony as our clue we constantly define the rights of the individual in terms of the common good, and think of the common good in terms of the welfare of all the individuals who constitute a society. Thus in economics we avoid the confusion of liberty with competition, and see no virtue in the right of a man to get the better of others. At the same time we are not led to minimize the share of personal initiative, talent, or energy in production, but are free to contend for their claim to adequate recognition.

7.9 JOHN ATKINSON HOBSON (1858–1940)

From *The crisis of liberalism: new issues of democracy,* P. S. King and Son: London, 1909, pp. xi–xii, 92–5, 162–8, 170–4.

Hobson, who was born in Derby, was one of the founders of the *Progressive Review.* He never secured a university post – probably because of his unorthodox economic views – and earned a living by means of journalism. The message of *The crisis of liberalism* was that the Liberal Party could not survive unless its members abandoned any lingering commitment to *laissez-faire* and endorsed instead a radical programme of economic and social reform.

No one who follows the new crystallisation of Liberal policy, as displayed in the anti-destitution and insurance proposals of the Government, to which substance is already given in Old Age Pensions, Wages Boards, and Labour Exchanges, in the public provision for the development of our natural resources, in the Small Holdings and Town Planning policy, and in the financial claims of the State to participation in 'unearned increments,' can fail to recognise a coherency of purpose, an organic plan of social progress, which implies a new consciousness of Liberal statecraft.

The full implications of this movement may not be clearly grasped, but Liberalism is now formally committed to a task which certainly involves a new conception of the State in its relation to the individual life and to private enterprise. That conception is not Socialism, in any accredited meaning of that term, though implying a considerable amount of increased public ownership and control of industry. From the standpoint which best presents its continuity with earlier Liberalism, it appears as a fuller appreciation and realisation of individual liberty contained in the provision of equal opportunities for self-development. But to this individual standpoint must be joined a just apprehension of the social, viz., the insistence that these claims or rights of self-development be adjusted to the sovereignty of social welfare.

How far the historical Liberal Party in the country is capable of the intellectual and moral re-orientation demanded for the successful undertaking of this new career, is the fundamental issue at stake ...

The negative conception of Liberalism, as a definite mission for the removal of certain political and economic shackles upon personal liberty, is not merely philosophically defective, but historically false. The Liberals of this country as a party never committed themselves either to the theory or the policy of this narrow *laissez faire* individualism; they never conceived liberty as something limited in quantity, or purely negative in character. But it is true that they tended to lay an excessive emphasis upon the aspect of liberty which consists in absence of restraint, as compared with the other aspect which consists in presence of opportunity; and it is this tendency, still lingering in the mind of the Liberal Party, that to-day checks its energy and blurs its vision. A more constructive and a more evolutionary idea of liberty is needed to give the requisite *élan de vie* to the movement; and every cause of liberation, individual, class, sex, and national, must be recharged with the fresh enthusiasm of this fuller faith.

Liberalism will probably retain its distinction from Socialism, in taking for its chief test of policy the freedom of the individual citizen rather than the strength of the State, though the antagonism of the two standpoints may tend to disappear in the light of progressive experience. But it will justify itself by two great enlargements of its liberative functions. In seeking to realise liberty for the individual citizen as 'equality of opportunity,' it will recognise that, as the area and nature of opportunities are continually shifting, so the old limited conception of the task of Liberalism must always advance. Each generation of Liberals will be required to translate a new set of needs and aspirations into facts. It is because we have fallen so far short of due performance of this task that our Liberalism shows signs of enfeeblement. We must fearlessly face as our first, though not our only question, What is a free Englishman to-day? If we answer this question faithfully, we shall recognise that it comprises many elements of real liberty and opportunity which have not been won for the people as a whole. Is a man free who has not equal opportunity with his fellows of such access to all material and moral means of personal development and work as shall contribute to his own welfare and that of his society? Such equal opportunity at least implies an equal access to the use of his native land as a workplace and a home, such mobility as will enable him to dispose of his personal energies to the best advantage, easy access to that factor of capital or credit which modern industry recognises as essential to economic independence, and to whatever new form of industrial power, electric or other, may be needed to co-operate with human efforts. A man is not really free for purposes of self-development in life and work who is not adequately provided in all these respects, and no small part of constructive Liberalism must be devoted to the attainment of these equal opportunities.

But all such distinctively economic liberties are evidently barren unless accompanied by a far more adequate realisation of spiritual and intellectual opportunity than is contained in our miserably meagre conception of popular education. For education in the large meaning of the term is the opportunity of opportunities, and the virtual denial to the majority of the people of any real share of the spiritual kingdom which is rightly theirs must remain for all true Liberals an incessant challenge to their elementary sense of justice, as well as the most obvious impediment both to the achievement and the utilisation of every other element of personal liberty ...

Finally, though Liberals must ever insist that each enlargement of the authority and functions of the State must justify itself as an enlargement of personal liberty, interfering with individuals only in order to set free new and larger opportunities, there need remain in Liberalism no relics of that positive hostility to public methods of co-operation which crippled the old Radicalism. When society is confronted, as it sometimes will be, by a breakdown of competition and a choice between private monopoly and public enterprise, no theoretic objections to the State can be permitted to militate against public safety. Just in proportion as education guides, enriches, and enlightens the will of the people, and gives spiritual substance and intellectual power to democracy, the presumption which still holds against the adequacy of public as compared with private co-operation will be weakened, and Liberalism will come more definitely to concern itself with the liberation and utilisation of the faculties and potencies of a nation and a municipality, as well as with those of individuals and voluntary groups of citizens ...

There are two fundamental causes of poverty, related in their nature, but here distinguished for convenience of argument:
1. Waste of human power.
2. Inequitable distribution of opportunities ...

Economists are fond of dwelling upon the delicate and elaborate mechanism of industry and commerce, working by intricate adjustment of parts to make and distribute commodities over the face of the earth. In point of fact the machine works very clumsily, with countless dislocations, innumerable wastes of power, and almost intolerable creaking.

Much of this waste is visible. Wherever we look we find during long periods of time great quantities of capital and labour lying idle –

unemployed, under-employed, or mis-employed. Everywhere the waste of duplication, new factories built where the existing plant is excessive, new shops arising to divide the custom of established shops, the endless multiplication of agents, branches, commercial clerks, and travellers, the constantly growing proportion of human energy drawn off from effective production to wasteful competition. I do not say all competition is wasteful: our present system requires competition. But where six competing grocers in a neighbourhood do the distributing work which could be done by two, the work of the other four is costly waste. This is the normal state over large areas of manufacture and of commerce.

But the invisible wastes, due to a failure to apply existing funds of knowledge to the actual work of production, are still greater. Anyone acquainted with the sciences of chemistry and mechanics, who knows what is being done in various parts of the world by an intelligent application of these sciences to the arts of manufacture, by improved machinery, utilisation of waste, economies of power, will perceive that lack of efficient education, ignorance, and apathy, absence of keen direction and bold experiment, weigh down enormously the productivity of our nation ...

Is it not pretty clear that if England could stop these visible and invisible wastes, could organise her actually available resources for the production of wealth, she could treble or quadruple her output of material wealth without any increase of human strain?

It is evident that poverty is not any longer necessary because the nation cannot make enough wealth to 'go all round.'

Indeed, it is probable that this analysis of waste appears to some readers irrelevant to the main issue. 'What has all this talk about insufficient production to do with poverty? There is plenty produced; poverty is obviously due to bad distribution of the wealth that is produced.' Now, no one is more fully alive than I am to the defects of distribution; but I nevertheless hold it to be of the first importance to realise the mistake of fastening the responsibility of poverty upon bad distribution as the sole sufficient cause ... The quantity of wealth available for distribution chiefly depends upon the stimulus afforded to the productive energies of man: this stimulus in its turn depends chiefly upon the opportunity open to every member of the community to do his best work.

The main cause of poverty is inequality of opportunity, because such inequality implies a waste of productive power upon the one hand, bad distribution or waste of consuming power upon the other.

'Equality of opportunity' as a cure for poverty is a familiar enough form of words, but to many it sounds vague and barren. I want to make its meaning plainer. But in explaining poverty as due to inequality of opportunity I must first brush aside one widely prevalent fallacy to which the personal vanity of lucky or successful men gives vogue.

Poverty, these are never tired of telling us, is due to personal inefficiency. Go down among the poor, what do you find? Most of them are ignorant, untrained, feeble, shiftless, thriftless, shirking hard steady work – often drunkards, wastrels, cadgers upon charity. There is, they tell us, no real lack of opportunity. Opportunities abound for energetic, honest, and industrious persons: the schoolmaster is abroad – emigration is cheap – willing, responsible workers can always get good work and a chance to 'rise' – and then actual instances are cited of capable and steady men who have risen from the lowest grades of labour into comfort and independence. In personal efficiency, education, moral elevation of individual character lies the slow but only cure for poverty!

Now, while it is quite true that no cure for poverty will be really effective unless it raises personality, it is most unprofitable to identify degraded personality as the cause of poverty.

For such analysis ignores the roots and the soil of personal efficiency. The factors of personal efficiency, industry, sobriety, energy of will, quickness of intelligence cannot be got out of ill-born and ill-nurtured children.

The slum-child who personifies the problem of poverty, born with low vitality, reared by ignorant and poor parents on bad food, breathing bad air, exposed to countless degrading influences, physical and moral, such a child growing to manhood or womanhood has commonly lost the power to grasp those opportunities which are said to lie within its reach. Except in rare instances of favoured stock, personal efficiency cannot grow in such a soil. Bad seed sown in poor earth will not grow into flourishing and fruitful plants, even if carefully watered, pruned, and protected as it grows. The material conditions of poorer working-class life are hostile to the attainment of personal efficiency: they not merely stunt physical and intellectual growth, but, still more detrimental, they maim the human will, sapping the roots of character.

This moral injury is the greatest sin committed by society against the poor.

But we must go further. Granting his attainment of a fair standard of personal efficiency, it is not true that an ordinary worker has a reasonable security against poverty.

Individual efficiency cannot produce wealth. The 'self-help' commonly imputed to individuals, the ability to earn 'an independent livelihood' when closely inspected, is seen to be illusory.

Economically, no man liveth to himself: we are all members of one another. Put in its simplest terms, this means that the worker requires the use of land, tools, and plant, the co-operation of other labourers, and the skilled organisation of industry to give any value to his individual efforts.

Poverty arises from the unfair terms upon which he gets these things. If he enjoyed *equal access* to all these requisites he could get his fair share of wealth, and his poverty, when it occurred, might be imputed reasonably to some personal defect or misfortune on his part.

Practically he has equal access to no one of them. Take, first, land, 'the mother of wealth.' Not merely is he born in a country the whole of which is marked out as 'private property,' but he cannot even buy or hire land in order to put his labour into it, except at a prohibitive price, and upon terms which give him no security that he will get the good of his labour. The English land system is the worst in the civilised world: excluding the ordinary labourer from advantageous work upon the land it is a perpetual breeder of poverty. If a poor man wants land, either to work it or for a dwelling, he must always bargain for its use with an owner who is economically stronger and can rackrent him. Decade after decade the burden of housing falls heavier upon the working-class population of our towns, and is a main factor in city poverty. In our villages the housing question is not less serious, for there the land-monopoly gives to one man, or a few, the power to determine whether men and women shall live at all in the place where they are born and bred, or shall be driven out to sojourn among strangers.

The use of some capital is another essential to economic independence. No man can work for himself either on the land, in a handicraft, or in any other business, unless he can get on easy terms some small capital or credit when he needs it. Everywhere for lack of cheap credit the poor are entangled in debt to money-lenders, shopkeepers, or other richer persons, who can take advantage of their extremity of need to drive hard bargains. Again, the ordinary labourer, untrained in business life, cannot set up for himself in any business, or co-operate with his fellows to produce goods which he can sell at a profit in the general market. He cannot buy the services of an organiser or business man so as to utilise his labour-power for his own gain, but is practically obliged to sell his labour-power piecemeal at a 'sacrifice' to a business man to be used for profit to the latter.

The labourer, then, cannot get high personal efficiency, and must sell his low efficiency cheap. Poverty, of course, is primarily due to the terms of sale of the labour-power, which is the only means of living for the great mass of the people in countries where there is no 'free' land. The worker who sells his labour-power for a living ordinarily bargains for its sale at a disadvantage: he must sell it or he and his family starve; the employer who buys it will not starve, but only lose some 'profit' if he fails to buy it. This difference between starvation and loss of profit means a perpetual handicap to the worker in bargaining for wages. He is a weak seller of a perishable commodity, which he must sell continuously in a fluctuating market.

As he sells his labour-power at a disadvantage so he buys the goods he needs at a disadvantage. Free Trade, with its cheap load and its more or less cheap meat, mitigates and hides this truth. But it is none the less true that the general fall of prices which has taken place since 1870 has benefited the poorer grades of the working classes less than any other grade of the community, the high prices of shelter, fuel, dairy, and vegetable produce in the towns taking a larger share of their small incomes than in the case of the well-to-do classes. The very poor notoriously pay the highest prices for the worst qualities of goods, compelled to buy in small quantities, and often 'tied' to certain credit shops.

The great mass of the low-skilled workers and their families still lie on or below the margin of poverty, subject to conditions of the labour market which preclude them from any reasonable hope of comfort, security, or independence. The 'Iron Law of Wages,' slightly abated in its rigour, still holds them down ...

The idea that the poor can help themselves, either as individuals or collectively, without mastering and using the public organisation called Government, can only be maintained by those who refuse to analyse the conditions of poverty. For the evil conditions which preclude the poor from gaining personal efficiency, which oppress them when they seek to sell their labour-power, and when they seek access to land or capital or skill or knowledge, are fastened upon them by *laws* relating to the ownership and use of the material and intellectual resources of the nation ...

It is true, that State action in changes of law will not in itself cure poverty, but it can enable poverty to cure itself by securing liberty for all to use their powers to the best advantage for their own gain and for the common good.

There is something pathetic in reading the history of the great Chartist movement to recall the enthusiastic confidence of the workers of that day in the immediate efficacy of mere political machinery. Give us, they said, shorter Parliaments, ballot, etc., and the will of the people will find free expression in legislation for the common good. Most of the six points of the Charter, not all, have been won, but now we need a new People's Charter with six new points:–

(a) The value and the use of land for the People. Public ownership or full control of the city by the citizens, the village by the villagers, and powers for local government to acquire agricultural land at reasonable prices and to let it to small holders with fair conditions of tenancy.

(b) Public ownership of the effective highways of the country, railways, tramways, canals, and suppression of the abuses of 'shipping conferences' controlling transport on our waterways.

(c) Public organisation of credit and insurance, essentials of modern business. The largest of our national wastes is the waste of public credit, and the practical abandonment of the monetary business, which rightly forms a State function, to private profitable enterprise.

(d) Full freedom of education: equal access for all to the social fund of culture and of knowledge. The right of the community to secure for every citizen the fullest and best use of his individual gifts and powers should be enforced even against the alleged rights of parents to keep their children in ignorance or to drive them prematurely into wage-earning.

(e) Equal access to public law. The entire cost of justice to be defrayed out of the public purse, and the machinery of the law courts free to all citizens. At present, whenever an issue arises between a rich and a poor man, the former enjoys a great advantage in utilising the machinery of the law, the result being that 'justice' is bought by the longer purse.

(f) The assertion of the popular power to tax or control any new form of monopoly or inequality which may spring up in the changing conditions of modern communities. This point covers those changes in the machinery of government required to depose the existing 'class government' and to substitute an effective democracy. It may be called 'socialisation of government' to correspond with the 'socialisation of law' which was just named.

No improvements of individual efficiency by education, temperance, technical instruction (important as these things are), no private co-operation under the existing political-economic system, can extirpate or greatly reduce poverty – except so far as it helps in working for political and legal reforms which shall secure the essential conditions for evoking individual efficiency and for supporting it by social opportunity.

This equal opportunity of self-development and social aid, so as to live a good and happy life, is practicable Socialism. It differs from what may be called full or theoretic Socialism in the following respects:–

It aims primarily not to abolish the competitive system, to socialise all instruments of production, distribution, and exchange, and to convert all workers into public employees – but rather to supply all workers at cost price with all the economic conditions requisite to the education and employment of their personal powers for their personal advantage and enjoyment ...

Once realised, this condition brings not only a better distribution of existing wealth, but a prodigious increase of national productivity. Closed opportunities mean torpid minds, slack effort, routine activity: open opportunities stimulate energy, rouse initiative, stir progress. We boast of the pace of modern industrial progress, but this pace is slow compared with what it would become if every man had a full stimulus applied to evoke his best thought and liberate the spark of talent which lies hid in every soul. Here is the great waste that would be saved by securing for every man a fair chance in life. Equality of opportunity would not merely stir individual energy, it would fertilise with fresh accessions of science and of skill large barren or backward tracts of industry.

7.10 JOHN ATKINSON HOBSON

From *Imperialism: a study* (1902). 3rd edn, George Allen & Unwin: London, 1938, pp. 85–7.

Hobson first formulated his theory of underconsumption or oversaving in *The physiology of industry,* published in 1889, which he wrote in collaboration with A. F. Mummery. He extended the theory into an explanation of imperialism in response to the Boer War in South Africa, which Hobson experienced first-hand as a special correspondent for the *Guardian.*

The fallacy of the supposed inevitability of imperial expansion as a necessary outlet for progressive industry is now manifest. It is not industrial progress that demands the opening up of new markets and areas of investment, but mal-distribution of consuming power which prevents the absorption of commodities and capital within the country. The over-saving which is the economic root of Imperialism is found by analysis to consist of rents, monopoly profits, and other unearned or excessive elements of income, which, not being earned by labour of head or hand, have no legitimate *raison d'être.* Having no natural relation to effort of production, they impel their recipients to no corresponding satisfaction of consumption: they form a surplus wealth, which, having no proper place in the normal economy of production and consumption, tends to accumulate as excessive savings. Let any turn in the tide of politico-economic forces divert from these owners their excess of income and make it flow, either to the workers in higher wages, or to the community in taxes, so that it will be spent instead of being saved, serving in either of these ways to swell the tide of consumption – there will be no need to fight for foreign markets or foreign areas of investment.

Many have carried their analysis so far as to realise the absurdity of spending half our financial resources in fighting to secure foreign markets at times when hungry mouths, ill-clad backs, ill-furnished houses indicate countless unsatisfied material wants among our own population. If we may take the careful statistics of Mr Rowntree* for our guide, we shall be aware that more than one-fourth of the population of our towns is living at a standard which is below bare physical efficiency. If, by some economic readjustment, the products which flow from the surplus saving of the rich to swell the overflow streams could be diverted so as to raise the incomes and the standard of consumption of this inefficient fourth, there would be no need for pushful Imperialism, and the cause of social reform would have won its greatest victory.

It is not inherent in the nature of things that we should spend our natural resources on militarism, war, and risky, unscrupulous diplomacy, in order to find markets for our goods and surplus capital. An intelligent progressive community, based upon substantial equality of economic and educational opportunities, will raise its standard of consumption to correspond with every increased power of production, and can find full employment for an unlimited quantity of capital and labour within the limits of the country which it occupies. Where the distribution of incomes is such as to enable all classes of the nation to convert their felt wants into an effective demand for commodites, there can be no over-production, no under-employment of capital and labour, and no necessity to fight for foreign markets.

* *Poverty: a study of town life.*

8.1 JOHN MAYNARD KEYNES (1883–1946)

From *The end of laissez–faire,* Hogarth Press: London, 1926, pp. 39–42,
46–9.
Keynes, the most influential economic theorist of this century, was the
son of a Cambridge University lecturer in logic and political economy.
Keynes himself was a Cambridge economist until becoming a wartime
civil servant in the Treasury, which he represented at the Paris Peace
Conference. This experience prompted him to condemn the harsh
reparations policy of the Treaty of Versailles in *The economic
consequences of peace,* published in 1919. Keynes now began the task of
laying the theoretical foundations for a fundamental reform of
capitalism. *The end of laissez-faire,* an early example of his endeavours
to transform economic doctrine, combines a brilliant polemic against
free-market ideologues with practical proposals for securing national
prosperity.

Let us clear from the ground the meta-physical or general principles
upon which, from time to time, *laissez-faire* has been founded. It is *not*
true that individuals possess a prescriptive 'natural liberty' in their
economic activities. There is *no* 'compact' conferring perpetual rights
on those who Have or on those who Acquire. The world is *not* so
governed from above that private and social interest always coincide.
It is *not* so managed here below that in practice they coincide. It is *not*
a correct deduction from the Principles of Economics that enlightened
self-interest always operates in the public interest. Nor is it true that
self-interest generally *is* enlightened; more often individuals acting
separately to promote their own ends are too ignorant or too weak to
attain even these. Experience does *not* show that individuals, when
they make up a social unit, are always less clear-sighted than when they
act separately.

We cannot therefore settle on abstract grounds, but must handle on its merits in detail what Burke termed 'one of the finest problems in legislation, namely, to determine what the State ought to take upon itself to direct by the public wisdom, and what it ought to leave, with as little interference as possible, to individual exertion.'* We have to discriminate between what Bentham, in his forgotten but useful nomenclature, used to term *Agenda* and *Non-Agenda,* and to do this without Bentham's prior presumption that interference is, at the same time, 'generally needless' and 'generally pernicious.'† Perhaps the chief task of Economists at this hour is to distinguish afresh the *Agenda* of Government from the *Non-Agenda;* and the companion task of Politics is to devise forms of Government within a Democracy which shall be capable of accomplishing the *Agenda.* I will illustrate what I have in mind by two examples.

(1) I believe that in many cases the ideal size for the unit of control and organisation lies somewhere between the individual and the modern State. I suggest, therefore, that progress lies in the growth and the recognition of semi-autonomous bodies within the State – bodies whose criterion of action within their own field is solely the public good as they understand it, and from whose deliberations motives of private advantage are excluded, though some place it may still be necessary to leave, until the ambit of men's altruism grows wider, to the separate advantage of particular groups, classes, or faculties – bodies which in the ordinary course of affairs are mainly autonomous within their prescribed limitations, but are subject in the last resort to the sovereignty of the democracy expressed through Parliament.

I propose a return, it may be said, towards mediaeval conceptions of separate autonomies. But, in England at any rate, corporations are a mode of government which has never ceased to be important and is sympathetic to our institutions. It is easy to give examples, from what already exists, of separate autonomies which have attained or are approaching the mode I designate – the Universities, the Bank of England, the Port of London Authority, even perhaps the Railway Companies ...

(2) I come next to a criterion of *Agenda* which is particularly relevant to what it is urgent and desirable to do in the near future. We

---

*Quoted by M'Culloch in his *Principles of political economy.*
†Bentham's *Manual of political economy,* published posthumously, in Bowring's edition (1843).

must aim at separating those services which are *technically social* from those which are *technically individual*. The most important *Agenda* of the State relate not to those activities which private individuals are already fulfilling, but to those functions which fall outside the sphere of the individual, to those decisions which are made by *no one* if the State does not make them. The important thing for Government is not to do things which individuals are doing already, and to do them a little better or a little worse; but to do those things which at present are not done at all.

It is not within the scope of my purpose on this occasion to develop practical policies. I limit myself, therefore, to naming some instances of what I mean from amongst those problems about which I happen to have thought most.

Many of the greatest economic evils of our time are the fruits of risk, uncertainty, and ignorance. It is because particular individuals, fortunate in situation or in abilities, are able to take advantage of uncertainty and ignorance, and also because for the same reason big business is often a lottery, that great inequalities of wealth come about; and these same factors are also the cause of the Unemployment of Labour, or the disappointment of reasonable business expectations, and of the impairment of efficiency and production. Yet the cure lies outside the operations of individuals; it may even be to the interest of individuals to aggravate the disease. I believe that the cure for these things is partly to be sought in the deliberate control of the currency and of credit by a central institution, and partly in the collection and dissemination on a great scale of data relating to the business situation, including the full publicity, by law if necessary, of all business facts which it is useful to know. These measures would involve Society in exercising directive intelligence through some appropriate organ of action over many of the inner intricacies of private business, yet it would leave private initiative and enterprise unhindered. Even if these measures prove insufficient, nevertheless they will furnish us with better knowledge than we have now for taking the next step.

My second example relates to Savings and Investment. I believe that some co-ordinated act of intelligent judgment is required as to the scale on which it is desirable that the community as a whole should save, the scale on which these savings should go abroad in the form of foreign investments, and whether the present organisation of the investment market distributes savings along the most nationally productive channels. I do not think that these matters should be left entirely to the chances of private judgment and private profits, as they are at present.

8.2 JOHN MAYNARD KEYNES

From 'Liberalism and industry' (1927), in H. L. Nathan and H.
Heathcote Williams (eds), *Liberal points of view*, Ernest Benn: London,
1927, pp. 205–09, 211–12.

The Liberal Party, according to Keynes, embodied the intellectual talent
and 'middle way' moderation needed to transform capitalism in an
orderly manner. He participated in Liberal Party affairs throughout the
1920s, and 'Liberalism and industry' was initially given as an address at
the National Liberal Club to the London Liberal Candidates
Association.

I am sure that the recent malaise in the Liberal Party has been due to
something much more important than personalities, and, rightly
considered, much more encouraging. It is due to the fact that the
subject-matter of Liberalism is changing. The destruction of private
monopoly, the fight against Landlordism and Protection, the
development of personal and religious liberty, the evolution of
democratic government at home and throughout the Empire – on all
those issues the battle has been largely won.

To-day and in the years to come the battle is going to be fought on
new issues. The problems of to-day are different, and, in the main,
these new problems are industrial or, if you like, economic. Now, this
change, which will be a disturbing thing for all the historic parties, is
partly a result of the victory of democracy, and of the new self-
consciousness and the new organisation of the wage-earning classes.
But it is not entirely psychological in its origins. It is due also, as I
believe, to the arrival of a new industrial revolution, a new economic
transition which we have to meet with new expedients and new
solutions.

The main political problem of to-day is the safe guidance of the
country through this transition and towards the establishment of an
economically efficient and economically just society in the changed
conditions. There is a dual aim before the statesman – a society which
is just and a society which is efficient; and more and more in terms of
our old solutions we are feeling ourselves confronted with a dilemma, a
seeming contradiction very often between the policy which appears to
be just and the policy which seems to be in the interests of efficiency.

On these issues between the Tories and Labour there is a sharp
cleavage on both points. They disagree as to what is just; they disagree
as to what is efficient; and so they can engage with conviction and
enthusiasm on the business of cutting one another's throats.

But Liberals are in a more difficult position. They are inclined to sympathise with Labour about what is just, but to suspect that in the ignorant blind striving after justice Labour may destroy what is at least as important and is a necessary condition of any social progress at all – namely, efficiency.

It is useless to suppose that we can pursue ideal justice regardless of ways and means in the economic world. No one can look at the evolution of society and not admit to himself that some measure of social injustice has often been the necessary condition of social progress. If society had always been strictly just, I am not at all sure that we might not still be monkeys in a forest.

The task of the statesman is to see to it that the best possible compromise is achieved between our ultimate aims and our practical means of reaching them. The great danger of to-day, as I see it, is lest the immense destructive force of organised Labour should, in its blindness and ignorance, destroy the opportunity for the contrivings of science and constructive industry before these have had time to guide the transition along sound lines. The Labour Party is organising an immense force to ends which may be right, but by dubious paths which may lead not to construction but to a destructive loss of the opportunities which would otherwise exist.

It is the task of Liberals, as I conceive it, to guide the aspirations of the masses for social justice along channels which will not be inconsistent with social efficiency; and a party which pursues that task with sincerity and devotion will exercise an influence over the future of this country altogether disproportionate to its numerical strength or to its Parliamentary position.

The very extreme Conservatives, led by Sir Ernest Benn and his friends – with whom, I am afraid, some so-called Liberal leaders may partly sympathise – Sir Ernest Benn and his friends would like to undo all the hardly-won little which we have in the way of conscious and deliberate control of economic forces for the public good, and replace it by a return to chaos. I cannot believe that that can be the policy of the Liberal Party if its aspirations are as I have described them.

The more moderate Conservatives, under Mr. Baldwin, try to temper the same logic with mercy and expediency; but the result is that they have no plan, which leaves them at the mercy of the noisy anti–Trade Union, anti–Communist, anti–everything man who has always been the muscle and brawn of their Party.

The Labour Party has got tied up with all sorts of encumbering and old–fashioned luggage. They respond to anti–Communist rubbish with anti–capitalist rubbish. I do not believe that class war or nationalisation is attractive or stimulating in the least degree to modern minds. I was talking to a prominent Labour politician not long ago somewhat on these lines, and I ventured to say that perhaps the old gag about the Conservatives being the stupid party ought now to be applied to Labour. 'No,' he said, 'not the stupid party – the silly party.'

The consequence of all this is that, whether in or out of Office, the business of orderly evolution seems likely to remain in Liberal hands. If we cannot carry out our policies ourselves, we can at least develop them and hope with some confidence that others will steal them.

What are the great changes of which I have been speaking, which have made this alteration of programme so essential? They are partly psychological and they are partly material. The industrial wage-earning classes are now, as a delayed result of the franchise reforms of the last two generations, on the road to political power, which means that they are able to force to the forefront of practical politics the industrial problems which especially concern them individually, just as each previous class which has attained political power in this country has made its own problems the dominant problems of the age.

It is not only that. It is also that the optimistic Zeitgeist of the nineteenth century has given way to a pessimistic Zeitgeist. The spirit of the age is not optimistic as it used to be. We are disappointed with the results of our existing methods of carrying on. We used to think that private ambition and compound interest would between them carry us to paradise. Our material conditions seemed to be steadily on the up-grade. Now we are fully content if we can prevent them from deteriorating; which means that the working classes no longer have sufficient hopes in the general trend of things to divert their attention from other grievances. We no longer have sufficient confidence in the future to be satisfied with the present.

But it is not only psychological changes which are responsible; there are also great changes in the world of things associated with these changes in the world of feelings and of desires. The old picture, the old schematism as to the actual nature of the economic world we live in is hopelessly out of date; the picture of numerous small capitalists, each staking his fortune on his judgment, and the most judicious surviving, bears increasingly little relation to the facts . . .

What is the remedy for the serious evils which we are suffering consequent upon our failure so far to adapt ourselves to the economic transition in which we are living? Certainly not backward to chaos. Certainly onwards towards order, towards society taking intelligent control of its own affairs. But equally it is not to class war, it is not to spoliation, it is not to the highly centralised system of State Socialism.

We need the maximum degree of decentralisation which is compatible with large units and regulated competition.

8.3 JOHN MAYNARD KEYNES

From *The general theory of employment, interest, and money*, Macmillan: London, 1936, pp. 377–83.

The general theory, the classic text of Keynesian economics, was a sustained critique of the traditional doctrine that full employment resulted from the operation of free-market forces. As in his earlier writings, however, Keynes blended economic theory with an analysis of the political dangers of unreformed capitalism.

In some other respects the foregoing theory is moderately conservative in its implications. For whilst it indicates the vital importance of establishing certain central controls in matters which are now left in the main to individual initiative, there are wide fields of activity which are unaffected. The State will have to exercise a guiding influence on the propensity to consume partly through its scheme of taxation, partly by fixing the rate of interest, and partly, perhaps, in other ways. Furthermore, it seems unlikely that the influence of banking policy on the rate of interest will be sufficient by itself to determine an optimum rate of investment. I conceive, therefore, that a somewhat comprehensive socialisation of investment will prove the only means of securing an approximation to full employment; though this need not exclude all manner of compromises and of devices by which public authority will co-operate with private initiative. But beyond this no obvious case is made out for a system of State Socialism which would embrace most of the economic life of the community. It is not the ownership of the instruments of production which it is important for the State to assume. If the State is able to determine the aggregate amount of resources devoted to augmenting the instruments and the basic rate of reward to those who own them, it will have accomplished all that is necessary. Moreover, the necessary measures of socialisation can be introduced gradually and without a break in the general traditions of society.

Our criticism of the accepted classical theory of economics has consisted not so much in finding logical flaws in its analysis as in pointing out that its tacit assumptions are seldom or never satisfied, with the result that it cannot solve the economic problems of the actual world. But if our central controls succeed in establishing an aggregate volume of output corresponding to full employment as nearly as is practicable, the classical theory comes into its own again from this point onwards. If we suppose the volume of output to be given, i.e. to be determined by forces outside the classical scheme of thought, then there is no objection to be raised against the classical analysis of the manner in which private self-interest will determine what in particular is produced, in what proportions the factors of production will be combined to produce it, and how the value of the final product will be distributed between them ...

The central controls necessary to ensure full employment will, of course, involve a large extension of the traditional functions of government. Furthermore, the modern classical theory has itself called attention to various conditions in which the free play of economic forces may need to be curbed or guided. But there will still remain a wide field for the exercise of private initiative and responsibility. Within this field the traditional advantages of individualism will still hold good.

Let us stop for a moment to remind ourselves what these advantages are. They are partly advantages of efficiency – the advantages of decentralisation and of the play of self-interest. The advantage to efficiency of the decentralisation of decisions and of individual responsibility is even greater, perhaps, than the nineteenth century supposed; and the reaction against the appeal to self-interest may have gone too far. But, above all, individualism, if it can be purged of its defects and its abuses, is the best safeguard of personal liberty in the sense that, compared with any other system, it greatly widens the field for the exercise of personal choice. It is also the best safeguard of the variety of life, which emerges precisely from this extended field of personal choice, and the loss of which is the greatest of all the losses of the homogeneous or totalitarian state. For this variety preserves the traditions which embody the most secure and successful choices of former generations; it colours the present with the diversification of its fancy; and, being the handmaid of experiment as well as of tradition and of fancy, it is the most powerful instrument to better the future.

Whilst, therefore, the enlargement of the functions of government, involved in the task of adjusting to one another the propensity to consume and the inducement to invest, would seem to a nineteenth-century publicist or to a contemporary American financier to be a terrific encroachment on individualism, I defend it, on the contrary, both as the only practicable means of avoiding the destruction of existing economic forms in their entirety and as the condition of the successful functioning of individual initiative ...

The authoritarian state systems of to-day seem to solve the problem of unemployment at the expense of efficiency and of freedom. It is certain that the world will not much longer tolerate the unemployment which, apart from brief intervals of excitement, is associated – and, in my opinion, inevitably associated – with present-day capitalistic individualism. But it may be possible by a right analysis of the problem to cure the disease whilst preserving efficiency and freedom.

I have mentioned in passing that the new system might be more favourable to peace than the old has been. It is worth while to repeat and emphasise that aspect.

War has several causes. Dictators and others such, to whom war offers, in expectation at least, a pleasurable excitement, find it easy to work on the natural bellicosity of their peoples. But, over and above this, facilitating their task of fanning the popular flame, are the economic causes of war, namely, the pressure of population and the competitive struggle for markets. It is the second factor, which probably played a predominant part in the nineteenth century, and might again, that is germane to this discussion.

I have pointed out in the preceding chapter that, under the system of domestic *laissez-faire* and an international gold standard such as was orthodox in the latter half of the nineteenth century, there was no means open to a government whereby to mitigate economic distress at home except through the competitive struggle for markets. For all measures helpful to a state of chronic or intermittent under-employment were ruled out, except measures to improve the balance of trade on income account.

Thus, whilst economists were accustomed to applaud the prevailing international system as furnishing the fruits of the international division of labour and harmonising at the same time the interests of different nations, there lay concealed a less benign influence; and those statesmen were moved by common sense and a correct apprehension of the true course of events, who believed that if a rich, old country were to neglect the struggle for markets its prosperity would drop and fail. But if nations can learn to provide themselves with full employment by their domestic policy (and, we must add, if they can also attain equilibrium in the trend of their population), there need be no important economic forces calculated to set the interest of one country against that of its neighbours. There would still be room for the international division of labour and for international lending in appropriate conditions. But there would be no longer be a pressing motive why one country need force its wares on another or repulse the offerings of its neighbour, not because this was necessary to enable it to pay for what it wished to purchase, but with the express object of upsetting the equilibrium of payments so as to develop a balance of trade in its own favour. International trade would cease to be what it is, namely, a desperate expedient to maintain employment at home by forcing sales on foreign markets and restricting purchases, which, if successful, will merely shift the problem of unemployment to the neighbour which is worsted in the struggle, but a willing and unimpeded exchange of goods and services in conditions of mutual advantage.

8.4 THE YELLOW BOOK

From *Britain's industrial future being the report of the liberal industrial inquiry,* Ernest Benn: London, 1928, pp. xviii–xx, 63.

The first annual Liberal Summer School met in 1921 with the intention of formulating an alternative industrial policy to that of the Labour Party. For one week each year throughout the 1920s the Schools provided a forum in which politicians, businessmen and academics could exchange ideas about the social reconstruction of Britain. The Schools attracted 'the educated bourgeoisie', as Keynes put it in an address to the School of 1925, who advocated social reform while rejecting 'the slogans of class war'. The Yellow Book, which emerged from a Summer School inquiry established in 1926, incorporated the aims of the liberal intelligentsia in an extensive analysis of Britain's social and industrial problems. Some of its proposals to reform capitalism were implemented by post-war Labour and Conservative Governments.

When it is asked how far it is the business of the State to attempt to set things right, we hold that the answer cannot be given in a phrase or a sentence. We are not with those who say that, whatever may be our present difficulties, the intervention of the State would only increase them. Nor do we share the views of the dwindling band who think that the right course is to hand over to the State the maximum of productive activity and industrial control. We have no love for State intervention in itself. On the contrary, we attach the greatest importance to the initiative of individuals and to their opportunity to back their opinion against that of the majority and to prove themselves right. But the methods of production have been subject of late to great changes. The theory that private competition, unregulated and unaided, will work out, with certainty, to the greater advantage of the community is found by experience to be far from the truth. The scope of useful intervention by the whole Society, whether by constructive action of its own or by regulating or assisting private action, is seen to be much larger than was formerly supposed ...

Liberalism stands for Liberty; but it is an error to think that a policy of liberty must be always negative, that the State can help liberty only by abstaining from action, that invariably men are freest when their Government does least. Withdraw the police from the streets of the towns, and you will, it is true, cease to interfere with the liberty of the criminal, but the law-abiding citizens will soon find that they are less free than before. Abolish compulsory education: the child, and perhaps his parent, will no longer be forced to do what they may perhaps not wish to do; but the adults of the next generation will be denied the power to read, to think, to succeed, which is essential to a real freedom. Repeal, to take one more example, the Shops Acts: short-sighted shopkeepers will be allowed to trade for longer hours, but other shopkeepers and the whole class of shop-assistants will be robbed of their proper share of the leisure without which life is a servitude. Often more law may mean more liberty.

But not of course always. The principle may be pushed too far. There is such a thing as a meddlesome, unjustified officious interference, against which we have to be on our guard. The fact remains that there is much positive work that the State can do which is not merely consistent with liberty, but essential to it. The idea of the extreme individualist, that in proportion as State action expands freedom contracts, is false.

Equally false is the idea that because State action on the widest scale is favoured by Socialists, those who are not Socialists must oppose any and every extension of State action. It will lead, it is said, to Socialism in the long run. It is a partial surrender to false and flimsy theories.

True that the Socialist is inclined to welcome extensions of State activity for their own sakes; he regards them all as stages on the road to an ideal which he cherishes. But the fact that we do not share his ideal, and do not favour particular measures merely because they might be steps towards it, is no reason why, out of prejudice, we should close our eyes to whatever merits those measures may possess in themselves. If no one had ever generalised about Socialism, or used the word, or made it the rallying cry for a party, these measures might have been universally welcomed. It would be folly to reject what is right because some would have it lead to what is wrong ...

The choice between 'Individualism' and 'Socialism' in the form in which it occupies the controversialists of the Conservative and Labour Parties is, in the main, a distorted, and indeed an obsolete, issue, based on a picture of the financial and industrial world of England as it was fifty or more years ago. As we shall attempt to show quantitatively, the evolution from these conditions is already far advanced. Change has been going on at a great rate. It is not a choice between nailing to the mast the Jolly Roger of piratical, cut-throat individualism, each man for himself and the devil take the rest, or, on the other hand, the Servile Society of a comprehensive State Socialism. Nor is the alternative between standing still and violent change. The world moves on anyhow at a smart pace; it is only the ideas of Conservatives and Socialists which remain where they were. The task is one of guiding existing tendencies into a right direction and getting the best of all worlds, harmonising individual liberty with the general good, and personal initiative with a common plan – of constructing a society where action is individual and knowledge and opportunity are general, and each is able to make his contribution to the efficiency and diversity of the whole in an atmosphere of publicity, mutual trust, and economic justice.

8.5 HUBERT PHILLIPS (1891–1964)

From *The liberal outlook,* Chapman and Hall: London, 1929, pp. 187–90.

Phillips, who had been economic adviser to the Liberal Industrial Inquiry, used *The liberal outlook* to summarize the proposals of the Yellow Book. Towards the end of his book, as this extract reveals, he conveyed the optimism of the people associated with the Inquiry: the belief that managed capitalism could create real equality of opportunity and so eliminate traditional class hostilities.

A time will come when poverty is no more than a legend, as the plague, so familiar once, is no more than a legend now. Security of livelihood, to which, to-day, only the well-to-do can lay claim, will be the common birthright of every citizen. The abolition of poverty, like the abolition of war, will put an end to jealousy and fear – to the jealousy that exists between class and class, to the poor man's fear of the rich, and to the rich man's fear of the poor. For only in a State from which the dread of poverty is absent can men live lives which are free from greed, from mutual hatred, from a degrading servility. And the liberation of the spirit of man from the bondage which to-day threatens to crush it must go forward side by side with the elimination of these evils.

A time will come when the environment in which men and women live their lives is not, as it largely is to-day, an offence to their self-respect – a conscious acceptance of conditions that are mean and unwholesome because to perpetuate them is the easiest and cheapest way. The slum will be known for what it is, an obscene outrage against civilisation itself. The failure to plan our towns will be recognised as wasteful, as the failure to plan our lives, and the lives of our children, is recognised as wasteful; spatially, as temporally, we shall learn to adjust harmoniously the claims and counter-claims of individuals and social groups. For upon this too the liberation of man's spirit must very largely depend.

These things will be possible because, with the march of science, we shall be able, without difficulty, to arrive at, and to maintain, a healthy balance between the making of the things we need and the using of them. Work will not be pursued, as it is pursued to-day, in servitude of spirit and under the lash of fear – a fear that is rooted in the dread of hunger. It will be pursued, by each of those concerned in the industrial complex, as the conscious expression of the faculties which he is best fitted to exert. With the disappearance of a social order based upon insecurity and want, a wider range of incentives will bring themselves to bear: not only the appeal to self-interest, but the appeal to good-will, the appeal to civic pride, the appeal to men's and women's creative instincts. The distinction between getting and spending will gradually become blurred, and the processes of creation and enjoyment, at present so sharply differentiated, will merge ultimately in one another.

A time will come, therefore, when to be an employer, as opposed to being employed, will imply, not a difference of status, but merely a difference of function. The terms 'capitalist' and 'wage-earner' will have no significance, for every wage-earner will be a capitalist and every capitalist a wage-earner. Organisation for production, like organisation for government, will be based upon ordered consultation and a recognition of the significance of the individual. For only on this basis shall we avoid those class-antagonisms which are as wasteful economically as politically they are dangerous.

And finally, a time will come when there will be no denial, to any human being, of the opportunity of giving full expression to the powers that are latent in him. Just as we shall cease to waste (as to-day we do waste) the greater part of the energy which the physical world makes available, so, in time, we shall cease to waste the capacities – artistic intellectual, spiritual – of the sons and daughters whom we bear. We shall learn that in the one field, as in the other, to waste opportunity is to destroy wealth – the wealth that in a sanely-planned economy is identified with life itself. The distribution of livelihood in the community will not, as now, cut across its educational processes, but will be the crown and the consummation of them.

Then, and not until then, shall we appreciate to the full the meaning of the possibilities of liberty, with which Liberalism and Liberal policy have always been identified – liberty to serve, but not liberty to enslave; liberty to enjoy, but not liberty to monopolise; liberty to create, but not liberty to destroy.

8.6 THE LIBERAL WAY

From *The liberal way: a survey of liberal policy, published by the authority of the National Liberal Federation,* with a foreword by Ramsay Muir, George Allen and Unwin: London, 1934, pp. 221–2.

The liberal way was a little more than a competent summary of the themes in the Yellow Book. Again, however, there was the promise that the liberal middle way between individualism and collectivism would lead to a community of self-governing citizens.

What we have attempted to do is not to describe a distant Utopia, but to set forth the steps that can now be taken to mend things as they are so as to bring us nearer to things as they ought to be. We do not and we cannot know what the ultimate destiny of our people and of the civilised world is to be. We know only the mixed good and evil that surrounds us; and it is our duty to work, under the inspiration of an ideal, for the removal of the evil and the strengthening of the good.

These chapters have been ill-written if the ideal of Liberalism has not been implicit in them, and shone through them. Its aim is to create a nation, not of humble though kindly treated workers dependent upon a small rich class who alone can enjoy the full benefits of a civilised life; and not of proletarians regimented, controlled, and provided with standardised comforts by a group of dictators or bureaucrats acting in the name of the State; but a nation of free, responsible, law-abiding, and self-reliant men and women – free from the grinding servitude of poverty and (so far as is possible for men) from the tyranny of circumstance; with healthy bodies and alert and trained minds; enjoying a real equality of opportunity to make the most and the best of their powers for their own advantage and that of the community, and to choose the way of life for which they are best fitted; having a real share of responsibility for regulating the management of their common affairs and the conditions of their own life and work; and secure of sufficient leisure to live a full life and to enjoy the delights of Nature, letters, and the arts.

8.7 WILLIAM BEVERIDGE (1879–1963)

From *Why I am a Liberal,* Herert Jenkins: London, 1945, pp. 7–10, 16, 18–19, 32–7, 62–3.

Beveridge, who was born in India, pursued a varied career after leaving Oxford University – as a social worker, journalist for the *Morning Post,* official at the Board of Trade, author of a standard book on *Unemployment,* and for eighteen years as Director of the London School of Economics. His wartime reports on *Social insurance and allied services* (1942) and *Full employment in a free society* (1944) transformed him from a little known academic into a national folk-hero. In *Why I am a Liberal* – which contains speeches and articles from the period when Beveridge was campaigning as a Liberal candidate for Parliament – 'the people's William' presented his plans for full employment and social security as means of extending the freedoms of ordinary people.

With two brief intervals the Conservatives were in charge of the country from 1922 to 1939. In domestic affairs this meant failing to take new steps to deal with the changed economic conditions of the world, accepting mass-unemployment as part of the order of nature. In international affairs conservatism meant reliance on national arms and on self-regarding policies, in place of collective security through the League of Nations. Of course, there are progressive elements in the Conservative Party: some of them ready for large changes. But also there will be found in the Conservative Party all those who want little change, and experience shows that these elements are likely to predominate; the Tory Reformers do not get their way in the Conservative Party. We cannot survive a revolutionary period in the history of the world, without being prepared for great changes, and we ought to have a Government that is not afraid of changes.

The Labour Party is on the whole a party of change. But I do not want change for the sake of change; I want it in a particular direction and, for several reasons, the direction in which the Labour Party will tend to move does not seem to me the best direction.

First, the Labour Party is formally committed to Socialism. I am no more a Socialist to-day than I was in the days when, for all my friendship for the Webbs, I did not feel able to join the Fabian Society or be more than an interested spectator of what they were doing. It is true that many, if not most, of the leaders of the Labour Party now spend much of their time in issuing carefully-expurgated editions of their creed of Socialism, in saying that if they were in power they would not think of nationalising all the means of production, distribution and exchange. But it does not seem to me a good plan to join a party and trust that it will not carry out what is the central plank of its platform. In any case, the Labour Party will have a Socialist bias, causing it to extend State control in doubtful cases. As a Radical, I am not afraid of State Control or public ownership where either of these is necessary to cure evils which cannot be cured without them, but my bias is against them, not for them. I am prepared to bring particular industries under unified public control for special reasons, but the reason has to be proved up to the hilt in each case. And I do not start out with an assumption that all working for profit is wicked.

Second, the Labour Party depends both for its funds and for its voting strength largely on the trade unions. I have nothing but admiration for the trade unions in their own field and for the purposes for which they were established, of securing fair wages and working conditions for all by brotherly co-operation. But after all they do represent one section only of the people and they represent people in their special aspect of producers. For political action, I want something wider; I want to see represented all the people, the general interest, the consumers even more than the producers ...

The Labour Party's primary concern, though not of course its sole concern, is to improve the material standard of living of the mass of the people and bring about greater economic equality. The Liberal Party wants to do both these things – of raising the standard of living and diminishing inequality – but its primary concern is to increase liberty for all. At one time it appeared that the greatest danger to liberty came from the arbitrary power of Governments. To-day, though it is still necessary to be on guard against arbitrary power of Governments, we all realise that this is only half the story. As I said at the Liberal Assembly:–

'Liberty means more than freedom from the arbitrary power of Governments. It means freedom from economic servitude to Want and Squalor and other social evils; it means freedom from arbitrary power in any form. A starving man is not free, because till he is fed, he cannot have a thought for anything but how to meet his urgent physical needs; he is reduced from a man to an animal. A man who dare not resent what he feels to be an injustice from an employer or a foreman, lest this condemn him to chronic unemployment, is not free.'

In many practical measures for improving the material conditions and the security of the masses of the people, Liberal and Labour men will go together, as with them will go many Tory Reformers. But as distinct from Labour, Liberals will always have more consciously in mind as their aim, not material progress but spiritual liberty; they will emphasise the importance of the individual and the need to let each man develop on his own line, so long as he does not harm others. And in distinction from many if not most Conservatives, Liberals will be concerned with those liberties which can be won and shared by all; they will be less concerned with liberties which cannot be general, and which become in the last resort the privileges of the few ...

My reason for desiring to take the opportunity that may be offered to enter Parliament is that there are many things which I should like to see done to make a New Britain after the war, and that I believe profoundly that the appropriate machinery for getting things done in this country is Parliament.

My reason for desiring to enter Parliament as a Liberal is that I believe that the things that I most desire to see done are essentially Liberal things – a carrying forward into the new world of the great living traditions of Liberalism.

What are the things that most need doing? To my mind there are three things above all that every citizen of this country and, indeed, of the world needs as conditions of a happy and useful life after the war. He needs freedom from Want and fear of Want; freedom from Idleness and fear of Idleness enforced by unemployment; freedom from War and fear of War.

The first of these freedoms is the aim of the Report on Social Insurance and Allied Services which I made to H.M. Government nearly two years ago. That Report sets out a plan for Social Security to ensure that every citizen of the country, on condition of working and contributing while he can, has an income to keep him above want when for any reason – of sickness, accident, unemployment, or old age – he cannot work and earn an income sufficient for the honourable subsistence of himself and all who depend on him, an income sufficient though he has nothing else of his own and not cut down by any means test if he has anything of his own.

Freedom from Idleness enforced by unemployment is the subject of a second Report on Full Employment in a Free Society, ... setting out a plan by which Full Employment at all times can be maintained without interfering with any of the essential British liberties. That plan is designed to make impossible any return to the mass unemployment which marked the interval between the Wars.

Freedom from War and fear of War is the most important and the most difficult of the three freedoms to attain. It depends on the kind of peace that we make and the organisation that we set up to establish the rule of law between nations instead of the rule of force and violence ...

In regard to each of these three problems, it is to me obvious that the action required is essentially Liberal. To win Freedom from Want means building on the structure of Social Insurance begun in 1911 by Mr. Lloyd George in the great Liberal administration of that time. Freedom from Idleness means prevention of unemployment. In the bad period between the two wars, the Liberal Party in 1929 was the only party which made serious proposals for dealing with unemployment. They didn't get the chance of trying those proposals and, to-day, we shall have to go beyond them: but when these proposals were made, they were far ahead of anything contemplated by the other parties: they went at least as far as the Employment Policy of the Government of to-day. As regards freedom from War, that cannot be obtained either by pacifism or by nationalism; it depends upon carrying into the international field essentially Liberal ideas of the rule of law, and of making the world safe for small nations by justice and the policeman ...

If you want Liberalism at once and in full, if you want a New Britain free of the giant social evils of Want, Disease, Ignorance, Squalor and Idleness, free at the same time of every needless restriction on individual liberty, you can get these things best through a strong Liberal Party with a Radical Programme ...

The execution of a Radical Programme involves an extension of the responsibilities and functions of the State. It means at the same time more individual liberty, not less. That is because Liberal radicalism avoids the errors both of the so-called individualists, who treat every liberty as equally important and of the collectivists who desire extension of state activity for its own sake.

Liberal radicalism in relation to liberty may be defined by three propositions:-

1. Certain citizen liberties are essential, and must be preserved at all costs. These are, on the one hand, the intimate personal liberties (worship, speech, writing, study, teaching; spending of personal income; choice of occupation) and on the other hand, the political liberties (assembly and associations for industrial and political purposes) which are necessary to prevent the establishing of arbitrary power.

2. Subject to preservation of these essential liberties, the power of the State should be used so far as necessary to protect citizens against the social evils of Want, Disease, Ignorance, Squalor and Idleness, as it is used to protect them against robbery and violence at home and against attack from abroad.

3. The power of the State should not be used except for purposes which cannot be accomplished without it. That is to say, liberties

outside the list of essential liberties can and should be allowed to continue, so long as they are exercised responsibly and in such a way as not to hurt others.

All liberties are not equally important. The error of the individualists is to treat them as if they were. The essence of Liberalism is to distinguish between essential liberties to be preserved at all costs and lesser liberties which should be preserved only so far as they are consistent with social justice and social progress.

The error of the individualists can be illustrated by a passage in a recent book – the *Road to serfdom,* by Professor Hayek. This passage is the opening of Chapter V on page 42. The chapter is headed by a quotation from Adam Smith, saying that for any Government to interfere with individuals in the application of their capitals would be presumptuous and tyrannous. Professor Hayek then proceeds as follows:–

'The various kinds of collectivism, communism, fascism, etc., differ between themselves in the nature of the goal towards which they want to direct the efforts of society. But they all differ from liberalism and individualism in wanting to organise the whole of society and all its resources for this unitary end, and in refusing to recognise autonomous spheres in which the ends of the individual are supreme.'

The simple answer to this is that Liberal radicalism, as defined above, does recognise autonomous spheres in which the ends of the individual are supreme, but that it does not recognise among these spheres, as Professor Hayek does, the investment of capital. That is a secondary liberty, desirable in itself but only so long as its exercise does not harm others. In fact, investment of capital, as it has been practised by individuals in the past without guidance in the general interest, has resulted in grave social evils.

(1) The allowing of business men before the war to place their factories just where they thought best for themselves has led to the endless harmful growth of great cities, with congestion, squalor, a cramped home for the housewife, and interminable journeys for the worker. Between 1932 and 1936 five-sixths of the new factories built in Britain were placed in the London area, that is to say, the area of greatest congestion and strategic danger. To allow businessmen to go on like this, means forcing squalor and unemployment on others; control of business men in the location of their factories is the alternative to direction of labour and creation of depressed areas.

(2) To allow business men freely to order factories, machines, raw materials when they want and not when they do not want, has meant in the past, and will continue to mean in the future, perpetual fluctuation

in the demand for labour. If business men continue to order a million tons of shipping one year and 500,000 tons of shipping a year or two later, or if they are allowed to build 100,000 houses one year and 30 or 20 thousand a year or two later, unemployment is inevitable. To stabilise the process of investment, by interfering so far as necessary with business men, is the only alternative to destroying human beings in unemployment and subjecting them to the misery of a dole, with or without means test. Only by sacrificing some of the less important liberties of the past can we preserve the essential liberties and increase their effective enjoyment by all.

Those who talk most of liberties have seldom taken the trouble to define these liberties. If they did, their case would fall to the ground in ridicule. Professor Hayek's argument, at this point, leads to one or other of two conclusions, each of which is ridiculous. Either he must assert that the liberty of a business man to place his factory where he likes or to order machinery just when he likes is as essential as any of the intimate personal liberties (which it obviously is not). Or he must assert that though liberty of investment may not be essential in itself, it is impossible to interfere with it without going on to interfere with essential liberties. That is like saying that no one can walk one mile without going on to walk a hundred miles.*

Let us get back to common sense. To interfere with the quite unimportant freedom of a few business men in the location of factories or the ordering of investment is the way to preserve the essentials of healthy, self-respecting life for thousands of others. We cannot end the social evils and injustices which have marred Britain in the past unless we are prepared to substitute a planned economy guided by social purpose for an unplanned market economy driven hither and thither by pursuit of individual interests. But planning must be planning for freedom. Planning can and should increase freedom, not diminish it. We increase liberty by use of the organised power of the community to stop crime by establishing the rule of law. We can increase enjoyment of liberty no less certainly by using the organised power of the

---

*Professor Hayek's book contains, of course, many arguments more valid than the one that is criticised here. It includes a useful criticism of totalitarianism, and a recognition of the need for some social measures to deal with social evils. But, in so far as it lends support to the view that 'liberty is indivisible,' and that you cannot interfere anywhere without interfering everywhere, it gives support to anarchy and privilege. As was pointed out by John Stuart Mill in his classic work *On liberty* more than eighty years ago: 'All that makes existence valuable to any one depends on the enforcement of restraints upon the actions of other people.'

community to put an end to Want, Disease, Squalor, Ignorance and mass-unemployment.

We can and should use the organised power of the community to increase the rights of individuals. Take one example: by having compulsory social insurance with benefits adequate for a subsistence, we can assure to all men the right to adequate care in youth, and to an honoured old age without dependence on the young, without charity, without subjection to a means test.

Take another example – of full employment. The liberal radical doctrine is that the State exists for the individual. Therefore, 'a State which fails in respect of many millions of individuals to ensure them any opportunity of service and earning in accordance to their powers or the possibility of a life free from the indignities and inquisitions of relief, is a State which has failed in a primary duty. Acceptance by the State of responsibility for full employment is the final necessary demonstration that the State exists for the citizens – for all the citizens – and not for itself or for a privileged class.'

In pursuance of full employment, the State may and should do anything necessary for that end, except interfere with essential liberties. But it should not do anything that is not yet proved to be necessary for that purpose, such as suppression of private enterprise in industry or of the practice of collective bargaining. These liberties – though not essential – should be left, to be exercised responsibly, so long as they do not block the way to full employment ...

Employment depends upon spending. Full Employment, defined as more paid jobs than men and women looking for jobs, requires that the total of spending should always be enough to set up a demand for the services of all the men and women in the country who are available for paid employment. It must become a responsibility of the State to ensure that spending in total is adequate for full employment, because no other body in the community has sufficient powers for the purpose and adequate spending will not come automatically. But spending, in addition to being adequate, must be spending to advantage, not digging holes and filling them up again, and not spending on luxuries and trivialities while any substantial proportion of the people go short of essentials. That is why in my Report on Full Employment, I spoke, as a rule, not of 'spending,' but of 'outlay.' The two words mean much the same, but 'outlay' is better, because it suggests design, the careful laying out of money for a purpose, rather than just getting rid of money, whatever the object.

Spending to advantage means putting first things first; it means laying out money on a long term programme of attack on the giant evils of Want, Disease, Ignorance, and Squalor and at the same time laying out money to raise our standard of living by increasing our output per head. The way to that lies in improving the capital equipment of the country.

While maintenance of adequate outlay in total must become a responsibility of the State, that does not mean that all or even a large part of the total of outlay is directly undertaken by the State. In a free community most spending will be that of private citizens spending for consumption according to their taste. In a community with any substantial proportion of private enterprise in business, there will be private investment. The national Budget will determine directly what is spent by public authorities and will influence by taxation the spending of private citizens.

The main instrument of a full employment policy is thus a new type of Budget based on man-power. With this must go many subsidiary measures ... to guide the location of industry, without which one may get depressed areas and local unemployment; to guide the free movement of labour from job to job and from area to area; to set up collective outlay guaranteeing a market and price in meeting essential needs; to regulate and steady the process of private investment; to extend the public sector of industry, wherever extension is needed for special reasons.

The policy proposed here for adoption by the Liberal Party is not Conservative, for it breaks new ground altogether, and it is not Socialist for, while it accepts nationalisation of particular industries for special reasons, it starts with no bias in favour of nationalisation and it leaves much the greater part of industry to private enterprise.

Part Nine
A DECENTRALIZED STATE

9.1 GEORGE ELLIOTT DODDS (1889–1977)

From 'Liberty and welfare', in George Watson (ed.), *The unservile state: essays in liberty and welfare*, George Allen and Unwin: London, 1957, pp. 14–15, 17–22, 25–6.

The unservile state was described on the jacket as 'the first full–scale study of the attitudes and policies of contemporary British Liberalism since the famous Yellow Book published under Lloyd George's inspiration in 1928'. It was certainly the first concerted attempt by post-war liberals to tread a distinctive path between the extremes of individualism and collectivism. Elliott Dodds set the tone of the book with his concept of a decentralized 'welfare society' which cushions its members against economic insecurity without undermining their individuality. Dodds was vice–president of the Liberal Party and editor of the *Huddersfield Examiner*.

As time has passed ... British Liberalism has become increasingly identified with Welfare – or, as one might put it, with 'economic liberty' in its modern sense. The first steps in establishing what has come to be known as the Welfare State were taken by Whig or Liberal Governments – e.g. the Factory Acts of 1833 and 1847, the legalization of trade unions (Trade Union Act, 1871), the 'liberalization' of taxation through graduation according to ability to pay, death duties, supertax, etc., the funds thereby raised being used to finance social improvement; the initiation of Old Age Pensions (1908) and of Health and Unemployment Insurance (1911). While the Liberal Party, during its sojourn in the wilderness, has been opening up new ground in the study of economic and social problems (for example, the famous Yellow Book of 1928 and the more recent reports on Trade Unionism, Co-ownership in Industry, Education and the Problem of the Aged), it may fairly be claimed that everything which other Parties have subsequently done in the way of Welfare has been merely a development of its achievements when it was last in office.

Thus in Liberal thought and action Liberty and Welfare have gone together, but during the period in which Liberalism has been in eclipse there has been an increasing tendency to set them over against each other. The 'new freedoms (economic) are contrasted with the 'old' (civil and political), and in some quarters which make much of the former there is a disposition to devalue the latter. This tendency, which vitiates much of Socialist thought, is seen at its logical extreme in Communism. 'Libertarians', on the other hand, are apt to deny that the new freedoms are freedoms at all, to dwell on the restrictions their establishment has involved, and to use 'Welfare State' as a term of disparagement.

Liberalism – true Liberalism – repudiates this antithesis ...

We argue that Welfare is actually a form of Liberty inasmuch as it liberates men from social conditions which narrow their choices and thwart their self-development as truly as any governmental or personal coercions. At any rate both, in the Liberal view, have this in common that they should be regarded as means to the full and harmonious development of persons. But the 'new' freedoms differ from the old in that they call for positive measures, whereas the 'old' freedoms require simply the abolition of restraints. Their establishment, though in many ways extending the field for free action, involves restrictions which did not exist before. A great machine is needed to administer them and more machinery still to prevent their abuse – an extensive system of rules and regulations, a vast amount of red tape and an army of officials who cost a great deal to maintain and whose bureaucratic methods are often strongly and rightly resented.

Nor is this all. A not unimportant liberty is the liberty to get and spend one's income as one likes. This is seriously curtailed by the heavy taxation required to finance the social services and the contributions required from 'insured persons', who benefit from the ways in which their money is used but have no choice in its spending.

Once again the conflict of claims arises – 'Who shall be free to do what?' The question is whether, taking the members of society as a whole, the net effect of the means adopted to spread Welfare more widely is to increase or diminish their scope for self-direction and responsibility. Under totalitarian systems, where civil and political liberties are reduced to zero and the benefits (such as they are) are liable to be withdrawn if their recipients show any sign of independence, there is plainly an overwhelming surplus on the debit side. In free societies, though so far in Britain there can be little doubt that the pursuit of Welfare has resulted in a net increase in effective liberty, a constant watch is needed lest the balance should tip against it. It has been inevitable that as the range of the State's concern for the Welfare of its citizens has increased, so has its control over their lives. But has not this gone unnecessarily far? Is not the control both too pervasive and too detailed? That many abuses exist is unquestioned. How are they to be remedied without weakening the structure itself? ...

Again, it is sometimes alleged that 'all this spoon-feeding' is sapping the British character – that when the State does so much for the citizen he loses the impulse to do things for himself. Is this true – and if so how true is it? The gloomy conclusion that security is fatal to initiative and enterprise is certainly unjustified. History attests that. But it is undeniable that some of the present symptoms warrant anxiety, and these, coupled with the inescapable fact that more State provision means more State control, prompt yet a further question.

Are the social services to be regarded as crutches, necessary while so many are unable to walk freely as they would like, but to be discarded as soon as they are able to use their own legs? Or are they to be considered as permanent features of a Liberal Society? With the value they attach to self-direction, Liberals must naturally desire that people should be able to make more adequate provision for themselves than many can do now, instead of relying on the State to make it for them. They certainly do not regard the present structure of the social services as sacrosanct, and favour substantial changes in organization and administration. On the other hand they are keenly concerned for the less fortunate and passionately believe in the principle of mutual responsibility. With these considerations in mind, is it possible or desirable to cut down the provision which the State now makes? If not, when? and to what extent? How far would it be practicable to introduce more choice in the State-run systems – in health insurance, for instance, or in education? These questions, bristling with difficulty, are also examined in subsequent chapters. If the results may be anticipated and summarized, we may say that while whole-heartedly approving of Welfare (i.e. of some social arrangement that will ensure subsistence and protect the citizen against economic misfortune) our aim is a 'Welfare Society' rather than a 'Welfare State'.* We recognize that the State must remain responsible for those for whom other sources of Welfare are not available; but in a Liberal

---

* For this distinction we are indebted to Lord Beveridge, and for his permission to use it (apparently for the first time) in print.

society we should look increasingly to the release and stimulation of private endeavour and voluntary agencies of service and mutual aid to diminish the role of the state. Eventually society, i.e. individuals and groups of individuals, would be able and ready to provide most of its welfare for itself.

In the introduction to his *Full employment in a free society: a report* (1944)* Lord Beveridge has stated that his purpose was 'to propose for the State only those things which the State alone can do or which it can do better than any local authority or than private citizens either singly or in association, and to leave to those other agencies that which, if they will, they can do as well as or better than the State' (p. 36). Wilhelm Ropke has extended this principle, which he calls 'the principle of subsidiarity', to apply to the whole hierarchy of society, from the individual through family, parish, district or county up to the central Government.† This is the principle by which we propose that the existing Welfare State should be transformed by stages into a Welfare Society.

In the past many social organizations have undertaken the task of providing Welfare. In the Middle Ages there was a Welfare Church. The Reformation, by sequestering Church property, made it imperative for some other body to step in: this was the (lay) Welfare Parish. But social changes put an increasing strain on the parish, and the Industrial Revolution rendered it completely incapable of these functions, limited though they were. This fact was recognized by the Poor Law of 1834, which set up the 'Union' in place of the parish. But the Union became a name of odium and Bumble the personification of its central feature, the workhouse. There followed a period in which attempts were made to humanize the administration of the Unions, and in which a variety of private Welfare organizations – friendly societies and insurance companies, with trade unions and co-operative societies fulfilling some similar functions – sought to mitigate the hardships caused by uncontrolled social and economic developments; but these proved quite insufficient and, while the Royal Commission in 1909 recommended drastic reforms in the Poor Law system which were not carried out until after the first World War, the Liberal Parliament in 1911 borrowed a leaf from Bismarck and his Prussian Welfare State in initiating National Health and Unemployment Insurance. Thus the foundation of our own Welfare State was laid.

This was a notable advance: but as the years have passed and the

* London: Allen & Unwin.
† Wilhelm Ropke, *Civitas humana* (1948), p. 90.

system thus initiated has assumed such comprehensive proportions it has become evident that a State monopoly in Welfare has certain illiberal consequences, and our conviction is that the time has come to provide, not Welfare merely, but a varied and competitive Welfare. Much can be done by devolution (back to the parish, as it were): and more, we claim, in a dynamic and expanding economy, by encouraging personal effort and by some reversion to the spontaneous Welfare organizations in which the nineteenth century put too early and too complete a trust.

Set, here as everywhere, on creating conditions favourable to the development of personality, Liberals are necessarily distributists. Concentration, which has grown so portentously in so many fields, is the great robber of personal dignity and significance. Liberals therefore seek to spread wealth, ownership, power and responsibility as widely as possible. Thanks largely to their initiative, much has already been done to spread income. It is arguable that this process has gone too far: that in the laudable effort to level up, levelling down has reached danger-point. Certainly the inordinate tax burden weighs with particular unfairness on some of the most talented elements in the nation. Little or nothing, however, has been done to spread property; yet this ... is vital to the spreading of choice and the creation of greater equality of opportunity.

'Greater equality of opportunity' – not equality of possession. The distinction is crucial. Equality of possession, whether in property or income, is not practicable, or at least only practicable in a totalitarian society. On the other hand, equality of opportunity is, in a rough sense, feasible, and is essential if all citizens are to have a fair chance of developing themselves to the full. But we should face the evident fact that greater equality of opportunity is likely to tend to less, not more, equality of possession, since talents previously condemned to 'fust unused' will be set free and will earn greater rewards; and watch will have to be kept lest a new inequality of opportunity should result at next remove owing to the effects of inheritance.

Other aspects of the distributism which is such a distinguishing mark of Liberal thought and policy ... are devolution from Westminster; the energizing of local government; the re-distribution of population; the breaking down of monopoly; the regionalizing (where possible) of the nationalized industries and services and the institution of competition between the various units; and the spreading of co-ownership in industry.

Welfare has to be paid for. The extent to which it can be financed depends on the national wealth, and this emphasizes the need for greater dynamism in our society ... It is true that a free economy, though it may maximize national wealth, does not necessarily promote the spreading of the product and thus the creation of greater equality of opportunity. A nation, indeed, may grow very rich as an entity, yet its wealth may be so maldistributed as to frustrate the self-development of many – and also, by way of nemesis, to create frictions which impede the wealth–producing process. But the antithesis of a free versus a planned economy is false, thus crudely stated. A totally planned economy is, of course, irreconcilable with freedom; but planning at certain central points is necessary in order to maintain the institutional framework favourable to liberty and even to preserve the freedom of the economy itself. A free economy needs to be upheld by law (which means denying freedom to those, e.g. some monopolists, who would pervert it), and steps must be taken to 'redress the balance of private actions by compensating public actions'.* ...

The Liberal purpose – let it be said again – is 'the creation of opportunity for men and women to become self-directing, responsible persons'. This means the simultaneous pursuit of Liberty and Welfare – or, if that way of putting it is preferred, of Welfare as an element in Liberty. It is because Welfare has come to be dissociated from Liberty, or set in antithesis to it, that Liberty has lost so much of its appeal; that Liberalism, falsely identified with Liberty as against Welfare, has suffered decline: and that the Statist parties (Communist and Socialist) have gained such unwarranted prestige with progressives. The business of Liberals today is to show by a practical and relevant programme how Liberty and Welfare can be consistently pursued with the aim of giving 'more abundant life' to the individual person – Liberty conceived as not merely freedom from restrictions, but as the enlargement of scope for the exercise of responsible citizenship: Welfare conceived, not merely as cash and comfort, but as providing opportunity for moral, intellectual and cultural development such as is frustrated when men are obsessed by anxiety about the bare business of living; and both encouraging adventure, experiment, colour, variety and eccentricity. Thus may Liberals re-establish themselves in their natural position as the acknowledged leaders of the Left – a consummation towards which we hope in this volume to make a contribution.

---

* Walter Lippmann, *The method of freedom* (1934), p. 46.

9.2 HARRY COWIE (b. 1930)

From 'Introduction' to *Partners for progress*, Liberal Publications
Department: London, 1964, pp. 7–8.

Partners for progress was issued as a handbook for Liberal candidates
and speakers. Cowie was Director of the Liberal Research Department.
In arguing that Britain should prepare for a technological revolution, he
was articulating a theme that cut across party divisions. In 1964 Harold
Wilson shaped the theme into a highly successful electoral strategy for
the Labour Party.

Britain cannot take advantage of what modern life has to offer so long
as the country is divided. Under Labour and Conservative
Governments class barriers have become more rigid, regional
differences have been exacerbated and our society and its social justice
has been slowly smothered by not one but many establishments. The
sham of Britain in 1964 is that not only are we left behind in the
technological race, but we are still suffering under social barriers
inherited from another age which cripple our society.

Liberal policies are designed to replace the class struggle of British
politics by a new sense of purpose based on a social partnership. The
Liberal programme is not therefore an attempt to outbid the other
parties in promises but a challenge to the social conscience of the
nation to remove the injustices which still exist in our society, to
replace privilege by a sense of participation, and build up a new
partnership in power based on a greater equality of wealth and
opportunity.

All parties promise more wealth. Even the Conservative Party
promises to modernise Britain. But practical achievement will depend
on the extent to which reforms can be made in the way we run our
affairs. We shall never mobilise Britain without reforming our system
of Government and giving people a greater say in the decisions that
affect their lives. Parliament and the Civil Service must be revitalised
and power decentralised from London to Regional Councils. This
would allow Ministers, their advisers, and Parliament to concentrate
on the right priorities – a broad strategy for economic expansion and
social reform – while at the same time creating new centres of political
and economic growth in the rest of the country.

The spreading of power would also permit more and more people to
participate in the organisation of their work and life by means of
community endeavours either through revived local government,
works councils, parent-teacher associations, or local consumer
organisations.

This is the way to get Britain moving. The building up of a real partnership of power will mobilise initiative today in the same way as nineteenth century Liberalism permitted the maximum outlet for the individual dynamic of the last century. We live in a new technological revolution but it is just as important to have a Government in power which is sympathetic to the innovators of the age – the scientists, the technologists, the young executives, and managers. At present this key group is frustrated and disillusioned. More state control, as proposed by the Labour Party, would only clutter up the desks of top civil servants even more, at a time when they should be cleared for action. It would certainly not spread power in our society. Without a voice, in the way we run our affairs, more scientists and other research workers will continue to be attracted abroad.

On the shop floor, the Liberal industrial proposals will go a long way towards creating a sense of partnership in industry. Whatever Government is in power, the attempt to achieve an incomes policy will fail until the class struggle on the factory floor can be replaced by a real partnership of power.

At home, therefore, Liberals have positive policies to reshape Britain and create a new spirit of partnership. Abroad they seek to apply the same spirit of partnership to the construction of international communities with their neighbours as a first step towards world order, peace and prosperity.

9.3 JOHN MALCOLM RAE (b. 1931)

From 'Liberalism means liberty, but it also means business', in *The Times*, 13 September 1976.

If most liberals perceive themselves as 'lefties' emancipated from socialist obsessions with class warfare, a minority still tend to view freedom in a negative, pre-T. H. Green sense. Rae's concern is to drive a wedge between liberty and equality in order to condemn the 'totalitarian' tendencies of 'state socialism'. The problem for a liberal who adopts this sort of individualist perspective, of course, is that liberals themselves were the intellectual architects of collectivism.

The Liberal Party ceased to be an effective political force in 1931. Since that date it has sought but failed to find a political identity that would give it once again a power base in the electorate. Its survival at all is remarkable, though whether this has real significance or is no more than a curiosity, like the headless chicken that continues to run round the farmyard in defiance of death, is not clear. Why then do men not now abandon this party that has neither an identity nor a prospect of power?

For some Liberals there is an almost constitutional reluctance to adopt any other political stance: they are repelled equally by the hard faces on the right and by the dogma and demagoguery on the left. For others the Liberal Party provides a convenient medium for publicizing themselves and their causes. For myself the reasons are simple. I want my children to grow up in a country that is a place of hope not of frustration, defeatism and despair. The one quality that neither Socialists nor Tories are able to communicate is hope; expectation, yes, but not hope. More specifically, much that I love in my country has been nurtured by the liberal tradition; I see that tradition threatened as never before and I look to the Liberal Party to counter that threat.

But here lies the predicament. Has the Party got what might be called the moral energy to undertake this task or has it long since lost the will to seek and wield power? If the latter, then it cannot expect to command the loyalty of those who believe in the importance of the liberal tradition in the destiny of the country.

This liberal predicament can only be understood in its historical context. The liberal tradition and the Liberal Party are not synonymous but for half a century from the formation of the first Liberal Ministry to the end of the First World War, the Party was the authentic champion of that tradition. Though the tradition was fed by different sources, its principal characteristics were clear. The struggle between Parliament and King in the seventeenth century had established the foundations: 'the principles of civil and religious liberty, the rule of law and the freedom of the press, the institutions of parliamentary government, limited monarchy and an independent judiciary.'

In the evolution of the tradition the concept of liberty was always central. Conflicts were about the right interpretation of the role of liberty: between Fox and Burke over the French Revolution; between the Whig aristocrats and the thrusting new men who represented the manufacturing interest; between the manufactures *laissez faire* and the broader, more humane interpretation of liberty that recognized the need for state initiative to create equality of opportunity. But always, liberty is the issue, how you ensure it for the individual, how you adapt it to changing social and economic conditions, how you reconcile it with social justice. This centrality of liberty is the touchstone of the liberal tradition, playing the same role as equality in the socialist tradition.

To claim that this liberal tradition is threatened as never before must appear both sweeping and rather glib, yet the evidence is there. The threat to liberty always comes from too great a concentration of power. In this century we have placed in the hands of government and of corporate bodies, powers that an absolute monarch would not have dared to take. We have pursued a socialist utopia with little regard for the liberties we were surrendering because we have been persuaded that the demands of equality are paramount. The result is that we are well on the way to establishing a maternalistic state in which the individual citizen must do what he is told because mother knows best: he must leave the complexities of government to the experts and bureaucrats; he must learn that he cannot cope without the services of the state from the cradle to the grave, he must bow to the big battalions because they are 'the important people in the country' and he must develop those social attitudes that ministers tell him are for the general good.

The threat to liberty comes from state socialism. It is characteristic that liberty should be redefined exclusively in terms of the group. The Benthamites' over-individualistic view of liberty is taken to the opposite extreme: the freedom of the group to exclude the non-conformist individual is put forward as the true meaning of liberty. Closed shop legislation is only the most obvious example. Thus the liberal tradition is threatened by an Orwellian perversion of itself.

Neither the Labour nor the Conservative Party will counter this threat to liberty. Labour's unwillingness hardly needs explaining: as a socialist party (despite attempts to project a social democratic image) it is committed to equality as the priority in politics. In the natural conflict between equality and liberty, there is no doubt which principle Labour will be prepared to sacrifice.

As defenders of liberty, the Tories are not so much unwilling as unconvincing; a large part of the electorate will always suspect them of being interested in liberty, not for its own sake, but as a means of supporting privilege. History supports such suspicions: the Tories track record on liberty, from Anglican discrimination against non-conformists to land-owners' fierce hostility to Lloyd George's radical budget, is not impressive. Knowing that this is so inhibits the Tories from taking action to defend liberty. They are prepared to sacrifice liberty for the sake of power . . .

What is true, I believe, is that many Liberals are politically disorientated, their attitude to political issues is ambivalent. Historically, their enemy has always been on the right. If asked, they will say they are 'left of centre' and they are still inclined to see the left as the party of generosity and humanity. They are deeply reluctant to admit that the real enemies of the liberal tradition are now on the left. But unless they do admit this and accept its implications, they will never re-establish a political identity.

If Liberals mean business, therefore, when they talk about defending liberty they must grasp the opportunity that now exists to establish themselves as the principal political force defending the liberal tradition against the protective totalitarianism of the left. At the moment that role is played by the Tory Party but inadequately because as defenders of liberty the Tories are always unconvincing. It follows that Liberal strategy should be to challenge the Tories for the leadership of all those who sense that the energies and talents of the British people can only be released if the nation re-asserts the importance of liberty. That is where political identity can be found.

9.4 JOSEPH GRIMOND (b. 1913)

From 'Community politics', in *Government and opposition*', vol. 7, Winter 1972, pp. 135, 144.

Born into a St Andrews textile family, Jo Grimond was educated at Eton and Balliol College, Oxford. He was Member of Parliament for Orkney and Shetland from 1950 to 1983, and Liberal Party leader between 1956 and 1967 and, temporarily, in 1976. Grimond's hope as leader was that his party would become the focus for a realignment of the Left around radical policies intended, *inter alia*, to reverse the growth of bureaucratic centralism.

There is some failure of orthodox politics. They fail to deal satisfactorily with the matters which face a modern community. They fail also to give people satisfaction or to make them feel that their wishes are adequately expressed ...

I do not believe that it is healthy when the left, who traditionally explore new ideas in politics, become bereft of political theory. The only attempt at such theory of recent years has come from the conservatives. It has, I think, been misunderstood. It has been regarded as a return to *laissez-faire*. But I would rather say that it is a reassertion of paternalism. A paternalism which tries to draw a distinction between those children in need of care and support and those which are thought to be capable of standing on their own feet.

As against this I believe that the left should assert what I would call fraternalism – the involvement of more and more people in the decisions which affect their lives. And I would end by saying that I believe this not only, or even principally, because I believe both in the inalienable right of people to be offered an effective opportunity to play some part in politics, but because I believe that it is only by getting the right blend of experts and democrats that you get good decisions. I believe decision-making in this country has not been good enough of recent years. I believe this is because of the distortions of the system and the preponderance of bureaucratic attitudes. I believe we want a reassertion of democracy, but in the context of wider social organizations.

9.5 BERNARD GREAVES (b. 1942) AND GORDON LISHMAN (b. 1947)

From *The theory and practice of community politics*, Association of Liberal Councillors Campaign Booklet no. 12: Hebden Bridge, 1980, secs. 4–10, 15.

This pamphlet was commissioned, according to the editor of ALC booklets, 'in the hope that more Liberals will contribute to the growing body of theory underlying the community politics action, and in the hope that many of the activists we have gained in recent years will gain a greater understanding of that theory. If we have a greater awareness of where we are heading it is all the easier to make decisions about the direction and priorities of our campaigning.' Both authors are former vice-chairmen of the National League of Young Liberals.

The Liberal view is based on the moral imperative that all people have an equal right to take part in the process by which decisions that affect their lives are taken. The greatest threat to that right is the concentration of power. Democracy is dependent as much on the dissemination, distribution and control of power as it is upon the ballot.

The objective of community politics is not the welfare of communities themselves. Communities are not in themselves an end. The end is the quality of the experience of each individual within them. The justification for community politics lies in the belief that the key to releasing the potential of each person as a unique individual lies in bringing together all individuals in voluntary, mutual and co-operative enterprise within relevant communities.

We have produced world-wide a society of mass production, mass marketing and mass consumption in which choice, participation and creativity are minimal. This approach and the values that have led to it, pervade every facet of human endeavour from industry, politics and commerce to recreation, sport, the arts and eating and drinking. It is a society that operates in a similar but not identical way, irrespective of the professed ideology of the political group who are in control in any particular place at any particular time. All such political groups, some in good faith and some in bad, profess to be promoting the welfare of all. Most usually do so at the expense of each.

Societies of such mass uniformity not only deny individuality to their members. They are vulnerable. Faced with changes in the factors upon which they are based, they must either adapt themselves as a whole or be faced with tensions which they may not survive. Indeed our current society is approaching just such a crisis. It has created an economy dependent upon the accelerating consumption of non-renewable resources, that inevitably cannot continue. So it must adapt and change or go out of existence. Yet a mass and uniform society is by its nature inflexible.

The alternative is a society made up of many varied and different communities. Such a society offers the individual a wide range of personal choice of social role and life-style. Such a society has a dynamic inbuilt tendency to change and develop.

New ideas can be tried out on an experimental basis within a community where they could not within the whole of society without endangering it if they failed. So, it makes sense in terms of the resilience and survival of society to reverse the trends towards centralisation and uniformity, and to encourage decentralisation and variety.

But our perspective is primarily political. We are concerned with the distribution and control of power *within* communities *and* with the manner in which decisions, attitudes and priorities emerge from the full range of smaller communities to govern larger and larger communities. That process of confrontation, conflict, negotiation, co-operation, change and law-making is the way in which societies should be run. The concept of pluralism is central to our view of politics, just as the concepts of free choice and diversity are central to our view of personal development. Pluralism is not a neat prescription or an easy concept: it is, however, essential to the alternative society which we are advocating.

We are not just concerned with the creation of communities, but also with their interaction, with the capacity of communities and the individuals who make them up for influencing the world around them and the decisions which affect or involve them. Our view is also outward looking and inclusive: we are not community chauvinists. We are all involved in mankind.

Our aim is therefore the creation of a political system which is based on the interaction of communities in which groups have the power, the will, the knowledge, the technology to influence and affect the making of decisions in which they have an interest. Even more, we want those communities to initiate the debate, to formulate their own demands and priorities and to participate fully in agreeing the rules by which their relationships are regulated ...

Community politics is quite incompatible with the centralisation of power at the level of the nation-state. Indeed, it is incompatible with the concentration of power at any level.

The most conspicuous and serious absence in Britain is of any structure of neighbourhood government. This is the level that most directly affects the everyday lives of everyone and it is the level of government in which everyone can take part directly. It is only in small, geographically coherent neighbourhoods that everyone can take a direct part in the making of decisions and the exercise of power. At any level above this, some form of indirect democracy involving representative government is needed.

Almost as serious in Britain is the lack of effective power and independence in local government. Local government, by virtue of the control exercised over it by the state through the control of its finances, has in effect become little more than devolved administration exercised by locally elected representatives carrying out the policies of the central government ...

The impact on people of the lack of neighbourhood government and the failure of local government is immediate and clearly identifiable. The lack of regional government and of effective and democratic authorities at a continental, a sub-continental and a world level is more intangible in its effects but equally serious. It is the absence of regional authorities that has created much of the stultifying bureaucracy of British internal administration. It is the lack of supranational authorities that has failed to bring about effective arms control, has allowed exploitation by multi-national corporations to go unchecked and has maintained the inequitable distribution of the benefits of the world's natural resources and the proceeds of industrialisation.

Supra-national government is bedevilled by the idea that international democracy means 'one nation one vote', and by the concept of national sovereignty that demands that each country has a veto on any crucial decision.

National sovereignty is a perniciously dangerous concept that subverts the independence of lower levels of government and prevents the exercise of effective power by authorities at a higher level. There is nothing special, sacrosanct or intrinsically superior about the authority of national governments. It is their unbridled exercise of power that is the greatest threat to the ideal of community politics.

Power wherever exercised must be limited. It must be held in check by a framework of constitutional relationships backed by effective enforcement. Above all, the use of power must be held in check by the vigilance and activity of communities with the habit and techniques of participation. Communities at every level have a legitimate claim to exercise power within a defined and limited area. That area of power must be safeguarded against the encroachments of other levels of government. The central concern of politics should be the definition and protection of legitimate spheres of power as exercised by different authorities: that is to say with the evolution, introduction and enforcement of a multi-layered federal structure. Community politics implies federalism.

It is a mistake to think of communities solely in geographical terms. A place is not the only sort of entity that can exist as an organised community and possess a degree of power to run its own affairs. We should be thinking equally of different functions of government and administration as arenas for the promotion of community politics.

In particular, community politics is applicable to the running of industry and other places of work. It is also applicable to the running of education, the health services, and other public services. The establishment of the claims of the communities involved in these fields to run their own affairs is no different in principle from the claims of members of a neighbourhood residential community.

In practice the problems may be more complex. The differing and sometimes competing interests of different groups of workers and consumers must be reconciled. This is not easy and has been used as a justification for rejecting the idea altogether. Of course it is not! It is much more an indication of the need to experiment with a variety of different approaches. Even that at present is premature. It is the claim by communities of both workers and consumers to the control of their own destinies that must be promoted as a valid demand.

Community politics is relevant both as a policy and as a process. In policy terms, we are looking for co-operative production, bringing direct and representative democracy into the planning, organisation and management of productive work. In terms of process, we are talking about the organisation and management of industrial communities which can take decisions and can interact in organising production just as any other democratic political community should do.

In the public services, we are looking for co-operation, involving not only workers and representatives of the public interests, but also the recipients, the victims, of the services they provide. Health, education and transportation are a long way from any form of democratic control, and even further from any realisation of a role for consumers. There is a need for the policy of decentralisation and co-operation ...

The Liberal vision of community politics is dependent upon the universal safeguard of civil liberties. Unless a community respects and upholds the liberty of the individual, of minority groups, and indeed of majority groups, no community, however well organised, however strong in group identity, can enhance the quality of experience of each and every individual who makes it up. Community politics is dependent upon the universal guarantee within each community of full democratic rights to all its members. This includes a fair voting system. The forms may vary according to the size and circumstances of the particular community but the principle itself is invariable.

Communities which sacrifice the liberty of the individual and democratic self-determination to whatever other objective, are intrinsically no better than any other form of government. But communities can be the most complete way of safeguarding that liberty and freeing the full potential of their members for self-expression.

There are two distinctively liberal aspects of community politics which afford protection to civil liberty and democratic practice. The first lies in our belief that with the increasing exercise of power goes an increasing responsibility for its application. When power is spread, it is in everyone's interest to use their power to maintain the civil liberty of others lest it be their turn next. The price of liberty is eternal vigilance – not only for one's own freedoms, but for others.

The second guarantee lies in the acceptance of personal moral responsibility to defend the liberty of oneself and others. In a society which is based on the habit and techniques of participation, in which civil disobedience can be a moral imperative, the difficulties of repression can be greater than the benefits. Tyranny depends not on the consent but on the apathy or despair of its subjects: in a society based on active consent, tyranny is impossible.

If the essence of community politics is to afford the maximum choice to each individual, that ideal cannot be realised if some of the most basic choices are denied to some people. For that reason community politics implies a full system of social welfare.

The welfare state is in a crisis. The expectations created a generation ago of a constantly rising standard of living for everyone, financed out of a steady and constantly continuing rate of economic growth, have led to a level of public demand for welfare provisions which currently is not and perhaps cannot be met. At the same time, the agencies of public welfare provision have grown into vast, insensitive bureaucracies ...

These are not arguments against social justice or against a role for public authorities in meeting social need. They are arguments against the particular method of achieving social justice and competent, caring support for those in need.

The current ideology of social welfare is based on a limited and limiting view of the central role of the paid professional in providing support. That view is also inaccurate: it remains true that, in most areas of welfare, most support is provided by families, friends, neighbours and, above all, self-help. We believe that it is possible to base a strategy for social welfare on the community politics approach. The emphasis will be on self-help and mutual aid, on the sharing of skills and knowledge amongst those who provide care in the community ...

Community politics poses a direct challenge to the social democratic ideology of centralised state welfare provision and its consequent undermining of the role of the community. Over the last 75 years, the ideology of bureaucracy, centralism and paternalism has developed to the point of suffocating its victims. Community politics offers the opportunity for a caring, competent alternative.

Social need is not confined within the boundaries of the nation state. There are whole populations in the Third World whose lives never rise above total and abject poverty. The remedies of international aid and the promotion of industrialisation have signally failed to work. With the current pattern of regular world recessions and a growing shortage of natural resources it is evident that they never will. Real solutions are dependent on effective controls to prevent exploitation by international companies and freeing aid from the shackles of national self-interest. Both require supranational institutions pursuing a programme to promote social justice on a world scale. Community politics embraces a commitment to social justice embodying a supranational dimension.

We must be clear, however, that we do not equate justice with equality. Social equality leads to a dull uniformity and an unacceptable degree of compulsion. That we reject. But without social justice the degree of diversity and choice that we advocate is not possible.

Central economic planning is one of the many threats to the independence of local communities. Just as local government has been effectively transformed into an agency of national government through expenditure controls, so economic planning centralised at a national level could, and indeed currently does, suppress the independent exercise of power by other communities within society.

To act independently a community must be able to determine its own level of expenditure. How the revenue is raised is of secondary importance. If one accepts this, it follows that centralised control of public expenditure is incompatible with community politics.

Further, the development of fully co-operative industrial enterprises on a community politics model makes the concept of a national prices and incomes policy both a nonsense and unenforceable. The need for such controls is based on the breakdown of the direct relationship between wages, prices and productivity. It is the rigidity and conservatism of Britain's industrial structure, and of our system of industrial relations, that lie at the root of our problems. It causes a vicious spiral which divorces the key elements of production from each. In a system of *co-operative* production, income is related to productivity – to profit. Liberals have been far too shy about the economic implications of worker participation and co-operatives. The participatory economy is the alternative to the immobility of the present.

The regulation of the economy has created a centralised bureaucracy second only to that involved in the management of the welfare state. For all its monitoring and control, that apparatus has failed to create prosperity. Both in absolute terms and by comparison with other states, our economic management has not worked. It has not worked because it has substituted detailed interference for control of the framework within which interaction takes place, because of the stultifying effect of the controls themselves, and because it has generally been incompetent even in its own terms.

In the field of government and politics, we advocate freedom and interaction between communities within an agreed framework. In just the same way, we advocate economic freedom, with some decisions necessarily taken at a higher level, involving a group of communities coming together as one larger community. Such a group of communities will need to protect itself against unfair competition from elsewhere and will need in the real, imperfect world to play a role in monetary and fiscal policy. The obvious example of such a larger community is, of course, the nation-state. It is not, however, the best example or the most relevent level.

The concentration of economic power at national level has distracted attention from economic relations between groups of nations. The crucial failure of most policies for regional economic development has stemmed from the obsession with central planning and subsidies to the direct detriment of any policy to develop regions as economic entities. A single currency and a lack of exchange controls between regions of one country may well prevent central planners even from considering such key factors in regional imbalance as the flight of capital and enterprise. Within regions, the same principle applies to smaller depressed areas such as the inner cities. From a logical point of view as well as from an ideological community politics perspective, the relevant larger economic units for our own country's future are summed up in the phrase 'Europe of the regions'.

The two keys to economic development and the conservation of resources are co-operative production and competitive distribution, operating within a clear and firm framework of protection for freedom and enterprise. The two major steps forward will be the re-structuring of industry into co-operative units, and the breaking down of the scale of operation of industrial production. As in the political system, the essence of our view is based on self-managing communities, freely united in a federal system which establishes a just framework. The philosophy of community politics is also the political economy of freedom ...

We have not used Liberal thinkers and activities of the past merely as a starting point. Rather we have developed our own ideas, we have discovered common themes in Liberal history, and we have read and interwoven their ideas and approaches with our own. Liberalism has no single Bible to be followed; it has instead a rich and varied series of contributions on and around continuing themes.

The principle of government by consent, of a constitutional and judicial framework to guarantee liberty, goes back to Hobbes and Locke and beyond. The commitment to the principles of civil, social and personal liberty, the concept of the tyrannous majority, the belief in pluralism and diversity, the democratic basis of representative government are all best described by J. S. Mill. Professor T. H. Green takes the argument about liberty further, developing the important idea of positive liberty which is enshrined in the preamble to the Liberal Party Constitution today.

The commitment to social liberty, the ideas of community, the belief in welfare service to free individuals is developed by Mill and then carried through thinkers and activists from Hobhouse and Lloyd George to Keynes and Beveridge. The belief in the capacity of a free community to exercise power responsibly is the underlying theme of the 'optimists', the 19th century Liberal reformers and leaders.

Fox's commitment to liberty, to self-determination, to an impartial judicial process marks the real start of organised liberalism. Gladstone carried those principles further into practice and principle. More recently, leading Liberals have maintained liberalism's record as the defender of liberty.